BEGINNER

STUDENT'S BOOK

HUGH DELLAR

ANDREW WALKLEY

Contents **3**

Contents 5

1

2

5

6

7

8

9

6

10

3

11

IN THIS UNIT YOU LEARN HOW TO:

- introduce yourself and other people
- understand simple questions with *be*
- answer questions with one or two words
- use numbers to say prices and times
- order in a coffee shop
- say the order is wrong

1 ▶ **1** Listen to the numbers.

1	one	5	five	9	nine
2	two	6	six	10	ten
3	three	7	seven	11	eleven
4	four	8	eight	12	twelve

2 ▶ **1** Listen again. Repeat the numbers.

WORDS FOR UNIT 1

3 Look at the words and photos.

1	**hus**band and **wife**	7	that's **right**
2	**what**?	8	fresh **o**range **juice**
3	**So**rry!	9	have **lunch**
4	a **ba**by **boy**	10	I don't **know!**
5	**tea** with **milk**	11	the **num**ber 19 **bus**
6	**food** and drink	12	a big **flat**

4 ▶ **2** Listen and repeat the words.

5 Work in pairs. Don't look at the words.

Student A: say the number.

Student B: say the word(s).

12

NICE TO MEET YOU

LISTENING

1 ▶ 3 Listen to the conversation.

Teacher: What's your name?
Student: Lara.
Teacher: Hi. I'm Greg.
Student: Nice to meet you.
Teacher: Yes. You too.

2 ▶ 4 Listen and repeat.

1 **What's** your **name**?

2 **Nice** to **meet** you.

3 Practise the conversation from Exercise 1 with other students. Say your names.

4 ▶ 5 Listen to Khalid introduce Lara and Dom.

Khalid: Lara, this is my friend Dom.
Lara: Hi. Nice to meet you.
Dom: Yes. You too.

5 Work in groups. Introduce other students.

DEVELOPING CONVERSATIONS

Checking names

A: *Who's she?*
B: *Aretha Franklin.*

A: *Who are they?*
B: *I don't know.*

A: *Who's he?*
B: *I don't know.*

6 Look at the people in File 1 on page 144. Check the names.

7 Work in pairs. Say all the names in the class.
A: *Lara, Khalid, ... Who's she?*
B: *I don't know. He's Joan. Who's he?*

VOCABULARY People

8 Look at the picture. Complete sentences 1–4 with the words from the box.

doctor	husband	son
friend	sister	teacher

1 Bob: Tina is my wife. She's a doctor. This is my daughter, Poppy. And he is my _____, Connor.

2 Tina: Bob is my _____. He's a teacher in an English school.

3 Poppy: My mother is a _____ and my father is a _____. Connor is my big brother.

4 Connor: Poppy's my _____. She's eight. Kevin is my best _____. We're in the same class at school.

9 ▶ **6** Listen and check.

10 ▶ **7** Listen and repeat the words.

my **bro**ther	my **fa**ther	my **mo**ther	a **tea**cher
my **daugh**ter	my **friend**	my **sis**ter	my **wife**
a **doc**tor	my **hus**band	my **son**	

11 Write the names of five people in your life.

Macu	Hugh
Matthew	Rebeca
Shirley	

12 Work in pairs. Give your names to your partner. Your partner asks questions.

A: *Who is Macu?*

B: *She's my wife.*

A: *Who is Matthew?*

B: *He's my friend.*

GRAMMAR

'm, 's, 're

am

I'm Andrew.	(= *I am*)

is

She's a doctor.	(= *She is*)
He's my brother.	(= *He is*)
My name's Ian	(= *My name is*)
This is my friend, John.	

are

You're Naomi, right?	(= *You are*)
We're your teachers.	(= *We are*)
They're in my class.	(= *They're*)

13 Complete the sentences.

1 A: Who is Maria?

  B: She_____ my wife.

2 A: Who is he?

  B: Greg. He_____ our teacher.

3 A: Lara. This _____ my sister, Katia.

  B: Hi. Nice to meet you.

4 A: You_____ Ana, right?

  B: No. I_____ Zeynep. She_____ Ana!

  A: Oh! Sorry!

5 A: Who are they?

  B: _____'re my children!

  A: Nice! What are their names?

  B: My son is Cristiano and my daughter _____ Inés.

14 ▶ **8** Listen and check the answers.

15 ▶ **8** Listen again. Practise the conversations.

G For more practice, see Exercises 1–4 on page 114.

CONVERSATION PRACTICE

16 Work in pairs. Say or ask who the people are. Choose 1 or 2:

1 Show photos on your phone.

2 Look at the photos in File 1 on page 144. They are your family and friends!

▶ **9** For more practice, listen to three more examples.

WHERE'S THE PARTY?

REVIEW AND SPEAKING

1 Work in pairs. Say words for people.

son, friend ...

2 Work in pairs. Read the conversations. Use your own names.

A: *You're Khalid, right?*
B: *No. I'm Ben.*
A: *Oh, sorry.*

A: *You're Joan, right?*
B: *Yes – and you're Harry.*
A: *Yes. How are you?*
B: *Good, thanks.*

A: *Sorry. What's your name?*
B: *Ben. And you?*
A: *Tina. How are you?*
B: *Fine, thanks.*

3 Check the names of other people in the class.

VOCABULARY Numbers 13–22

4 ▶ **10** Listen and repeat the numbers.

13	thirteen	18	**eighteen**
14	**fourteen**	19	nineteen
15	fifteen	20	twenty
16	sixteen	21	twenty-one
17	seventeen	22	**twenty-two**

5 ▶ **11** Listen. Write the numbers.

1 _____, _____, _____, _____ [?]
2 _____, _____, _____, _____ [?]
3 _____, _____, _____, _____ [?]
4 _____, _____, _____, _____ [?]

6 Work in pairs. Look at Exercise 5 again. What's the next number?

A: *What's the number?*   A: *What's the number?*
B: *It's eighteen.*   B: *I don't know.*
A: *Yes, that's right.*

7 ▶ **12** Listen and check.

VOCABULARY Question words

8 ▶ **13** Look at the photos. Listen and repeat.

1 Where?

2 What time?

3 How old?

4 How long?

5 Who?

6 How much?

9 ▶ **14** Write the question words. Listen and check.

1 _____ is she? My wife.
2 _____ is it? São Paulo in Brazil.
3 _____ is it? Eight o'clock.
4 _____ is it? Twenty-two dollars.
5 _____ is it? Fifteen minutes.
6 _____ is she? She's thirteen.

10 ▶ **15** Listen to some questions and answers. Choose the answer you hear (a, b or c).

1 How are you?
  a Good.
  b Fine, thanks.
  c OK.

2 How long is the class?
  a One hour.
  b Three hours.
  c Twenty minutes.

3 How old are you?
  a Thirteen.
  b Eight.
  c Nineteen. I'm twenty on Saturday!

4 Where are you from?
  a New York.
  b China.
  c Here!

5 Who's she?
  a My mother.
  b That's my daughter.
  c My friend, Amani.

6 How much is lunch?
  a Fourteen euros.
  b Seven twenty.
  c Sixteen dollars.

7 What time is it?
  a Five.
  b Three o'clock.
  c Ten.

8 What's your phone number?
  a 71 33 68 922
  b 022 193 548
  c 069 455 781

V For more countries, see page 139.

GRAMMAR

Questions with *be*

are

A: *How **are** you?*   B: *I'm OK.*

A: *Where **are** you from?*   B: *Japan.*

A: ***Are** you OK?*   B: *Yes, thanks.*

is

A: *How much **is** it?*   B: *Two pounds.*

A: *How old **is** he?*   B: *He's 18.*

A: *Who **is** she?*   B: *My teacher.*

A: ***Is** it nice?*   B: *Yes, it's good!*

11 Complete the questions with *are* or *is*.

1 Where _____ you from?

2 How _____ you?

3 Where _____ he from?

4 How long _____ the class?

5 How old _____ you?

6 What time _____ the party?

7 How old _____ your son?

8 _____ she nice?

9 Who _____ he?

10 How much _____ it?

G For more practice, see Exercises 1–4 on page 115.

12 ▶ **16** Listen and check. The questions are fast then slow.

13 Work in pairs. Practise the questions.

SPEAKING

14 Write answers to the questions. Use one or two words.

- What time is it?
- How are you?
- Where are you from?
- How old are you?
- How long is the coffee break?

15 Work in pairs. Ask and answer the questions.

GRAMMAR

his, her, our, their

Tia**'s** party	= **her** party
Pedro**'s** daughter	= **his** daughter
Tom and Peter**'s** flat	= **their** flat
Sara**'s** and my son	= **our** son

G For practice, see Exercises 1 and 2 on page 115.

READING

16 Read the invitations. Answer the questions.

1 What day is Tia's party?

2 What's Joe and Kate's phone number?

3 Where's Sara and Pedro's party?

4 Who is Santiago?

5 How long is Tom and Peter's party?

6 What number is Tom and Peter's flat?

Friday 15

Saturday 16

Sunday 17

17 Write five more questions about the parties.

1 How old is _____?

How old is Tia? / How old is Joe and Kate's daughter?

2 Where's _____?

3 What time is _____?

4 How long _____?

5 _____

18 Work in pairs. Ask and answer your questions from Exercise 17.

▶ **17**

INVITATION!
OUR DAUGHTER TIA IS 18

Come to her party at:
Selale Restaurant
25 Green Lanes
Friday 15th
9pm – 2am

Joe and Kate's phone: 121 786 5539

SARA AND PEDRO

HAVE A NEW BABY BOY!

Come to our party and meet Santiago
(and his sister Rebeca!)

The Spanish Centre 3 High Street	Saturday 16th 12pm – 6pm Lunch at 2pm

Mobile: 07311 762 4683

TOM AND PETER HAVE A NEW FLAT

COME TO OUR PARTY AT
Flat 6 Floor 3
19 Old Street

3pm – 8pm
This Sunday (17th)
email: tom@xmail.com

TIME FOR COFFEE

Coffee and cake

VOCABULARY Times and prices

1 ▶ 18 Listen and repeat the numbers.

20	twenty	60	sixty
21	**twenty-one**	65	sixty-five
30	thirty	70	seventy
32	thirty-two	76	**seventy-six**
40	forty	80	eighty
43	**forty-three**	87	eighty-seven
50	fifty	90	ninety
54	fifty-four	98	**ninety-eight**

Times

10.25	ten twenty five	
2.00	two	two o'clock
16.30	four thirty	sixteen thirty

Prices

£3.99	three ninety-nine	three pound**s** ninety-nine
€17.50	seventeen fifty	seventeen euro**s** fifty

2 ▶ 19 Listen. Write the time or price.

1 It's 3._____.

2 It's £15._____.

3 The class is at _____.

4 The coffee break is at _____.

5 A cappuccino is €_____.

6 Lunch is at _____.

7 Sandwiches are $_____.

8 My bus is at _____.

3 Work in pairs. Remember the questions from Exercise 2. Ask and answer the questions.

VOCABULARY In a coffee shop

4 ▶ 20 Listen and repeat words from a menu.

ameri**ca**no	es**press**o	**me**dium	**small**
cake	large	**o**range **juice**	tea
cappu**cci**no	latte	**sand**wich	**wa**ter

5 ▶ 21 Listen and repeat the words in sentences.

6 Work in pairs. Ask the prices. Complete the menu.

Student A: look at the menu on this page.

Student B: look at the menu in File 3 on page 145.

A: *How much is a medium cappuccino?*

MENU

	Large	Medium	Small
Hot drinks			
cappuccino	3.75	_____	2.90
latte	_____	3.40	_____
americano	_____	2.80	2.30
espresso	2.05	1.60	
tea	2.25	1.95	1.60
Cold drinks			
fresh orange juice	_____	3.95	3.45
Coke	2.15		
water	_____		
Food			
cakes	4.95	sandwiches	_____

7 Ask about prices.

How much is a cappuccino in your country?

How much is _____ in _____?

DEVELOPING CONVERSATIONS

Ordering and serving drinks
A: **What would you like?**
B: A large americano.
A: Americano. **Anything else?**
B: Yes – one medium orange juice.
A: OK. Anything else?
B: **No, thanks.**
A: OK. That's £7.05 (seven oh five).

8　▶ **22** Listen to the conversation.

9　Have similar conversations. Use the menu on page 12.

LISTENING

10　▶ **23** Listen to a man in a coffee shop. Tick (✓) the food and drink on the menu. How much is it?

11　▶ **24** Listen to part 2 of the conversation. What's the problem (a, b or c)?
- a It's not the right coffee.
- b It's not the right money.
- c It's not a large cappuccino.

GRAMMAR

not
It's **not** right.
It's **not** a black tea.
It's **not** fifty pounds.
It's medium – **not** large.
My tea – it's **not** hot!

12　Add not.
1 A: What's the problem?
   B: My tea – it's not right.
2 A: What's the problem?
   B: My coffee – it's a cappuccino.
3 A: Yes, sir. Are you OK?
   B: Sorry. It's a small tea – large.
4 A: Are you OK?
   B: No. It's coffee cake – chocolate.
5 A: Is everything OK?
   B: No. My tea's hot.
6 A: What's the problem?
   B: It's right. It's 35 euros. It's 29.

13　▶ **25** Listen and check.

14　▶ **26** Listen and repeat the answers.

15　Have similar conversations. Use the pictures.

1

A: What's the problem?　A: Are you OK?
B: My coffee, it's small –　B: It's not a large coffee.
　　not large.　　　　　　A: Sorry.
A: Sorry.

2 　　**3**

4 　　**5**

Ⓖ For more practice, see Exercise 1 on page 116.

SPEAKING

16　Have conversations. Take turns.

Student A: assistant	**Student B:** customer
Hi. How are you?	
What would you like?	
Anything else?	
That's	
	Here you are.
Are you OK?	No, ...
Oh, yes. Sorry. Here you are.	Thanks.

PRONUNCIATION AND REVIEW

17　▶ **27** Listen to the sentences. They are fast. Write the number.

This is my son, John.	_____
This is my friend, Don.	_____
Where are you from?	_____
What's her name?	_1_
What time is the class?	_____
What's your phone number?	_____

18　▶ **28** Listen and check the answers. They are slow then fast.

19　Work in pairs. Say the sentences. Reply.
　A: This is my son, John.　B: Hello. Nice to meet you.

Ⓖ For more pronunciation, see Exercise 1 on page 116.

2 LIVE, WORK, EAT

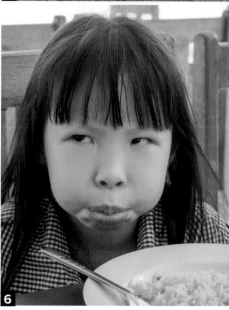

14

IN THIS UNIT YOU LEARN HOW TO:

- ask and say where you live
- ask about someone's job
- talk about people you know
- understand a menu
- say what you like / don't like
- answer a waiter and order food

WORDS FOR UNIT 2

1 Look at the words and photos.

1 a big **city**	7 some **meat**
2 **near** and **far**	8 a **ta**xi **dri**ver
3 a lot of **chil**dren	9 fresh **fruit**
4 it's ex**pen**sive	10 **work** in an **o**ffice
5 some **nur**ses	11 **walk** in the **park**
6 I don't **like** it	12 a small **vi**llage

2 ▶ 29 Listen and repeat the words.

3 Work in pairs. Don't look at the words.

Student A: say the number.

Student B: say the word(s).

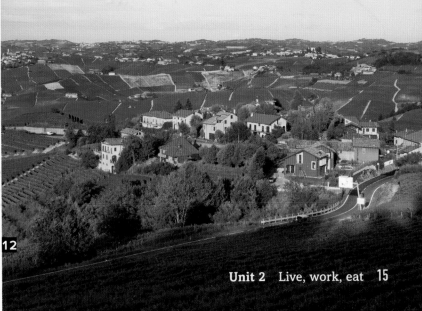

Unit 2 Live, work, eat 15

WHERE DO YOU LIVE?

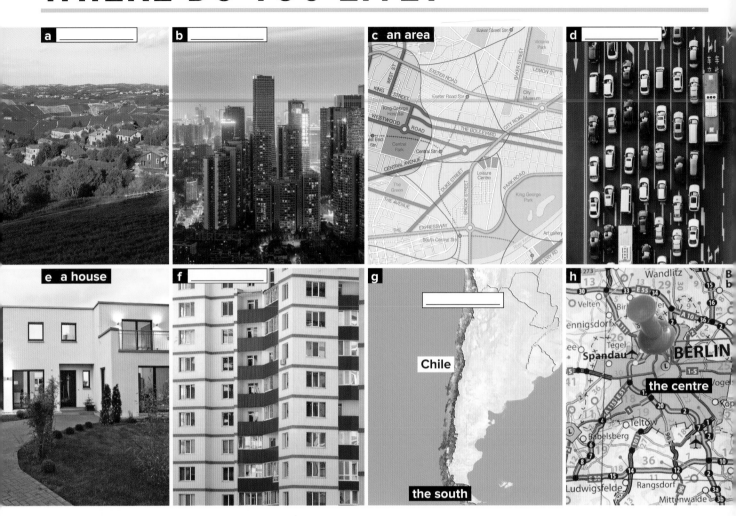

a _____
b _____
c an area
d _____
e a house
f _____
g _____ Chile / the south
h Wandlitz / BERLIN / the centre

LISTENING AND SPEAKING

1 ▶ 30 **Listen to Freya and Adam.**

F: Hi, you're Adam, right?

A: Yes. Sorry. What's your name?

F: Freya.

A: Oh yes. How are you?

F: Good. And you?

A: Yeah, I'm OK.

F: Where do you live?

A: Kings Heath. And you?

F: I live on New Road. Do you know it?

A: No. Is it near here?

F: Yes. I walk here. It takes ten minutes.

2 ▶ 31 **Listen and repeat.**

1 **Where** do you **live**?

2 Do you **know** it?

3 Is it **near here**?

4 It takes **ten mi**nutes.

3 **Work in pairs. Practise the conversation from Exercise 1. Change the words in red.**

VOCABULARY My home

4 **Write the words in the box with the correct photo.**

> a city   flats   the north   a road   a village

5 ▶ 32 **Listen and repeat.**

a **vil**lage	a **road**	the **north**
a **city**	a **house**	the **south**
an **area**	**flats**	the **cen**tre

6 ▶ 33 **Listen to Leo. Choose the correct word(s).**

My name's Leo.

I'm from [1] *Chile / Argentina.*

I live in a [2] *village / city* called Temuco.

Temuco **is in an area called** Araucanía. **It's in the** [3] *north / south* **of** Chile.

I live in a small [4] *house / flat* with my [5] *son / daughter* and [6] *my wife / my dog.*

It's on Los Leones **road.**

It's near [7] *a big park / the university.*

7 **Make the sentences from Exercise 6 true for you. Tell a partner.**

My name's ...

I'm from ...

GRAMMAR

Present simple

I	**live** near here.
You	**know** the city.
We	**like** Rio.
They	**walk** to the centre.
My mother and father	**have** a nice house.

He	live**s** near here.
She	know**s** the city.
My brother	like**s** Rio.
My friend Karen	ha**s** a nice flat.
It	take**s** ten minutes.

8 Tell the class about your partner.

His name's Leo.

He's from Chile.

He lives in a city ...

G For more practice, see Exercise 1 on page 116.

9 Write three sentences about friends and family. Use the verbs in the Grammar box or a dictionary.

*My mother **lives** with me.*

*My friend Fei **has** a Ferrari.*

*My sister **knows** our teacher. They're friends.*

10 Work in pairs. Say your sentences.

GRAMMAR

Present simple questions: *do you*

Where **do you** live?

Who **do you** live with?

Do you live near here?

Do you know it?

11 Put the words in the correct order. Make questions.

1 live / where / do / you / ?

2 with your brother / do / live / you / ?

3 who / you / live / with / do / ?

4 do / your / city / you / like / ?

5 you / know / my / name / do / ?

6 do / a / you / have / house / or / flat / a / ?

12 ▶ **34** Listen and check the questions.

13 ▶ **35** Listen and repeat the questions.

14 Work in pairs. Ask and answer the questions.

G For more practice, see Exercises 1–4 on page 117.

DEVELOPING CONVERSATIONS

And you?

We use *And you?* to ask the same 'you-question'.

A: *How are you?*

B: *Good, thanks. **And you?*** (= How are *you?*)

A: *I'm OK.*

A: *Do you like Tokyo?*

B: *Yes, it's great! **And you?*** (= Do *you* like Tokyo?)

A: *No, I don't like it. It's very big.*

15 Work in pairs. Take turns.

Student A: ask questions 1–6.

Student B: answer and ask *And you?*

Student A: answer.

1 How are you?

2 What's your name?

3 Where do you live?

4 How old are you?

5 Do you have any brothers or sisters?

6 Do you like grammar?

CONVERSATION PRACTICE

16 Complete the conversation.

and	it	live	~~name~~	to	takes
do	know	meet	on	you (x3)	~~your~~

A: Hi. Sorry, what's ¹___your___ ___name___?

B: Ali. And you?

A: Maria. Nice ²_____ _____ you.

B: You too.

A: So, Ali. Where ³_____ _____ live?

B: Clayton. It's a small village. Do you know it?

A: No. Is it far?

B: It takes thirty minutes by car. ⁴_____ _____? Where do you live?

A: I ⁵_____ _____ Havana Road. Do ⁶_____ _____ it?

B: Yes. It's near here, right?

A: Yes. I walk here. ⁷_____ _____ fifteen minutes.

17 ▶ **36** Listen and check.

18 Have similar conversations. Talk to other people in the class. Find someone who:

• lives near you.

• lives far from you.

Hi. Sorry, what's your name?

_____.

Nice to meet you.

_____

I'm _____.

And you?

You too. Where do you live?

[Continue]

 37 For more practice, listen to another example.

WHAT DO YOU DO?

REVIEW AND SPEAKING

1 Choose one or two:
- Look at the photos on pages 14 and 15. Test each other.
- Study the conversation in Exercise 1, page 16. Close your book and practise the conversation.
- Ask other students *Who do you live with?*

VOCABULARY Jobs

2 ▶ **38** Listen and repeat the words.

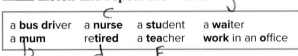

a **bus driver**	a **nurse**	a **stu**dent	a **wai**ter
a **mum**	retired	a **tea**cher	**work** in an **o**ffice

3 ▶ **39** Listen to eight conversations. What do they do? Write the letter of the photo.

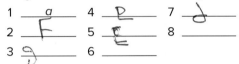

1   *a*   4   b   7   d
2   f   5   c   8 _____
3   g   6 _____

4 Work in pairs. Practise conversations. Student B close your book. Take turns.

Student A: ask *What do you do?*

Student B: say *I'm … / I work in …*

Student A: point to the correct photo.

SPEAKING

5 Work in groups. What jobs do people you know do? Use the jobs from Exercise 2.

My friend James is a …

My brother works …

My mother ….

6 Say which jobs are:

a great.   b good.   c OK.

GRAMMAR

Present simple: *don't (do not)*

*I **work** 50 hours a week.*	*I **don't work**. I'm retired.*
*I **walk** to school.*	*I **don't walk** to school.*
*You **like** the job.*	*You **don't like** the job.*
*We **have** a flat.*	*We **don't have** a flat.*
*They **have** a lot of money.*	*They **don't have** a lot of money.*

7 Make the sentences negative.

1 I work on Friday and Saturday.
2 I know.
3 You live near here.
4 I like it.
5 We have children.
6 They live in the centre.
7 I walk to class.
8 I go to a language school.

8 ▶ **40** Listen and repeat the negative sentences from Exercise 7.

G For more practice, see Exercises 1 and 2 on page 117.

9 Complete the sentences. Make them true for you. Use these verbs or others.

go	know	live	work	have	like	walk

- I don't _____
- I don't _____
- I don't _____
- I'm not _____

10 Tell a partner your sentences.

READING

11 Read about four people's jobs. Answer the questions.

1 Where are the four people from?
2 Which city do they all live in?

12 Read again. Write the names of the people.

1 I'm a taxi driver. *Ali*
2 I'm a nurse. *Jessica*
3 I'm a teacher. *Carlos*
4 I'm a student. *Rasa*
5 I like my job. *Carlos and Rasa*
6 I live near my job. *Rasa*
7 I work a lot of hours. *Ali*

13 ▶ **42** Listen to Carlos and read again. <u>Underline</u> two things that are different.

14 ▶ **43** Listen to the three other people and read again. Underline the two things that are different for each person.

GRAMMAR

Plural / no plural

Singular	Plural	No plural
a doctor	The doctors **are** nice.	The money **is** good.
a job	I have three jobs.	I don't have time.
an hour	The hours **are** good.	I have some money.
a person	The people **are** nice.	I have a lot of work.
a child	I have two children.	

G For practice, see Exercises 1–3 on page 118.

15 ▶ **44** Listen to the conversation. Who is it?

16 Work in pairs. Have similar conversations. Take turns. Who is it?

Student A: ask the questions *What do you do? Do you like it? Why? / Why not?*

Student B: answer the questions. You are Ali, Jessica, Rasa or Carlos.

WRITING AND SPEAKING

17 Change the words in red so the sentences are true for you. Use a dictionary to help you.

I'm a teacher. I work in a university. I like my job. The hours are good. The people are nice. The money's good.

18 Ask other people in the class the questions from Exercise 16 about their real jobs.

THE WORLD IN ONE CITY

▶ **41**

My name's Carlos. I'm from Mexico, but now I live in London. I live in north London and I work in a university in the centre. It takes thirty minutes by train. The job's great. I like my students and the money's OK.

My name's Jessica. I'm from Australia, but I'm a nurse here in London. My job's OK, but I don't like the hospital. It's big and I don't live near it. It's an hour by car from my house. The other nurses are nice, but I don't like some doctors.

My name's Rasa. I'm from Lithuania, but now I live and work in Tooting – an area in south London. I work in a coffee shop. It's OK. I like the people and the hours are good for me. I work from nine to three and then I go to university.

My name's Ali. I'm from Turkey. I work for a taxi company. I don't like my job. London traffic is bad. The money is bad and I work a lot – 70 or 80 hours a week. I don't have time with my wife and two children.

TABLE FOR TWO

VOCABULARY Food and drinks

1 ▶ **45** Listen and repeat.

chicken	**fish**	**ice** cream	**meat**	**sa**lad
drinks	**fruit**	**juice**	**rice**	

2 Complete the menu on page 21 with the words from Exercise 1.

GRAMMAR

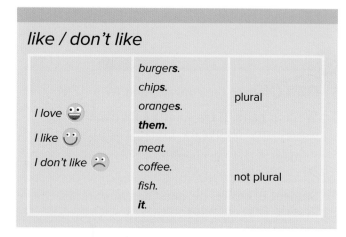

like / don't like

	burgers. chips. oranges. **them.**	plural
I love 😃 I like 🙂 I don't like 🙁	meat. coffee. fish. *it.*	not plural

3 ▶ **46** Work in groups. Listen to the example.

A: I love meat.

B: I don't like it. I only eat fish or vegetables.

C: I like chicken, but I don't like bacon.

A: I love chips.

B: Me too! I love chips.

C: I don't like them.

4 Say the food and drinks you love / like / don't like. Find one thing you all:

• love.   • don't like.

G For more practice, see Exercise 1 on page 118.

SPEAKING

5 Work in pairs. Look at the words in the box. Then read the examples.

more = ↑	less = ↓

A: *Fruit juice?*	A: *Beef burger?*	A: *Salmon?*
B: *Three euros 50.*	B: *Fourteen euros.*	B: *Ten euros.*
A: *OK.*	A: *No.* **Less.**	A: *No.* **More.**
	B: *Twelve euros.*	

6 It's your restaurant. Decide the prices. Have similar conversations to the examples in Exercise 5. Write the prices for each dish on page 21.

7 Change partner. Ask about prices. Say *It's expensive, It's OK* or *It's cheap.*

A: *How much is your kebab?*

B: *Sixteen euros.*

A: *Oh. It's expensive.*

B: *Our kebab is good. Very nice!*

LISTENING الله ؟ ريف

8 ▶ **47** Listen to a waiter and family. Tick (✓) the drinks the family orders on the menu.

9 ▶ **48** Listen. Tick (✓) the food they order.

10 ▶ **49** Listen. Complete the conversation with one word in each space.

A: Do you have a table for ¹ __3__ ?

B: Yes. Would you like a menu in ² _English_

A: Please.

B: Would you like some drinks?

A: Yes. Two orange juices, a Coke and ³ _____ water.

...

B: Are you ready to order?

A: Yes. A kebab with rice for ⁴ _____.

B: OK. And for ⁵ _____?

C: Chicken, please.

B: With ⁶ _____ or chips?

C: Chips, please.

B: And you?

D: Prawns with rice.

B: Anything ⁷ _else_ ? A salad?

C: How much is the tomato salad?

B: ⁸ _Fifteen_ euros.

C: Oh. It's expensive. No, ⁹ _____.

B: So, that's one kebab and rice, one chicken and chips, and one prawns with rice.

DEVELOPING CONVERSATIONS

Ordering food

A Coke and some water, **please**.

Chicken **for me** *and a kebab for my son.*

11 Work in threes. One person is the waiter. Ask and answer the questions.

• Would you like some drinks?

• Are you ready to order?

• What would you like?

• And you?

كباب و دؤاجه و تنبس سلاطط تماطلو

SPEAKING

12 Work in pairs. One person is the waiter. Practise the conversation. Change the information in **red**.

A: *Do you have a table for* four?

B: *Yes. Would you like a menu in English?*

A: *Please.*

B: *Would you like some drinks?*

A: *Yes, please.* One coffee, two orange juices.

13 Work in groups of four. Close your books. Practise similar conversations to the one in Exercise 10. Choose your food and drink.

رايس بسكرية

PRONUNCIATION AND REVIEW

14 ▶ **50** Listen to the sentences below. They are fast. Write the number.

Where do you live?	_____	They have a nice house.	_____
I don't know it.	_____	It's in the north.	_____
I don't live near here.	_____	He's a student at university.	_____
I like it here.	_____	I don't like it.	_____
It's a nice area.	*1*	She's a teacher in a language school.	_____

15 ▶ **51** Listen and check the answers. They are slow then fast.

16 Practise saying the sentences.

17 Work in pairs. In one minute:
- write words for jobs and work.
- write words for food.

G For more pronunciation, see Exercises 1 and 2 on page 118.

MENU

burger
kebab
2 _____ curry
grilled chicken
hot bacon sandwich

VEGETARIAN DISHES

cheese pizza   vegetable curry

3 _____ AND SEAFOOD

cod

salmon

prawns

8

water
coffee
Coke
tea
fresh orange 9_____

SIDE DISHES

bread	green 5 _____
chips	tomato salad
4 _____	vegetables

DESSERTS

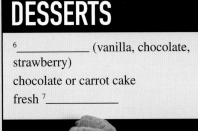

6 _____ (vanilla, chocolate, strawberry)
chocolate or carrot cake
fresh 7 _____

PEOPLE

1 Look at the photo. Where are the people from? Use the words on page 139 to help you.

2 ▢**1** Watch the video. Number the sentences when you hear them.

   a This is us. People. Nice to meet you.   _____

   b This is us. Lots of people from different countries.   _____

   c We meet as a family. We talk.   _____

   d We meet on the train. We talk.   _____

   e We meet in the street. We talk.   _____

   f We are friends. We do the same things.   _____

3 Are the sentences true (T) or false (F)?

   1 The baby is a boy.

   2 The baby is two years old.

   3 The two old women are sisters.

   4 The woman doesn't like the book.

   5 The man knows the book.

   6 The women want a coffee.

   7 The boy is nine.

4 ▢**1** Watch the video again and check.

5 Complete the sentences with one word in each space.

   1 We are friends. _____ do the same things.

   2 _____'s a boy. _____ name's Josh.

   3 Her daughter _____ a son. _____'s two.

   4 The book. Do you like _____?

   5 Would _____ like a break?

   6 You'_____ ten!

6 Work in groups. Answer the questions.

   • Do you have any friends from another country? Where are they from?

   • What times do you have a break in the day? How long are your breaks?

SPEAKING

7 Work in pairs. Ask and answer questions about people. Use the photos on page 18 or page 144 or photos of people on your phone. Change the words in red.

Who's she?	My sister.
What's her name?	Juana.
What does she do?	She's a nurse.
How old is she?	23.
Where does she live?	Mexico City. She lives with me.

REVIEW 1

_a p l9_

1 Choose the correct word(s).

1 How old *is / are* you?

2 What *is / are* her name?

3 Where *are you / you are / do you* live?

4 She *has / have* a new car.

5 We have three *childs / children* – two *son / sons* and a daughter.

6 Do you know Andrew? This is *his / their / our* wife.

7 Who *are / do / is* you live with?

8 Where *is / are / do* they from?

9 We *not / don't / are not* live here.

10 *I'm not / I don't / I not* like meat.

2 Rewrite the sentences as negatives (–) or questions (?).

1 It's expensive. (–)

2 His mother is retired. (?)

3 They have a lot of money. (–)

4 You work near here. (?)

5 I have a sister. (–)

6 The teachers are nice. (?)

7 I know her brother. (–)

8 He likes English. (?)

3 Complete the sentences with one word in each space. Contractions (*I'm, don't*, etc.) are one word.

1 I like tea, but I _____ like coffee.

2 It's my husband's birthday on Saturday. Come to _____ party.

3 I walk to university. I _____ have a car.

4 Excuse me. This is _____ a cappuccino. It's a latte.

5 I like my job. The hours _____ OK and the money _____ very good.

6 It's not far. It _____ ten minutes by car.

7 I don't have time today. I have a _____ of work.

8 Where _____ you live? _____ it near here?

4 Write full questions to complete the conversation. Use the words in brackets.

A: [1]_____? (name)

B: Isabella.

A: And [2]_____? (from)

B: Cuzco. In Peru.

A: [3]_____? (old)

B: Twenty-seven.

A: [4]_____? (do)

B: I'm a doctor. I work in a hospital in the city centre.

A: [5]_____? (job)

B: Yes, I do. I love it. I like the people and the money is OK.

5 Match the verbs in the box with the correct groups of words (1–7).

have	know	like	live	take	walk	work

1 _____ in an office / forty hours a week

2 _____ ten minutes / twenty minutes by train

3 _____ in a village / near here

4 _____ a big house / children

5 _____ in the park / to school

6 _____ my job / fish and chips

7 _____ your name / the area

6 Put the words into three groups: food, drinks or jobs.

americano	fish	salad	teacher
chicken	nurse	sandwich	waiter
Coke	orange juice	taxi driver	water
doctor	rice	tea	

7 Replace the words in italics with their opposites from the box.

brother	daughter	small	wife
cheap	father	south	

1 This is my *husband*.
This is my wife.

2 This is my *sister*.

3 This is my *mother*.

4 This is my *son*.

5 It's in the *north*.

6 It's very *expensive*.

7 It's a *big* town.

8 Complete the text with the words from the box.

brother	flat	nice	park
city	name	north	student

My [1]_____ is Maryam and I'm a [2]_____. I'm from Oman. I live in a small [3]_____ called Khasab. It's in the [4]_____ of Oman. I live in a big [5]_____ with my mother, father and [6]_____. We live near a [7]_____. It's very [8]_____.

9 Match the questions (1–8) with the answers (a–h).

1 Who's he?

2 Where do you live?

3 How long is the class?

4 What time is it?

5 How old is she?

6 What day is the party?

7 How much is it?

8 What's your phone number?

a Twenty-three.

b Ninety minutes.

c 07781-336-454

d My father.

e Two euros twenty.

f Eight thirty.

g In Rome.

h Friday.

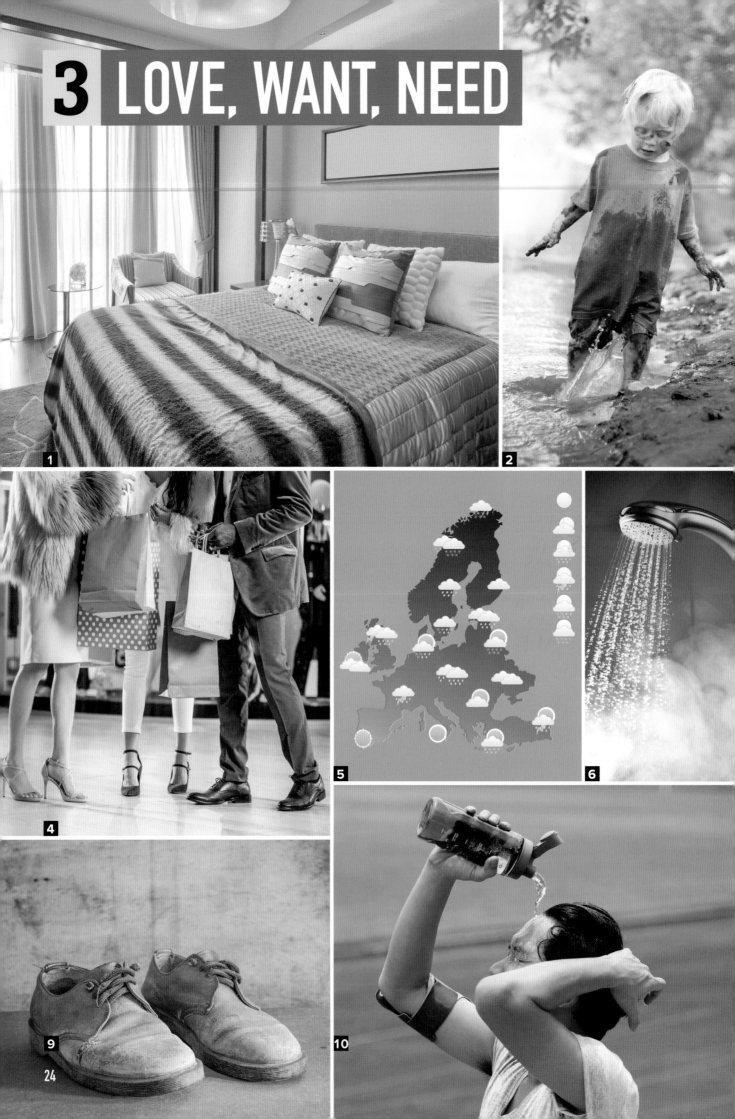

3 LOVE, WANT, NEED

3

IN THIS UNIT YOU LEARN HOW TO:

- ask how things are
- respond to good and bad news
- use adjectives to describe things
- ask and talk about things people have
- ask someone to repeat

WORDS FOR UNIT 3

1 Look at the words and photos.

1 a **ho**tel room	7 go on **hol**iday
2 he **needs** a **show**er	8 get **mar**ried
3 **read** a **book**	9 old **shoes**
4 buy **clothes**	10 very **hot**
5 **wea**ther	11 he's not **well**
6 a **show**er	12 take the **train** to **work**

2 ▶ **52** Listen and repeat the words.

3 Work in pairs. Don't look at the words.

Student A: say the number.

Student B: say the word(s).

7

8

11

12

HOW IS IT?

SPEAKING

1 ▶ 53 Listen to two conversations.

1

A: Hi. How are you?

B: Good, thanks. And you?

A: Yeah – not bad!

2

A: Hi. How are you?

B: Very good. And you?

A: I'm not very well.

B: Oh, I'm sorry.

2 Work in pairs. Practise the conversations from Exercise 1.

3 Ask other students in the class *How are you?*

VOCABULARY Adjectives

4 ▶ 54 Listen and repeat the adjectives. Tick (✓) the words you know.

bad	expensive	hungry	old
big	good	married	small
cold	great	new	tired
difficult	hot	nice	well

5 Say two or three adjectives for each photo.

6 Don't look at the adjectives in Exercise 4.
1) Complete sentences 1–6 with an adjective.
2) Complete the sentences with a different adjective.

1 It's **a/an** _____ **flat.**

2 It's **a/an** _____ **class.**

3 It's **a/an** _____ **hotel.**

4 It's _____ **weather.**

5 They're _____ **clothes.**

6 I'm _____.

---

a / an

a nice flat   an old flat

a big hotel   an expensive hotel

---

7 Compare your answers.

8 Write the correct numbers.

−15°C	98	78	0°C

1 It's cold. _____

2 It's very cold. _____

3 He's old. _____

4 She's very old. _____

9   **Work in groups. Say things you love / like / don't like.**

A: *I love very hot weather.*

B: *Me too.*

C: *I don't like very hot weather.*

A: *I like big cities.*

B: *I don't like them. I like small cities.*

C: *Me too.*

LISTENING

10 **Where are the people? Match the questions (1–4) with the places (a–d).**

1	How's the class?	a	in a hotel
2	How's the chicken?	b	in a restaurant
3	How's your room?	c	in a school
4	How's the weather?	d	on holiday / in a different country

11 ▶ **55** **Listen. What question from Exercise 10 do they ask in each conversation?**

Conversation 1: _____

Conversation 2: _____

Conversation 3: _____

Conversation 4: _____

12 ▶ **55** **Listen again. Choose the correct word(s).**

1 A: It's *not very / very* big.

B: The same. And it's *cold / old*!

2 English is *difficult / good*.

3 A: How's the fish?

B: It's *great / not very nice*.

4 A: It's *cold / hot*.

B: Oh no! It's normally *near / hot* there.

GRAMMAR

Negatives with *be*

'm not

*I***'m not** *well.*

're not

*We***'re not** *tired.*

*They***'re not** *in my class.*

*You***'re not** *English, right?*

's not

*He***'s not** *married.*

*She***'s not** *here.*

*It***'s not** *very difficult.*

13 **Make the sentences negative.**

1 She's my friend.

2 It's a big city.

3 We're married.

4 I'm very hungry.

5 They're from here.

6 The rooms are very expensive.

7 My job's very good. The money's great.

14 ▶ **56** **Listen and check. The sentences are fast then slow.**

15 **Work in pairs. Practise the sentences.**

16 **Work in pairs. Say true sentences about you and where you live.**

I'm not married.

My flat's not very big.

Moscow is very expensive.

G For more practice, see Exercises 1 and 2 on page 119.

DEVELOPING CONVERSATIONS

Responding to news

For good news

A: *The teacher's nice.*

B: **Oh, good.**

For bad news

A: *I'm not very well.*

B: **I'm sorry.**

17 ▶ **57** **Listen and repeat the phrases from the box.**

18 **Write *Oh, good* or *I'm sorry* after each sentence.**

1 It's not very expensive. _____

2 My room is nice and big. _____

3 It's very cold in my flat. _____

4 The weather here is great. _____

5 I love my English class. _____

6 The fish is very good. _____

7 My father's not very well. _____

8 I don't like my new job. The hours are very bad. _____

19 ▶ **58** **Listen and answer.**

20 **Work in pairs. Take turns.**

Student A: say a sentence from Exercise 18.

Student B: say *Oh, good* or *I'm sorry*.

CONVERSATION PRACTICE

21 **Write questions starting with *How's ... ?***

1 in a hotel

2 in a restaurant

3 at school

4 in a different country

5 about a new flat/house

22 **Have your own conversations.**

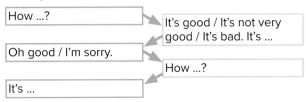

How ...?

It's good / It's not very good / It's bad. It's ...

Oh good / I'm sorry.

How ...?

It's ...

59 For more practice, listen to another example.

THINGS I WANT IN LIFE

REVIEW

1 Choose two:
- Write or say all the adjectives you know.
- Add eight different words to *I'm ...*

  I'm cold.

  I'm 16.
- Say five things about you and your things with *not*.

  I don't live near here.

  My flat is not expensive.

VOCABULARY *go, take, want*

2 Look at the sentences. Then match the verbs in the box with the groups of words 1–3.
- He / She takes the train to work.
- He / She wants a new car.
- He / She goes to the gym every day.

go	take	want

1 _____ the bus

   a photo

   a shower

   a long time

2 _____ to the park every day

   to the doctor

   on holiday

   shopping

3 _____ a coffee

   a new house

   to go to China

   to buy some clothes

3 ▶ **60** Listen to the phrases and repeat them.

4 Work in pairs. Take turns.

Student A: say a verb. *go*

Student B: don't look. Say a phrase. *go shopping*

GRAMMAR

Present simple: *doesn't*

wants	→	She **doesn't want** to go.
takes	→	It **doesn't take** a long time.
likes	→	He **doesn't like** coffee
goes	→	The bus **doesn't go** to the centre.

5 Complete the sentences with the verbs.

1 My sister _____*has*_____ two children. (have)

2 He _____ lots of money. (not have)

3 The number 30 bus _____ near my house. (go)

4 He _____ to university. (not go)

5 He _____ his job. (like)

6 My mother _____ big cities. (not like)

7 My dad _____ the bus to work. He walks. (not take)

8 My friend, Marc, _____ for Google. He _____ in San Francisco. (work / live)

6 Make six negative sentences about people you know. Use these verbs.

go	have	live	take	want	work

7 Work in pairs. Say your sentences.

G For more practice, see Exercise 1 on page 119.

WHAT DO PEOPLE WANT?

▶ 61

JOSH
I want a new mobile phone for my birthday. My phone is very old! I want some money to go shopping too. My mum buys my clothes, but I don't like them. They're for old people!

BETTINA
I have a good job. I love my husband. We have a big house and a nice car. We go on holiday to nice places. It's all great, but we don't have children and now we want a family.

MATTHIEU
I only work for two days a week – fifteen or twenty hours. I don't have a lot of money, but I don't want a lot of things. Money's not important to me. I have food. I only drink water. I have friends. I have some books to read. I have a lot of free time.

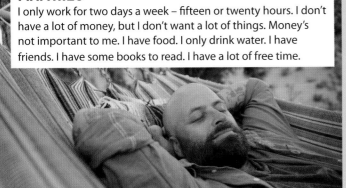

ANGELO
I'm a teacher. I live in the city, but I work in a village. I go by car and it takes me two hours. At the end of the day, I'm very tired. I want a job in the city. I want to walk to work and have more free time. But it's difficult.

READING

8 Read five things people want. Tick (✓) the things *you* want.

9 Read about the four people. Answer the questions.
1. What does Josh want for his birthday?
2. Does Josh like his clothes?
3. Is Bettina married?
4. Does Bettina have a daughter?
5. Does Matthieu work a lot?
6. Does Matthieu want more money?
7. What does Angelo do?
8. How long does it take Angelo to get to work?

GRAMMAR

Present simple questions: *does*
What **does he** do?

Why **does she** want a new job?

How long **does it** take to get to work?

10 Complete the questions with the name of people in the class. Use a different name in each sentence.
- What does _____ do?
- Does _____ have any brothers or sisters?
- Where does _____ live?
- Where does _____ work?
- How does _____ come to class?
- What food does _____ like?

11 Work in groups. Ask and answer the questions about people in the class.

A: *What does X do?*

B: *I don't know.*

C: *She's a teacher.*

 For more practice, see Exercises 1 and 2 on page 119.

WRITING

12 Write four sentences about things you have and things you want – and don't want – in your life. Say why. Use a dictionary if you need to.

DO YOU NEED ANYTHING?

 my **mobile**

 a **map**

 a **pen**

 a **towel**

 a **dictionary**

 a **brush**

 a **charger**

 a small **bag**

 a big **coat**

 lots of **clothes**

 **soap**

 some **cash**

 **som**ething to **read**

 food from **home**

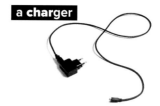 some **other shoes**

a **tooth**brush and **tooth**paste

VOCABULARY Things

1 What do you need on holiday? Tick (✓) the things you take with you.

2 ▶ 62 Listen and repeat the words from Exercise 1.

3 Work in pairs. Say what you take on holiday. Think about these times and places.

- a weekend in a city
- a week to visit friends or family
- two weeks in a hotel in a hot country

Aled

LISTENING

4 ▶ 63 Listen. Answer the questions.

1 Who are the people in the picture? Write the names.

2 Where is Wilton from?

5 ▶ 64 Listen to Part 2. Answer the questions.

1 How long does it take from Peru to the UK?

2 Is Wilton tired?

3 What food or drink does Wilton want?

4 What else does he need?

DEVELOPING CONVERSATIONS

Asking for help in conversation

When you don't hear a word

Sorry? **Can you say that again?**

When you don't know a word

How do you say batería *(in English)?*

6 ▶ 65 Listen to a conversation.

1 What's the woman's question?

2 What's the man's answer?

7 ▶ 66 Listen again. Then work in pairs. Practise the questions in the box. Use your own words.

8 Listen to the questions your teacher asks. Use the phrases from the box.

T: *What do you do?*

S: *Sorry, can you say that again?*

T: *Do you have a towel?*

S: *Sorry, can you say that again?*

9 Ask other students in your class. *How do you say [English word] in your language?* Use words from Exercise 1. Do the words sound the same or very different?

10 Work in groups. Think of three more things you take on holiday.

GRAMMAR

a and any

		towel?
	a	pen?
Do you have		towels?
Do you need		other clothes?
Do you want	***any***	money?
		toothpaste?
	anything (else)?	
	a	charger.
I don't have		other clothes.
I don't need	***any***	milk.
I don't want		
	anything (else).	

11 Say things from Exercise 1 you *don't* take on holiday. Why?

I don't take any towels on holiday. The hotel has towels.

I don't take a dictionary. I have one on my phone!

12 Complete the sentences with *a* or *any*.

1 A: Do you need _____ dictionary?

B: No, thanks. I understand the word.

2 A: Do you have _____ money? I only have euros.

B: Yes. How much do you need?

3 A: It's very cold here. Do you have _____ other clothes?

B: Yes. I have a big coat.

4 A: Do you need _____ towel?

B: No, it's OK. I have one.

5 A: Do you want _____ food?

B: Yes, please. I'm hungry.

6 A: Do you have _____ brothers or sisters?

B: Yes. One brother and three sisters.

13 ▶ 67 Listen and check.

14 Work in groups. Ask and answer six questions with *Do you have/want/need* .... Use words from Exercise 1.

 For more practice, see Exercise 1 on page 120.

SPEAKING

15 **Student A:** you are a student like Wilton. Write three questions on paper to ask your host.

Do you have a towel?

Student B: you are a host like Janet. Write three questions on paper to ask your student.

Do you want to have a shower?

16 Give your questions to your partner. Write answers to your partner's questions.

A: *Do you have a towel?*

B: *Of course. Wait here.*

A: *Do you need to have a shower?*

B: *No. I'm OK now. Later.*

17 Have conversations. Use your questions and answers.

A: *Hello. Are you ...?*

B: *Yes.*

A: *Hi. Nice to meet you! I'm ....*

B: *Hello .... Nice to meet you, too.*

A: *Come in. Leave your bag there.*

B: *OK.*

A: *...*

PRONUNCIATION AND REVIEW

18 ▶ 68 Listen to the sentences. They are fast. Write the number.

How's the weather? _____

How's your class? _____

It's not very expensive. _____

It's not very nice. It's very cold. _____

Do you have any brothers or sisters? _____

Do you have a pen? ___1___

Do you want to go shopping? _____

I don't have a lot of free time. _____

19 ▶ 69 Listen and check the answers. They are slow then fast.

20 Practise saying the sentences.

21 Work in pairs. In one minute, say:

• adjectives

• things you have

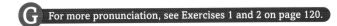 For more pronunciation, see Exercises 1 and 2 on page 120.

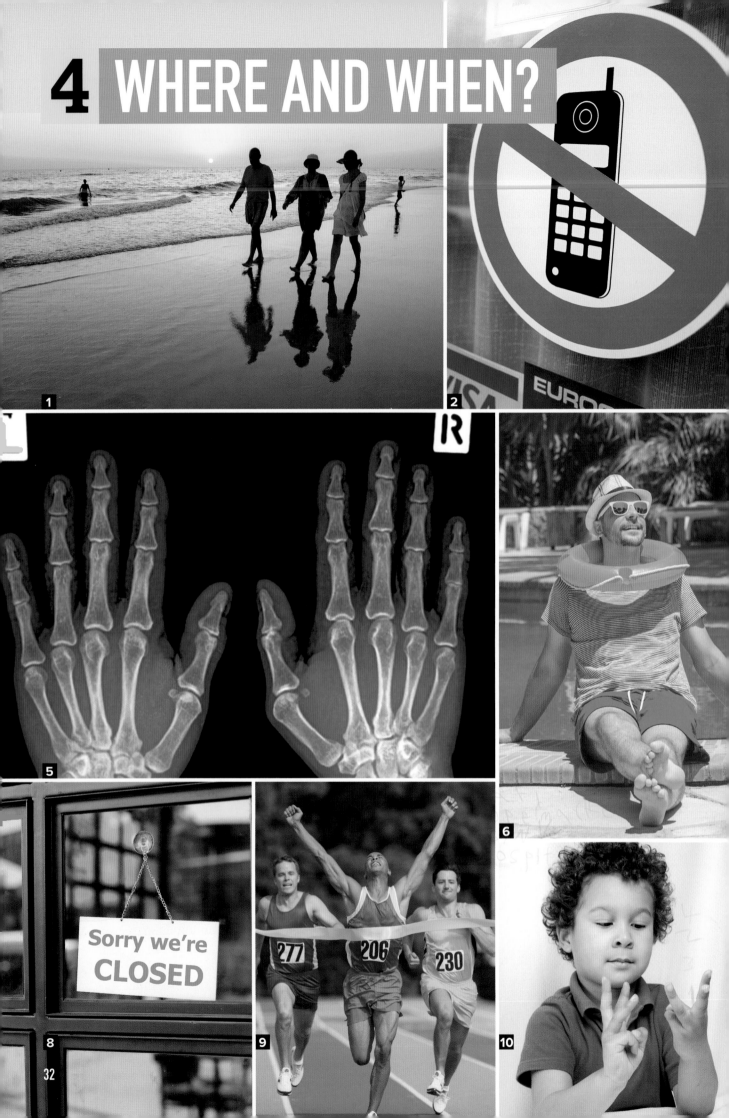

1

2 VISA EURO

5 R

6

8

Sorry we're **CLOSED**

9 277 206 230

10

3

IN THIS UNIT YOU LEARN HOW TO:

- ask about places and say what's there
- understand simple directions
- talk about your week
- ask for help / ask to do things in class

WORDS FOR UNIT 4

4

1 Look at the words and photos.

1 a **walk** on the **beach**	7 in the **train sta**tion
2 **turn off** your **phone**	8 it's **not o**pen
3 **get up ear**ly	9 **first** (1st), **se**cond (2nd) and **third** (3rd)
4 **see** a **film**	10 how m**any**?
5 **left** and **right**	11 **cash** ma**chines**
6 sit **next** to the **pool**	12 a **church** at **night**

2 ▶ **70** Listen and repeat the words.

3 Work in pairs. Don't look at the words.

Student A: say the number.

Student B: say the words.

7

self-servic

11

12

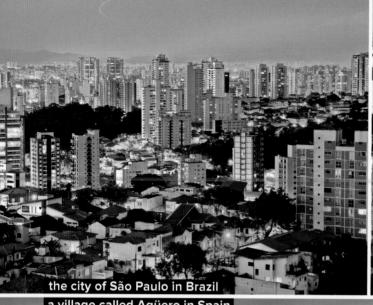

the city of São Paulo in Brazil

a town called Ludlow in the UK

a village called Agüero in Spain

IS THERE A BANK NEAR HERE?

VOCABULARY Places

1 Look at the three photos of places. Which places do you like / don't you like? Are they good places to live / go for a holiday?

2 Tick (✓) the words you know. Compare in pairs.

a **bank**	a **cinema**	a **park**
a **café**	a **clothes** shop	a **rest**aurant
a **car** park	a **hospital**	a **supermarket**
a **cash ma**chine	a **ho**tel	a **swim**ming pool
a **church**	a **market**	the **train sta**tion

3 ▶ 71 Listen and repeat.

4 What places in Exercise 2 are usually:
a in a village?
b in a town?   *is heer o*

5 ▶ 72 Listen to four questions. Write the places.
1 Is there a *café* near here?
2 Is there a *supermarket* near here?
3 Is there a *BANK* near here?
4 Is there a *hospital* near here?

6 ▶ 73 Listen and match the answers (a–d) with questions (1–4) from Exercise 5.

a Sorry. I don't know. I don't live here.   *4*
b Yes. There's one next to the train station.   *2*
c Yes. There's a Santander bank on this road. Down there. On the right.   *3*
d Yes. There's one on this road. Down there. On the left.   *1*

GRAMMAR

Is there ... ? There's ...

A: **Is there** a supermarket near here?

B: **There's** one next to the train station.

A: **Is there** a bank near here?

B: **There's** a Santander bank on this road.

A: **Is there** a bank near here?

B: No, **there isn't** (one).

7 Work in pairs. Try to remember the conversations in Exercise 6. Ask and answer the questions.

8 Work in pairs. Find five different things in the two pictures. Ask questions.

Student A: look at File 6 on page 145.

Student B: look at File 7 on page 146.

A: *Is there a bank?*

B: *Yes. Is there a cash machine?*

A: *No.*

G For more about prepositions, see page 120 and do exercises 1 and 2 on page 121.

WRITING

9 Write five sentences about the different things.

*There's a hotel in Picture A, **but** there isn't one in Picture B.*

*There's a man in Picture A, **but** there's a woman in Picture B.*

LISTENING

10 ▶ **74** Listen. Where do they want to go?

1 The woman needs a _____.

2 The man wants to go to a _____ called Gema.

3 The woman wants a _____.

11 ▶ **74** Listen again. Choose the correct word(s).

1 The cash machine is:

　a *100 / 200* metres down the road.

　b *in / next to* the supermarket.

　c on the *left / right*.

2 The pizza restaurant called Gema is:

　a on *this / the next* road.

　b the *first / second* restaurant.

　c on the *left / right*.

3 The car park is on London Road.

　a London Road is the *first / second* road.

　b She needs to go *left / right*.

　c The car park is on the *left / right*.

12 ▶ **74** Listen again and read the conversations on page 152 to check your answers.

13 Work in pairs. Practise the conversations from Exercise 12.

DEVELOPING CONVERSATIONS

called

We use *called* to say the names of things and places.

*Do you know a restaurant **called** Gema?*

*On Long Street, there's a bookshop **called** Bradley's.*

*There's a nice clothes shop **called** Looking Good.*

14 Complete the phrases with the names of places you know.

　a restaurant called _____

　a clothes shop called _____

　a bookshop called _____

　a hotel called _____

　a village called _____

　a town called _____

　a _____ called _____

15 Work in pairs. Use your ideas from Exercise 14. Have conversations like this.

A: *Do you know a restaurant called Gema?*

B: *Yes, I like it.*

A: *Do you know a restaurant called Gema?*

B: *No. Where is it?*

A: *It's on Peter's Road.*

B: *Is it far? / Is it nice? / Is it expensive?*

CONVERSATION PRACTICE

16 Think about the town or city you are in now. Write:

　• three questions with *Is there ... near here?*

　• one question with *Do you know ...?*

17 Work in groups. Ask and answer the questions.

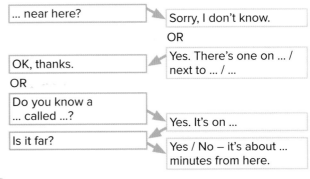

▶ **75** For more practice, listen to another two examples.

WHEN ARE YOU FREE?

REVIEW AND SPEAKING

1 Choose two.

- Look at the photos on pages 32 and 33. Test each other.
- Ask about: a cash machine, a supermarket, a swimming pool, a restaurant.
- Find out where people in the class work. What places from Exercise 2 on page 34 do they work in?

A: *What do you do?*   A: *What do you do?*

B: *I'm a teacher.*   B: *I work in a hospital.*

A: *Where do you work?*   A: *Where is it?*

B: *A school in Al Aln.*   B: *In Festival Street.*

VOCABULARY Days and times of day

2 ▶ **76** **Listen and repeat the days of the week.**

| **Mon**day | **Wednes**day | **Fri**day | **Sun**day |
| **Tues**day | **Thurs**day | **Sat**urday | |

3 Complete 1–10 with a day or a time.

1 To**day**: _____

2 Tomorrow: _____

3 Yes**ter**day: _____

4 Morning is from _____ to_____.

5 After**noon** is from _____ to _____.

6 Eve**ning** is from _____ to _____.

7 **Night** is from _____ to _____.

8 I have my English class on _____. It's from _____ to _____.

9 The bank is always **closed** on _____.

10 Supermarkets normally o**pen** at _____ in the morning.

4 Work in pairs. Discuss your ideas.

5 Write three days and times you are free.

Monday morning

Wednesday evening

Saturday afternoon

6 Ask people in the class when they are free. Find two people who are free at the same time as you.

A: *Are you free on Monday morning?*

B: *No, sorry. I'm busy. Are you free on Saturday afternoon?*

A: *Yes.*

B: *Great. Me too.*

GRAMMAR

Adverbs of frequency

	Mon	Tue	Wed	Thur	Fri	Sat	Sun
*I **always** go swimming in the morning.*	X	X	X	X	X	X	X
*I **normally** go swimming in the morning.*	X	X		X		X	X
*I **usually** go swimming in the morning.*	X	X		X		X	X
*I **sometimes** go swimming in the morning.*			X			X	
*I **never** go swimming in the morning.*							

7 Work in pairs. Ask and answer the questions.
- What days do you work / go to class?
- What days are you normally free?
- What time do you start work/classes?
- What time do you normally go to bed?
- What time do you usually get up?

G For more practice, see Exercises 1 and 2 on page 121.

READING

8 Read about weekends in different countries. Which place is the same as your country?

9 Look at the words in red. Guess what they mean. Check in a dictionary.

▶ 77

THE END OF THE WORKING WEEK

Different countries have different weekends. The days depend on the religion and traditions of the country.

In Saudi Arabia, the weekend is usually Friday and Saturday, but some companies only have Friday for their weekend. In Indonesia, people normally only have a free day on Sunday.

In Colombia, people usually work 48 hours a week and lots of people only have Sunday free.

In Italy, people work 40 hours a week. A lot of people have Saturday and Sunday free, but children usually go to school on Saturday morning.

In Russia, Sunday is always a free day. Government offices are always open on Saturday and closed on Sunday and Monday. Other people are usually free on Saturday and Sunday.

People relax in Colombia.

10 Read again. Which sentences are true?

1 Weekends are always two days.

2 Saudi Arabia and Indonesia have the same weekend.

3 People in Colombia work a lot of hours and have a short weekend.

4 Children in Italy normally go to school from Monday to Saturday.

5 In Russia, offices are never open on Saturdays.

SPEAKING

11 Work in groups. Discuss the questions.
- What's the normal working week and weekend in your country?
- How many hours do people usually work? 40? More? Less?
- What is *your* working week – what days and how many hours?
- How many free days do *you* have a year?

12 Say how often you do these things at the weekend. When do you do them?
- go shopping for clothes / go shopping for food
- go to the beach / go to the pool
- go to a supermarket / go to a market
- go to church / go to mosque
- go to a village / go to another town or city
- get up early / get up late
- watch a film / watch football
- study English / study for university

I sometimes go shopping for clothes on Saturday afternoon.

I always go to the beach on Friday morning.

I never go to the market at the weekend.

People go to mosque in Indonesia.

Government offices in Russia

CAN YOU HELP ME?

SPEAKING

1 ▶ **78** Listen to the questions.

CLASS QUIZ

1 What time does the class start?

2 How long is the class?

3 What's the name or number of your classroom?

4 What floor is your classroom on?

5 Do you have a break? How long is it?

6 What's the name of your book?

7 Do you know the names of all the students in the class?

8 What's the first name of the teacher? And the family name of the teacher?

9 Who is the youngest person in the class?

10 Do you need to do homework? One hour a week? More? Less?

11 Is there anywhere to get a coffee in the school?

12 Can you have food or drink in the class?

2 Work in groups. Discuss the questions. Can you answer all the questions?

GRAMMAR

Can ...?

A: **Can** we have food or drink in the class?
B: *Sorry, you can't.*
A: **Can** I use your pen?
B: *Sure.*
A: **Can** you do Exercise 3 on page 121 for homework?
B: *OK.*

 G For practice, see Exercises 1–3 on page 121–122.

3 Look at some questions people ask in an English class. Who asks questions 1–7? Write *T* (teacher) or *S* (student).

1 Can we have a break? *S*
2 Can we have five more minutes?
3 Can we have drinks in the class?
4 Can you close the window?
5 Can you do exercises six and seven?
6 Can you help me?
7 Can you wait a minute?

4 ▶ **79** Listen and repeat the questions from Exercise 3.

5 Work in pairs. Take turns.

Student A: ask the questions from Exercise 3.

Student B: give an answer.

A: *Can we have a break?*

B: *Sure/OK.*

6 Read these parts of five conversations. Complete them with the questions from Exercise 3.

1 Student: It's difficult. _____?
Teacher: Sure.

2 Student: _____? I'm cold.
Teacher: Is everybody else cold?

3 Student A: Do you want to go and have a coffee?
Student B: Sure. _____? I need to go to the toilet.

4 Student: I can't come to class on Thursday.
Teacher: OK. _____?

5a Student: We're tired. _____?

5b Student: _____?
Teacher: Sorry. You can't.
Student: OK. _____? We don't have time to drink our coffee.

7 ▶ **80** Listen to the full conversations and check.

38

VOCABULARY Classroom verbs

8 Match the phrases (1–8) with the pictures (a–h).

1 turn on the light   5 play it again
2 sit at the front   6 leave early
3 come in   7 write it on the board
4 use your tablet   8 share your book

9 Look at the situations (1–6). Write questions with *Can you* or *Can I* and phrases from Exercise 8.

1 I can't see the board. _____
2 I don't have my book. _____
3 Sorry, I'm late. _____
4 I don't feel well. _____
5 I don't know this word. _____
6 I don't understand. _____

10 Write more questions with *Can you* or *Can I* that:
• you ask the teacher
• the teacher asks you
• you ask another student

11 Work in pairs. Ask and answer your questions.

PRONUNCIATION AND REVIEW

12 ▶ **81** Listen to the sentences. They are fast. Write the number.

Is there a hospital near here?   _____
It's down this road on the right.   _____
It's at the end of this road on the left. _____
There's one on the third floor.   _____
Do you know a town called Atrani?   __1__
I normally work late on Mondays.   _____
Are you free tomorrow night?   _____
There's one near here. The first road
on the right.   _____

13 ▶ **82** Listen and check the answers. They are slow then fast.

14 Work in pairs. Practise the sentences.

15 Work in pairs. In one minute, say:
• days of the week and times of day.
• places in towns and cities.

 For more pronunciation, see Exercise 1 on page 122.

VIDEO 2

MORNING

1 Work in pairs. Answer the questions.
- Do you like mornings?
- Do you usually feel tired? Happy? Hungry? Good or bad?

2 ▶️**2** Watch the first part of the video (0:00–0:56). Tick (✓) the countries you hear.

Japan	●	Argentina	
America	🇺🇸	Italy	🇮🇹
Turkey	☪️	Brazil	🔷
Vietnam	★	Poland	
China		South Africa	▷

3 Read the sentences from Part 2 of the video. Which country or person do you think each sentence is about?

1 He has an important job in a bank.

A: The man from Argentina?

B: No, the man from Turkey. Nice clothes.

A: Oh, yes.

2 Paolo is her first child. _____

3 Children usually go to school on their own. _____

4 The building is a new block of flats. _____

5 He goes to the park every morning. _____

6 She sells flowers in the street. _____

7 The school gives the students breakfast for free. _____

4 ▶️**2** Watch the full video and check.

5 Work in pairs. Complete the sentences with the numbers.

1st	7.30	8	50	$490
5	200	10	73	13 million

a This is Maiko. She's _____. She gets up at 6. It takes _____ minutes to get to school.

b Paolo is her _____ child. He often wakes up at _____.

c In America, _____ children don't have breakfast.

d This is Serhat. He starts work at _____.

e This is Yang. He's _____. He goes to the park every morning.

f She has _____ flowers on her bike – or more!

g This is Diego. He starts work at _____. He gets _____ a month.

6 ▶️**2** Watch the video again and check.

SPEAKING

7 Work in groups. Ask and answer the questions. Use a dictionary if you need to.
- What time do you get up?
- What do you have for breakfast?
- Do children sometimes have breakfast at school in your country?
- Do you do exercise in the morning?
- What time do you start work/school/university?
- What things do people sell in the street in your town?

REVIEW 2

1 Choose the correct word(s).

1 Do you have *any* / *a* money?

2 *I don't* / *I'm not* well. I want to go home.

3 Can *you* / *we* help me? This is difficult.

4 I *sometimes* / *never* go to the cinema. I don't like it.

5 *Do you have* / *Have you* a pen?

6 *Is there* / *There is* a hospital in your town?

7 This bus *don't* / *not* / *doesn't* go to my area.

8 How long *it takes* / *does it take* / *it does take*?

2 Rewrite the sentences as negatives (–) or questions (?).

1 You have a mobile. (?)

2 There's a supermarket near here. (?)

3 They're French. (–)

4 It takes a long time. (–)

5 You need to do it today. (?)

6 She likes coffee. (–)

3 Complete the questions with *Can I* or *Can you*.

1 _____ use your pen?

2 _____ help me?

3 _____ do exercises 4 and 5 for homework?

4 I can't see the board. _____ sit at the front?

5 _____ wait a minute? I'm busy.

6 _____ help you?

4 Put the adverbs in the best place in the sentences.

1 Is the restaurant busy on Saturday night? (usually)

2 What time do you get up? (normally)

3 I go to the beach. I can't swim. (never)

4 I get up late on Sundays. (always)

5 I don't go out in the week. (normally)

6 I get the bus to work, but I get a taxi. (usually, sometimes)

5 ▶ 83 Listen and complete the sentences with one word in each space. Contractions (*I'm*, *don't*, etc.) are one word.

1 _____ she _____ _____ brothers or sisters?

2 I _____ _____ shopping _____ _____ _____ near here.

3 _____ _____ in my class at school.

4 Do you need _____ _____?

5 _____ _____ car park on the left.

6 ▶ 83 Work in pairs. Compare your answers. Listen again to check.

7 Match the verbs in the box with the correct groups of words (1–8).

get	share	take	use
go	sit	turn off	want

1 _____ your phone / the light

2 _____ a shower / a photo

3 _____ more free time / a new car

4 _____ next to the pool / at the front

5 _____ books / my food with you

6 _____ married / a coffee

7 _____ shopping / on holiday

8 _____ a dictionary / your tablets

8 Put the words into three groups: places, things or days / times of the day.

afternoon	charger	hotel	tomorrow
bag	church	map	toothpaste
bank	cinema	market	yesterday
brush	evening	Saturday	

9 Replace the words in italics with their opposites from the box.

busy	early	hot	morning
closed	good	left	new

1 The supermarket's *open*.

The supermarket's closed.

2 I'm *free* on Monday.

3 It's very *cold*.

4 I get up *late* on Sundays.

5 I go there every *evening*.

6 It's a *bad* film.

7 It's on the *right*.

8 They're my *old* shoes.

10 Complete the sentences with these adjectives.

difficult	hungry	married	tired
great	long	small	well

1 I'm _____ and I have two children.

2 Are you _____? Do you want a sandwich?

3 I like my flat, but it's very _____.

4 My homework is very _____. I can't do it.

5 Can I leave early? I'm not very _____.

6 I take the train to work. It usually takes a _____ time.

7 I'm _____. I need to have a break.

8 It's a _____ film. I love it.

5 GOING PLACES

3

6

IN THIS UNIT YOU LEARN HOW TO:

- talk about good places to go
- say how to get to places
- talk about journeys
- buy train tickets
- ask about and say your plans
- say where and when to meet

WORDS FOR UNIT 5

1 Look at the words and photos.

1 go **out** in the **eve**ning	7 the **main square**
2 **vi**sit a mus**eu**m	8 **wait** on the **plat**form
3 **use** the **ti**cket ma**chine**	9 a **bus stop**
4 **pay** by **card**	10 What **time's** the **flight**?
5 the **Old** Town	11 **sleep well**
6 **stay** at **home**	12 **play foot**ball

2 ▶ 84 Listen and repeat the words.

3 Work in pairs. Don't look at the words.

Student A: say the number.

Student B: say the words.

7

12

GOOD PLACES TO GO

Visitors look at packets of food in the noodle museum in Yokohama, Japan.

SPEAKING

1 Work in pairs. Where do you go to:

- buy new clothes? *a clothes shop, a market*
- go out in the evening? *an area called Vestebro*
- get some money?
- have something to eat?
- have a walk?
- go swimming?
- sit and have a coffee?
- see some interesting art?
- see a film?

2 Choose four activities from Exercise 1. Say where you usually do these things.

I normally sit and have a coffee in a café called Music and Beans. It's near my house.

I usually get some money from a cash machine near my office.

LISTENING

3 ▶ 85 Listen to five conversations. Match conversations 1–5 with places a–e.

Conversation 1	a a pool or a beach
Conversation 2	b a good museum
Conversation 3	c a cinema or the main square
Conversation 4	d an area called Cihangir
Conversation 5	e a street called Szeroka

4 ▶ 85 Listen again. Why do they want to go to each place? Choose an activity from Exercise 1.

5 ▶ 85 Listen again. Write the short words.

1 Are there any good shops _____ here?

2 There's a pool _____ this road. Or there's a beach _____ thirty minutes from here.

3 Not _____ the village. People go _____ the town. There are some nice places _____ the main square.

4 Try Ariel. It's _____ a street called Szeroka. _____ Kazimierz.

5 There's a good museum _____ the centre. It's _____ the station.

DEVELOPING CONVERSATIONS

> ### best
> We often use *best* to talk about one thing that is very good.
> *What's the **best** restaurant?*
> *Where's the **best** place to go?*
> *It's **best** to take a bus.*

6 Work in groups. Think about your town/city. What's the best:

1 restaurant?	3 area?	5 hotel?
2 museum?	4 park?	6 market?

GRAMMAR

> ### Are there ... ? / There are ...
> A: **Are there** any good shops near here?
> B: Yes. **There are** lots of nice places in Cihangir.
>
> A: **Are there** any places to go out in the evening here?
> B: Yes. **There are** some good places on South Street.

7 Choose the correct word(s).

1 A: I want to have a coffee. *Is there / Are there* a nice café near here?

  B: Yes. *There's / There are* four or five different places in Nova Street.

2 A: I want to have something to eat. *Is there / Are there* any good restaurants near here?

  B: Yes. Try Via Garibaldi. *There's / There are* some nice places there.

3 A: I need to get some money. Is there *a / any* bank near here?

  B: Yes, *there's / there are* one down this road.

4 A: I want to visit some places. Are there *a / any* interesting places near here?

  B: Well, *there's / there are* a museum in the Old Town. Lots of people go there.

8 ▶ 86 Listen to the sentences. They are fast then slow.

1 Are there any good shops near here?

2 Are there any nice places to eat?

3 Are there any markets in town?

4 There are some nice cafés in the main square.

5 There are lots of good places to go.

6 There are normally a lot of people there.

G For more practice, see Exercises 1–3 on page 122.

9 Work in pairs. Practise the sentences.

VOCABULARY Getting there

10 Match the phrases (1–8) with the pictures (a–h).

1 get off   5 walk to work

2 get a taxi   6 change trains

3 go home   7 wait for the bus

4 take the metro   8 take the red line

WRITING

11 Write true sentences about you and where you live. Use the ideas here. Change the words in red.

The metro in my town is very cheap.

I usually take the train to work.

I usually wait about ten minutes for the train.

To get to my house, take the metro. It's the blue line. Get off at *Rocafort*.

I never walk to the shops.

I sometimes get a taxi to go home.

CONVERSATION PRACTICE

12 ▶ 87 Listen to the complete conversations from Exercise 3. Answer the questions.

	How do you get there?	How long does it take?
1	walk	
2		30 minutes
3		
4		
5		

13 Work in pairs. You are in your partner's home. Write three questions to ask about places.

I want to buy some clothes. **Are there any good** *shops near here?*

14 Student A: give your questions to your partner.

Student B: think of answers and directions.

15 Have conversations. Take turns.

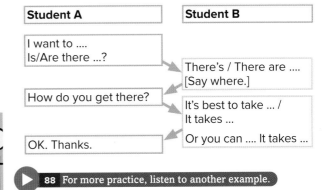

Student A

I want to ....
Is/Are there ...?

How do you get there?

OK. Thanks.

Student B

There's / There are ....
[Say where.]

It's best to take ... /
It takes ...

Or you can .... It takes ...

▶ 88 For more practice, listen to another example.

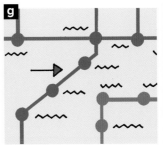

HAVE A GOOD TRIP!

REVIEW AND SPEAKING

1 Write two nouns next to each verb. Work in groups. Compare.

1 take _____   4 wait for _____

2 get off _____   5 buy _____

3 visit _____

2 Ask other students the questions. Add one more question.

How do you normally get here / to school / to work?

How long does it take?

READING

3 Read the first line of the text. Do you think trains are best? Why? / Why not?

4 Read about train travel. Match paragraphs 1–3 with photos a–c.

5 Match sentences a–c with paragraphs 1–3.

a A train journey can be a holiday.

b There are some beautiful stations.

c You can get great views from a train.

▶ 89

WHY I LOVE TRAIN TRAVEL

Planes are fast, buses are cheap, but trains are the best. Here are three reasons:

1 This is Grand Central in New York. It is more than 100 years old. It has 44 platforms and 750,000 people use the station every day.

2 You can sit and see the world outside. Sometimes you can see beautiful mountains or the sea. This is the train from Fort William to Mallaig in Scotland. This line is in the Harry Potter films. It takes 80 minutes and a single ticket only costs £7.50 ($10).

3 Some train journeys take a long time and you sleep on the train. You can travel for four days in Kyushu, Japan on the private Seven Star train. There are only 28 passengers. They can sit and talk and have dinner together. You can get off and visit some interesting places. It costs $14,000 for four nights. Or you can have a cheap holiday on the train from Moscow to Vladivostok in the east of Russia. It takes six days and seventeen hours. That's a lot of time to make friends and it only costs $160 in third class!

a

b

c

6 Read again. Answer the questions.

1 Where is Grand Central?

2 Where is Fort William?

3 Where is the Seven Star Train?

4 Which journey is very expensive?

5 Which journey is very long?

7 Look at the words in red. Guess what they mean. Check in a dictionary.

8 Work in pairs. Do you want to visit Grand Central or go on each train journey? Why? / Why not?

VOCABULARY Buying tickets

9 ▶ 90 Listen and repeat the words and phrases. Tick (✓) the words you know.

cash	a ma**chine**	re**turn**
change trains	the **next** train	**se**cond **class**
enter your **num**ber	**pay** by **card**	**sin**gle
first class	a re**ceipt**	a **ti**cket

10 Complete the conversation between an assistant (A) and a tourist (T). Use one word from the box in each space.

A: Do you want to buy a ¹_____?

T: Er ... yes.

A: You can use the ²_____ over here. You can pay by cash or ³_____ and you don't need to wait.

T: Oh, OK. Is the machine in German?

A: Yes, but I can help you. Come with me.

T: OK.

A: Where are you going?

T: Lausanne.

A: ⁴_____ or return?

T: Return.

A: For now, right?

T: Yes. And back on Monday.

A: Yes, fine. ⁵_____ class? Second class?

T: Second class is fine.

A: OK. Do you want a receipt?

T: Yes, please.

A: Put your card in here and enter your ⁶_____.

T: OK.

A: And here are your tickets and ⁷_____.

T: When's the ⁸_____ train?

A: 9.47. From platform 8.

T: Sorry. Which platform?

A: 8 – at 9.47.

T: OK. Thank you for your help.

A: You're welcome. Have a good day.

11 ▶ 91 Listen and check.

12 Work in pairs. Practise the conversation in Exercise 10.

DEVELOPING CONVERSATIONS

Where are you going?

A: *Where are you going?*

T: *Lausanne.*

A: *Single or return?*

A: *Is this the stop for the 98 bus?*

B: *Yes. Where are you going?*

A: *The museum.*

13 Think of the town or city you are in now. Write down five places you want to go to.

14 Work in pairs. Take turns. Have conversations like this.

A: *Where are you going?*

B: *The City museum.*

A: *You need to take the 73 bus. / You can walk there.*

SPEAKING

15 Work in pairs. Practise the conversation in Exercise 10 two more times. Take turns to start.

First time: Change the information in red.

Second time: Change the information in blue.

GOOD PLAN!

LISTENING

1 What do you normally do:
- after your class?
- after work?
- on holiday?

2 ▶ 92 Listen to three conversations about plans. Write the number of the conversations (1, 2 and 3) next to who is talking (a or b).

a friends at a hotel in the evening _____

b friends at the end of a class _____

3 ▶ 93 Listen to the sentences. Repeat them.

a I need some money. _____

b I need to study. _____

c I need to eat something. _____

d I'm going home. _____

e I'm going to bed. _____

f I'm going to have a coffee. _1_

g I'm going to meet a friend. _____

h I'm going to stay here. _____

4 ▶ 92 Listen to the conversations from Exercise 2 again. Write the number of the conversation next to each sentence (a–h) in Exercise 3.

5 In which conversations are the two people going to do:

a the same thing?   b different things?

GRAMMAR

Talking about plans: *I'm/We're going ...*

Plan	Where / What	When
I'm going *We're going*	*home* *to the gym* *to the cinema*	*now.* *this afternoon.* *at six.*
I'm going *We're going*	*to have a coffee* *to meet a friend* *to see a film* *to play football*	*tonight.* *tomorrow.* *on Saturday.* *after the class.*

6 Put the words in the correct order.

1 tonight / I'm going / to meet my brother

2 we're going / this afternoon / to the park

3 to the beach / we're going / on Sunday

4 now / to have a coffee / I'm going

5 tomorrow night / we're going / to have a party

6 I'm going / tomorrow morning / to the pool / with some friends

7 ▶ 94 Listen and check.

8 Work in pairs. Use the ideas from Exercise 6. Invite your partner.

A: *I'm going to meet my brother tonight. Do you want to come?*

B: *Sorry, I can't.* or B: *OK. Great!*

9 Write more plans. Use a dictionary if you need to.

_____ after the class.

_____ tonight.

_____ tomorrow.

_____ on Saturday.

_____ next week.

10 Work in groups. Say your plans.

11 Tell the class who is going to do the same thing.

We're all going for a coffee after the class!

Aslim *and I* are going to the park on Saturday.

 For more practice, see Exercises 1–4 on page 123.

GRAMMAR

Asking about plans: *going* and *doing*

	Are you **going**?
What time Where	**are** you **going**?
What	**are** you **doing** after the class? **are** you **doing** tonight?

12 Write the questions.

1 A: I'm going to the beach on Saturday. Do you want to come?

B: _____?

A: Five or six in the afternoon.

2 A: I'm going to have a walk later.

B: _____?

A: Around the Old Town.

3 A: _____ tonight?

B: I'm going to see a film. Do you want to come?

A: Sorry. I can't. I need to study.

4 A: _____ to Dieter's party tomorrow?

B: Yes. _____?

A: Yes. Do you want to share a taxi?

13 ▶ 95 Listen and repeat the questions in the Grammar box.

 For more practice, see Exercises 1 and 2 on page 123.

14 Work in pairs. Ask about plans from Exercise 9. Ask questions to know more.

DEVELOPING CONVERSATIONS

I'll meet you

We use *I'll meet you* to say where and when to meet.

I'll meet you here in ten minutes.

I'll meet you outside.

I'll meet you here at 6.

I'll meet you at the airport

15 ▶ 96 Listen. Choose the correct word(s).

1 I'll meet you at *the restaurant / the hotel*.

2 I'll meet you at *the airport / the station*.

3 I'll meet you *at the bus stop / outside* at six.

4 I'll meet you *here / there* in ten minutes.

5 I'll meet you here at *three / five* o'clock.

16 Say the sentences from Exercise 15 and answer.

A: *I'll meet you at the bus stop at six.*

B: *OK* or B: *Can we meet at six thirty?*

17 Ask other students about their plans. Invite someone to do something.

Student A	Student B
What are you doing [when]?	
	I'm going ... Do you want to come?
[Question]	
	[Answer]
OK.	
	Great. I'll meet you ...
Great.	

PRONUNCIATION AND REVIEW

18 ▶ 97 Listen to the sentences. They are fast. Write the number.

How do you get there? _____

What time are you going? _____

When's the next train? _____

Where are you going? _____

We need to get off at the next stop. _____

We need to change at Red Square. _____

I'll meet you at six. _____

I'm going to meet a friend. *1*

19 ▶ 98 Listen and check the answers. They are slow then fast.

20 Practise the sentences.

21 Work in pairs. In one minute, say:

• words for buying tickets and travelling by train

• things you are going to do next weekend

 For more pronunciation, see Exercise 1 on page 124.

6 AWAY FROM HOME

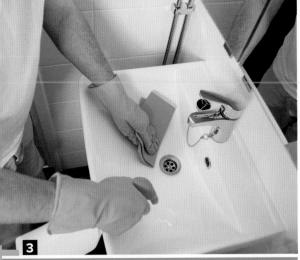

3

5

8

IN THIS UNIT YOU LEARN HOW TO:

- say there's a problem
- say *don't worry* and *that's OK*
- ask how something was
- check in to a hotel
- talk about your stay
- ask what people did

WORDS FOR UNIT 6

1   Look at the words and photos.

1 on the **top floor**	8 a lot of **traffic**
2 **keys**	9 make a **boo**king
3 **clean** the **bath**room	10 make **din**ner
4 **play mu**sic	11 **stay** in a **hos**tel
5 **right** and **wrong**	12 **what's** the **WiFi pass**word?
6 do **ex**ercise	13 a **busy street**
7 **take** the **lift**	14 **mo**dern **art**

2   ▶ **99** Listen and repeat the words.

3   Work in pairs. Don't look at the words.

Student A: say the number.

Student B: say the words.

9

10

14

a Rain on holiday

b People wait for their late flight.

HOW WAS YOUR FLIGHT?

VOCABULARY Problems

1 Look at the photos (a–d). Say if each is a big problem or a small problem.

2 ▶ **100** Listen and repeat the words. Tick (✓) the words you know.

late	**no**-one	**pro**blem	tir**ed**
noise	**no**where	rain	wrong

 For more about pronouns like *no-one* and *nowhere*, see page 140.

3 Complete 1–8 with the words from Exercise 2.

1 I have a _____ at work. I need to work late.

2 I can't sleep. There's a lot of _____ outside my room.

3 The weather's very bad. There's a lot of _____.

4 The flight is two hours _____. We need to wait in the airport.

5 We need help, but there's _____ here.

6 There are a lot of people here. There's _____ to sit.

7 I'm going to bed early. I'm very _____.

8 We're going the _____ way. This isn't the right train!

4 ▶ **101** Listen and check.

5 Look at Exercise 3 again. Choose one problem you often have, one problem you sometimes have and one problem you never have.

I need to work late: I often have this problem.

LISTENING

6 ▶ **102** Dana meets Bryan at the airport. Choose the correct word(s), then listen and check.

A: Bryan. Great to see you!

B: Hi, Dana. ¹*How / Who* are you?

A: Great.

B: Sorry ²*we're / I'm* late. There was a problem in London.

A: Don't worry. It was on the airport website.

B: Oh, good.

A: How was the flight?

B: ³ *Very / Not very* good. The weather was bad.

A: Oh, I'm sorry. Are you tired?

B: Yeah. Where are ⁴*you / we* going now?

A: To the hotel and then we can have something to eat.

B: Oh, sorry. I had dinner on the plane. ⁵*I'm / I'm not* hungry.

A: That's OK. ⁶*Do / Are* you want to stay in the hotel?

B: Is that OK? I did a lot yesterday and I went to bed late.

A: Of course! We ⁷*can / are* go out tomorrow.

B: Great. Thanks.

GRAMMAR

Past simple: common irregular verbs

Present	Past	
is	**was**	There **was** a problem in London.
are	**were**	We **were** late.
have/has	**had**	I **had** dinner on the plane.
go/goes	**went**	I **went** to bed late.
do/does	**did**	I **did** a lot yesterday.

7 ▶ **103** Listen and repeat the past forms in the box.

8 Work in pairs. Look at the verb list on page 138. Practise the conversation from Exercise 6.

9 Complete the sentences with *did, had, was, were, or went.*

1 A: How was your day?

B: Bad. I _____ a lot of problems at work.

2 A: How was your day?

B: Good. I _____ a lot of work.

3 A: How was your flight?

B: Bad. It _____ four hours late!

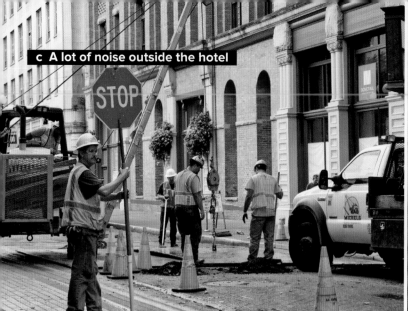

c A lot of noise outside the hotel

d Tired after a busy day

4 A: How was your journey?

B: Bad. We _____ the wrong way. There was a lot of traffic.

5 A: How was your holiday?

B: Great. We _____ very good weather. We _____ to the beach every day.

6 A: How was your hotel?

B: Great. The rooms _____ very nice.

7 A: I _____ shopping yesterday.

B: How was it?

A: OK. It was busy.

8 A: I _____ a party last weekend. I was 25.

B: How was it?

A: Great. All my friends were there.

10 Complete each sentence in two ways.

I went to _____ yesterday / last night.

I had _____ yesterday / last night.

11 Tell your partner your sentences. Your partner asks *How was it?*

A: *I went to the cinema yesterday.*

B: *How was it?*

A: *Good.*

G For more practice, see Exercises 1 and 2 on page 124.

DEVELOPING CONVERSATIONS

Don't worry / That's OK

A: *Sorry, I'm late! There was a problem in London.*

B: **Don't worry**! I know.

A: *Sorry. I'm not hungry.*

B: **That's OK**.

12 Put the words in brackets in the correct order to make a second sentence.

1 Sorry I'm late. (had / at work / I / a problem)

2 Sorry I'm late. (the wrong place / went to / I)

3 Sorry I'm late. (on the bus / was / there / a problem)

13 Take turns to say the sentences from Exercise 12. Reply with *don't worry* or *that's OK*.

14 ▶ **104** Listen and complete the sentences.

1 Sorry I _____ come to class on Monday.

2 Sorry. I _____ have any money.

3 Sorry. I _____ very early!

4 Sorry the room _____ very big.

5 Sorry. I _____ know the answer.

15 Complete your own sentences.

Sorry I'm late. _____.

Sorry I'm late. I had a problem at home.

Sorry. _____.

Sorry. I don't have my book.

16 Work in pairs. Say your sentences from Exercise 15 to different students. Reply.

CONVERSATION PRACTICE

17 Write an answer to the questions. Use a dictionary if you need to.

• How was your journey/flight?

• How was your day?

• How was your holiday?

18 Work in pairs. Have conversations like this.

Student A	Student B
Hi. How are you?	
	[Answer] And you?
[Answer]. Sorry I'm late.	
	[Answer].
How was _____?	
	[Answer] How was _____?
[Answer]	

▶ **105** For more practice, listen to another example.

WE LOVED IT

REVIEW AND SPEAKING

1 Test each other on the words on page 51.

2 Ask and answer six *How* questions.

How are you?	How was the last class?
How's work?	How was your weekend?
How do you get here?	How was your day yesterday?

VOCABULARY Hotels and checking in

3 Complete the sentences with these words.

ad**dress**	**break**fast	**lift**	**pass**word
bags	check **out**	**num**ber	**rooms**
booking	**key**	**pass**port	

1 Good evening. Do you have any _____ for tonight?

2 Hi. We have a _____. My name's Kim Jae-Sung.

3 Can I have your _____, please?

4 Can you write your name and _____ here? And sign here?

5 Do you need help with your _____?

6 Here's your key. Your room _____ is 351.

7 What time do we need to _____?

8 I'm sorry there's no _____. The stairs are over there.

9 What time is _____ in the morning?

10 What's the _____ for the WiFi?

4 ▶ **106** Listen and check your answers.

5 ▶ **107** Listen to someone checking in. Tick (✓) the sentences in Exercise 3 you hear.

6 ▶ **107** Listen again. What's the problem (a, b or c)?

a The restaurant is closed.

b He needs to pay for breakfast.

c They don't have his booking.

7 Work in pairs. Practise the conversation.

A: Hi.

B: Hello. How can I help you?

A: We have a booking. My name's [Name].

B: OK. Yes. Can I have your passport?

A: Sure.

B: Can you write your name and address here? And sign here?

A: Here? OK.

B: Here's your key. Your room number is [Number].

8 Work in a new pair. Practise the conversation again, then continue the conversation. Use one or two questions from Exercise 3.

READING AND GRAMMAR

9 Is each sentence (1–6) about a hotel or a hostel?

1 There were eight beds in each room.

2 We shared a bathroom.

3 It had four stars. It was $190 a night.

4 I talked to the other people in my room.

5 There was a swimming pool on the top floor.

6 We stayed in the best place in the city centre.

10 Look at the Grammar box on page 55. Notice how we form the regular past simple forms. Follow the rule to complete the other two sentences in the box.

Regular past simple endings

Present	Past	
stay(s)	stay**ed**	We **stayed** in the best place.
talk(s)	talk**ed**	He **talked** to us.
rain(s)	_____	It _____ a lot.
share(s)	shar**ed**	We **shared** a bathroom.
love(s)	_____	I _____ it.

G For more practice, see Exercises 1 and 2 on page 125.

11 Read about the three places in Costa Rica. Which do you like best?

12 Read again. Match sentences a–c with the three places in the text.

   a The weather wasn't very good one day.

   b There wasn't any noise.

   c There were lots of people and it wasn't expensive.

13 Look at the words in red. Guess what they mean. Check in a dictionary.

14 Work in groups. Answer the questions.

   • Do you want to go to Costa Rica? Why? / Why not?

   • What places do you want to go to: in your country? in a different country?

GRAMMAR

Past simple negatives

Positive	Negative
There **were** a lot of people.	There **weren't** a lot of people.
The weather **was** good.	The weather **wasn't** good.
It **had** a restaurant.	It **didn't have** a restaurant.
We **saw** a lot.	We **didn't see** a lot.

15 Make the sentences negative.

   1 It was a nice place.

   2 We had a car.

   3 We visited San José.

   4 There were a lot of hotels.

   5 There was a lot of noise.

   6 It rained.

G For more practice, see Exercises 1 and 2 on page 125.

WRITING

16 Write about a place you went to on holiday. Change the words in red. Add two more sentences with your own ideas.

I went to Cairo. I stayed there for five days.

I stayed in a hotel called the Safary.

It's near the centre.

It was cheap but nice.

The weather wasn't good. It was very hot.

A forest and beach in Nosara

Arenal volcano and lake near Fortuna

▶ 108

A HOLIDAY IN
COSTA RICA

Tell us about your stay in Costa Rica.

SELINA HOSTEL $9/night   4/5

I stayed in San José for six days. The hostel was good. It's near the city centre and the modern art museum. I shared a room with nine other people. The room was clean and the other people were nice to talk to. The café in the hostel was OK and sometimes there was a band.

TIERRA MAGNÍFICA $365/night   5/5

We went to Nosara last December. We stayed in this small five-star place. It's in a forest, but you can see the beach from the hotel. There weren't a lot of people. It was quiet. The service and the food were great. We loved it.

HOTEL REGINA $38/night   4/5

This great place is in the centre of Fortuna and we had a view of the Arenal Volcano from our room. We didn't have dinner in the hotel. There was a nice restaurant in the same street. One day, we did a tour of the volcano. It rained and we didn't see a lot. Another day we went swimming in a lake. It was beautiful.

WHAT DID YOU DO?

People dance in the streets of Buenos Aires in Argentina.

SPEAKING

1 Work in pairs. Say:
- the time of the day you like best: morning, afternoon, evening or night.
- one thing you usually do at each time of day and one thing you never do.
- the meal you like best: breakfast, lunch or dinner.
- one thing you usually have and one thing you always have for each meal.

LISTENING

2 ▶ 109 Lucy and Dom are in a hostel. Listen to the first part of their conversation. Choose the correct word(s).
1 It's the *morning* / *evening*.
2 They talk about their *breakfast* / *dinner*.
3 They talk about what Lucy did *during the day* / *last night*.

3 ▶ 110 Listen to the first and second parts of the conversation. Put Lucy (L) or Dom (D) next to sentences 1–8.
1 I went to bed late. _____
2 I went to bed early. _____
3 I didn't eat a lot for breakfast. _____
4 I didn't go out. _____
5 I walked round the Old Town. _____
6 I talked to some people after dinner. _____
7 I danced a lot. _____
8 I didn't feel well. _____

4 ▶ 111 Listen to the third part of the conversation. What are they doing today?
a They are going shopping after breakfast.
b They are going to the modern art museum together.
c Dom is going to the modern art museum and Lucy is going to the beach.

5 Work in pairs. Discuss the questions. When you are on holiday:
- do you talk to other people? Who? Where? When?
- do you usually stay in a hostel or a hotel? In the city or near the beach?
- do you like: walks in the Old Town? / dancing? / modern art? / other museums?

6 ▶ 112 Listen to the questions from the conversation. Complete each question with one word.
1 _____ I sit here?
2 How _____ your breakfast?
3 What did you _____?
4 How _____ you? Did you sleep well?
5 What _____ you do?
6 _____ did you go?
7 _____ was it?
8 _____ it busy?
9 And you? What did you _____ last night?
10 _____ you OK now?
11 So, what _____ you doing today?
12 _____ you want to go together?
13 When are you _____?
14 _____ time is it now?

GRAMMAR

Past simple questions

What		do (last night / yesterday)?
		have (for breakfast/dinner)?
Where	**did you**	go?
What time		go to bed?
		get here?
	Did you	sleep well?
		go out (last night)?
How **was** it?		
Was it busy?		
Were you tired?		

7 ▶ **113** Learn to say these questions. Listen and repeat what you hear.

What did you do last night?

What did you do yesterday?

8 Ask different people in the class the two questions from Exercise 7.

9 Who in the class did one of these things?

• went to work/classes
• stayed at home
• went out
• went shopping
• did some exercise/sport
• met a friend / some friends
• watched TV

Ⓖ For more practice, see Exercises 1–4 on page 125.

10 Complete the conversations about yesterday. Make questions with *did you or do you*.

1 A: I went shopping.
  B: _____ (What / buy?)

2 A: I went to work.
  B: _____ (Where / work?)

3 A: I went out.
  B: _____ (Where / go?)

4 A: I went to my classes at the university.
  B: _____ (What / study?)

5 A: I went to the beach.
  B: _____ (stay there all day?)

6 A: I stayed at home.
  B: _____ (What / do?)

7 A: I watched TV.
  B: _____ (What / see?)

8 A: I went to the gym.
  B: _____ (go every day?)

11 ▶ **114** Listen and check your answers.

12 Work in pairs. Take turns to start conversations from Exercise 10. Add answers to the questions.

1 A: *I went shopping.*
  B: *What did you buy?*
  A: *Some clothes.*

13 Think of your answers to these questions.

• What did you do yesterday? last weekend?
• What did you do on your last holiday?

14 Ask and answer the questions from Exercise 13. Ask other questions to get more information.

A: *What did you do yesterday?*
B: *I went to work.*
A: *What do you do?*

PRONUNCIATION AND REVIEW

15 ▶ **115** Listen to the sentences. They are fast. Write the missing word.

1 How was your _____?
2 I had a very busy _____.
3 We stayed in a _____.
4 We had a great view of the _____.
5 What's the password for the _____?
6 What did you do last _____?
7 I met some _____.
8 I went to the _____.

16 Work in pairs. Say the sentences from Exercise 15, but change the last word.

17 Try to remember the answers in Exercise 6.

18 Work in pairs. In one minute say:

• past verbs
• words about problems

Ⓖ For more revision and pronunciation, see Exercises 1–4 on page 126.

VIDEO 3

ANCIENT LAND

A very big library

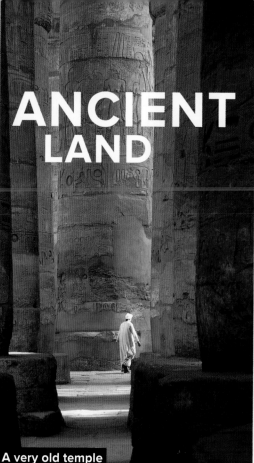

A very old temple

A great museum

1 **Look at the photos. Discuss the questions.**
- Do you know a country where you can see all these things?
- Do you know the place well?
- What else can you see there?

2 **▣ 3 Watch the video. Complete the table with the words.**

| Alexandria | cafés | great art | mosques |
| beach | Cairo | Luxor | pyramids |

City	Famous sight	Other things to see
	the museum	
	the library	
	the temple	

3 **▣ 3 Watch the video again. Are these sentences true (T) or false (F)? Correct the false ones.**
1 Around twelve million people live in Cairo.
2 You can see Pharaoh Tutankhamun at the Egyptian Museum.
3 There are seventeen pyramids in Egypt.
4 The pyramids at Saqqara are five thousand years old.

5 It takes four hours by train to get to Alexandria from Cairo.
6 The library has books in Arabic, French and German.
7 Luxor is in the north of the country.
8 Before it was called Thebes and it was the capital of Egypt.

4 **Match the verbs (1–6) with the words and phrases (a–f) to make phrases from the video.**

1 see   a on the beach
2 rent   b big temples
3 take   c great art
4 relax   d the sun go down
5 build   e a boat
6 create   f three hours to get there

5 **▣ 3 Watch the video again to check your answers.**

SPEAKING

6 **Work in pairs. Discuss the questions.**
- Do you want to visit Egypt?
- What are the three best towns or cities to visit in your country?
- What can you see and do in each place?

REVIEW 3

1 Choose the correct word(s).

1 *Is / Are* there any good places to eat near here?

2 There *is / are* a nice Italian restaurant in the main square.

3 *Did / Were* you go out last night?

4 What *you are doing / are you doing* after class?

5 I went to Denmark. The weather *wasn't / weren't / didn't* good.

6 It wasn't busy. There *weren't / wasn't / didn't* a lot of people there.

7 *There are / There is / Have* lots of good shops in this area.

8 I'm going *play / for to play / to play* football this afternoon.

2 Complete the text with the past simple of the verbs.

Last year I ¹_____ (go) on holiday to Tunisia. It ²_____ (be) great. We ³_____ (stay) in a small village near the beach. Our rooms ⁴_____ (be) very nice and there ⁵_____ (not / be) a lot of noise. There ⁶_____ (not / be) a lot of people there. Every evening we ⁷_____ (have) dinner in a very nice restaurant and it ⁸_____ (not / rain) for a week. We ⁹_____ (talk) to lots of very nice people. I ¹⁰_____ (love) it. I want to go again.

3 Write questions to complete the conversations. Use the words in brackets.

1 A: _____? (where / you / go)

   B: Home. I'm tired. I need to sleep.

2 A: _____ after class? (what / you / do)

   B: I'm going to meet a friend. We're going to see a film.

3 A: Kenzo is going to have a party on Friday.

   B: I know. _____? (you / go)

   A: Yes, I am.

4 A: _____ last night? (what / you / do)

   B: We went out. It was fun. I didn't sleep a lot!

   A: _____? (where / you / go)

   B: We went to see a band. They were great.

4 ▶ 116 Listen and complete the sentences.

1 _____ _____ _____ to the museum yesterday?

2 I'm _____ _____ _____ some friends this afternoon.

3 _____ _____ _____ good places to eat in Kalamaki.

4 _____ _____ _____ you _____ to bed last night?

5 We _____ good weather on Saturday. We _____ _____ the beach.

5 ▶ 116 Work in pairs. Compare your answers. Listen again to check.

6 Match the verbs in the box with the correct groups of words (1–8).

get	have	play	stay
go	need	see	take

1 _____ a film / some interesting art

2 _____ the blue line / the lift

3 _____ at home / in a hostel

4 _____ a walk / a party

5 _____ to bed late / swimming

6 _____ a taxi / a great view

7 _____ football / some music

8 _____ to study tonight / some more money

7 Put the words into three groups: buying tickets, hotels or problems.

a lot of rain	nowhere to sit	return
a lot of traffic	passport	second class
check out	password	single
key	platform	the wrong way

8 Complete the text with these words.

change	get off	long	take
costs	line	metro	wait

I usually ¹_____ the train to work. The ²_____ here is expensive, but it's good. I usually ³_____ three or four minutes for my train. I take the red ⁴_____ and then I ⁵_____ trains at Holborn. I ⁶_____ at Green Park. It doesn't take ⁷_____ – about thirty minutes most days – and it ⁸_____ about £150 a month.

9 Complete the sentences with these verbs.

clean	enter	sleep	walk
do	pay	visit	write

1 Is it far? Can we _____ there?

2 Is there a park near here? I want to _____ some exercise.

3 Here's the machine. Can you _____ your number, please?

4 Can you _____ your name and address here, please?

5 We're going to _____ the museum in the Old Town this afternoon.

6 I'm sorry. There's a problem with the bathroom. Can you _____ it, please?

7 Can I _____ by card?

8 Good morning. Did you _____ well?

1

2

5

6

7

10

11

SALE SALE SALE SALE SALE SALE
SALE
SALE
50% OFF
SALE
SALE SALE
SALE SALE

12

IN THIS UNIT YOU LEARN HOW TO:

- talk about activities you like
- say what you like doing or prefer
- talk about books, TV and music
- talk about people and things from other countries
- talk about clothes you want to buy
- ask and give opinions

WORDS FOR UNIT 7

1 Look at the words and photos.

1 **go** to a **con**cert	8 **read** a **sto**ry
2 **take** an e**xam**	9 **sell** ma**ga**zines
3 **sports**	10 her **fa**vourite **toy**
4 a **long dress**	11 **half price**
5 a **bas**ketball **play**er	12 an **I**talian **dish**
6 **give** someone a **pre**sent	13 **sing** a **song**
7 **try on** a **ja**cket	14 a **team**

2 ▶ 117 Listen and repeat the words.

3 Work in pairs. Don't look at the words.

Student A: say the number.

Student B: say the words.

4

8

9

13

14

I LOVE GOING OUT

SPEAKING

1 Work in pairs. What is the past form of the verbs in the box?

cook	go out	read something
do some exercise	go shopping	watch football
go on the internet	listen to music	watch TV

2 ▶ **118** Listen and check.

3 Work in pairs. Say which activities in the box you did. Check the verb table on page 138 if you need to.

* last night • yesterday • last weekend

I read something in the newspaper last night.

I went shopping last weekend.

VOCABULARY Words for activities

4 Match each group of words (1–9) with an activity from Exercise 1.

1 a favourite writer / stories / a magazine
   <u>read something</u>

2 a singer / a band / a song
   _____

3 Italian food / a favourite dish / make cakes
   _____

4 go running / play basketball / go to the gym
   _____

5 a game / my team / a great player
   _____

6 go to concerts / go dancing / go to the cinema
   _____

7 try on some clothes / buy something / like the design
   _____

8 a series / the news / a programme about art
   _____

9 look at Facebook / a website / watch videos
   _____

5 Complete the conversations with words from Exercise 4. Use one word in each space.

1 A: I love reading.
   B: Do you have a favourite _____?
   A: Yes. Arturo Pérez-Reverte. I love his books. They're great _____.

2 A: I like K-pop.
   B: Me too. My favourite _____ is Chungha.
   A: Yeah, she's OK. Her _____ 'Why don't you know' is good.

3 A: What do you normally cook?
   B: I make a lot of Mexican _____. My best _____ is tamales. It's very good!

4 A: Do you go out a lot?
   B: Yes. I love music. I go to a lot of _____ and I often _____ dancing at the weekend.

5 A: What did you do last night?
   B: I watched TV. I watched the _____ and then there was a great _____ about modern art.

6: A: I love football.
   B: Me too. Did you watch the _____ last night?
   A: Yes. I love Leroy Sané. He's a great _____.

6 Work in pairs. Ask and answer questions. Do you have a favourite:

* song? • team?
* band? • website?
* series? • shop?
* player?

GRAMMAR

like + -ing

I	like		
We	love	reading.	
They	don't like	listening to music.	
She/He	likes	doing exercise.	
My son	loves	watching football.	
Dan	doesn't like		
	Do you **like**	playing football?	Yes.
		cooking?	It's OK.
		reading?	Not really.

Remember we can also use *like* + noun. See page 20.

7 Tick the sentences that are right (✓). Change the sentences that are wrong.

1 I don't like coffee. ✓
2 Do you like walk? ✗ *Do you like walking?*
3 I love play football.
4 My daughter loves sport.
5 I love cooking.
6 Do you like drive?
7 Do you like your job?
8 My husband doesn't like go to the gym, but I love it.

8 Write six questions with *Do you like ...-ing?* Use a dictionary if you need to.

9 Work in groups. Take turns to ask and answer your questions.

 **G** For more practice, see Exercises 1–3 on page 127.

LISTENING

10 ▶ **119** Listen to the start of three conversations. What did each woman do last night?

1 _____
2 _____
3 _____

11 ▶ **120** Listen to the three conversations. Choose the correct information about the woman in each conversation.

Conversation 1

a She likes *cooking / going out* for dinner.
b She doesn't have a favourite dish, but she likes *Russian / Mexican* food.

Conversation 2

a She likes watching *the news / programmes about art*.
b She likes the series called *WarGames / The Crown*.

Conversation 3

a She plays basketball and she sometimes goes *running / swimming*.
b Her favourite team is *Real Madrid / Atlético Madrid*.

DEVELOPING CONVERSATIONS

Me too and I prefer

Me too means I like or do the same thing as you.

I prefer means I like a different thing more.

A: *I love cooking.*
B: **Me too**. *What do you cook?*

A: *I like Real Madrid.*
B: **I prefer** *Atlético Madrid.*

A: *Do you like playing sport?*
B: *I love it, but* **I prefer** *watching it.*

12 Complete the replies with *Me too* or *I prefer* ... .

1 I like Rihanna.
   _____. I love her songs.
2 I look at Facebook a lot.
   _____ Snapchat.
3 I go out a lot.
   _____ staying at home.
4 I love going shopping.
   _____. Where do you normally go?
5 My favourite food is Chinese.
   I like Chinese food, too, but _____ Mexican.

13 Work in pairs. Say the sentences in Exercise 12. Give true answers with *Me too* or *I prefer*.

CONVERSATION PRACTICE

14 Write what you did last night on a piece of paper. Give it to your partner.

15 Read what your partner did. Complete two or more of these questions to ask your partner.

Do you like ...?   Do you have a favourite ...?
Do you ... a lot?   What do you normally ...?

16 Have conversations like this.

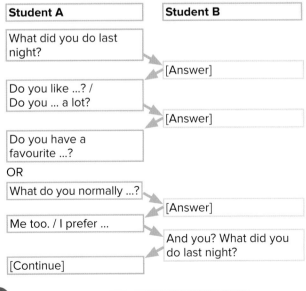

▶ **121** For more practice, listen to another example.

WHAT ARE YOU READING?

REVIEW AND SPEAKING

1 Work in pairs.

1 Say an activity (*cooking*). Your partner says three words to talk about the activity (*cook, food, dish*). Take turns.

2 Write something you:

- did last week.
- you normally do at the weekend.
- you are going to do next week / next month.

Take turns to tell your partner. Ask one or more questions about it.

LISTENING

2 ▶ **122** Listen. Match the conversations (1–4) with the pictures (a–d).

3 ▶ **122** Listen again. Tick (✓) the sentences that are true for the man in each conversation.

Conversation 1	a	I'm reading a magazine. ✗
	b	I read a lot.
Conversation 2	a	The band are very good.
	b	I usually listen to Spanish music.
Conversation 3	a	I'm watching a film.
	b	It's not very good.
Conversation 4	a	I'm studying.
	b	I have an important meeting tomorrow.

4 ▶ **122** Listen again and read the conversations on page 156 to check your answers.

GRAMMAR

Present continuous (*I'm* and *are you ...?*)

We use present continuous for activities **now** or **at the moment** (and not with *every day, always, usually,* etc.)

What	**are you**	do**ing**? read**ing**? watch**ing**? mak**ing**?	
	Are you	read**ing**	anything good at the moment?
	I'm **I am**	do**ing** watch**ing**	some work. TV.

5 Complete the questions. Use the present continuous form of the verbs.

1 A: What _____?   (you / listen to)

   B: Nicky Jam. Do you know him?

2 A: _____ a great series at the moment.   (I / watch)

   B: Oh yes? What's it called?

3 A: What _____?   (you / do)

   B: Nothing much. _____ at Facebook.   (I / look)

4 A: _____ dinner?   (you / make)

   B: Yes.

   A: What _____?   (you / cook)

   B: A vegetarian dish called ragu.

6 Work in pairs. Student A: look at File 4 on page 145.

Student A: act one of the activities. Don't say anything.

Student B: ask *What are you doing / reading / listening to / making,* etc.?

Student A: answer.

7 Student B: look at File 10 on page 147. Change roles and repeat Exercise 6.

G For more practice, see Exercises 1–3 on page 127.

VOCABULARY Country adjectives

*I'm listening to a **French** band called Superbus.*

 French = from France

*I listen to a lot of Bra**z**ilian music.*

 Brazilian = from Brazil.

8 ▶ **123** Listen and repeat the adjectives in the questions.

1 Do you know any Japa**nese** writers?

2 Do you know any Am**er**ican bands?

3 Do you know any **Bri**tish singers?

4 Do you know any Chi**nese** companies?

5 Do you know any **Spa**nish actors?

6 Do you know any E**gyp**tian cities?

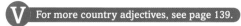

9 Work in groups. How many of the questions from Exercise 8 can you answer?

10 Write five similar questions with *Do you know…?* to test other groups in the class. (You need to know an answer!)

V For more country adjectives, see page 139.

11 Ask your questions. Which group gets the most points?

READING

12 Read what four people think about books. Match sentences 1–4 with the four people in the text.

1 I'm learning to read. _____

2 I prefer to read about real life. _____

3 I read when my teacher gives me a book, but I don't like it. _____

4 I'm reading two different books at the moment. _____

13 Find the name of three books in the text. Then answer the questions.

1 Do the people think they are good books?

2 Do you know the books? Do you like them?

14 Complete the sentences with one of the words in red. There are two you don't need.

1 I sometimes read books about politics or about _____ people.

2 At the _____, I'm reading a famous French book called *The Stranger* by Albert Camus.

3 At school, we read a book _____ *Matilda*. It was my favourite book. It's a story _____ a girl who loves reading.

4 It's a _____ good book, but it's very _____. It's about a man who's in prison.

SPEAKING

15 Work in groups. Discuss the questions.

• Do you read a lot?

• Are you reading anything at the moment? What? Is it good?

• What books did you read at school? Did you like them?

WRITING

16 Write three or four sentences about you and what you read or watch on TV.

I watch TV a lot.

I normally watch series.

At the moment, I'm watching an old series called *Orange is the New Black*. It's about some women in prison. It's really good.

My favourite programme is *Black Mirror*.

▶ **124**

ARE YOU A BIG READER?

CAMILA, ARGENTINA

I don't really like reading, but we need to read some books for school. At the moment, we're reading a famous book called *The Mad Toy*. It's by an Argentinian writer. I don't really like it. It's sad.

ZEYNEP, TURKEY

I love reading. I normally finish one book a week or more. I sometimes read two or three books at the same time. At the moment, I'm reading a book called *Three Daughters of Eve* by Elif Şafak. It's a story about a woman from Istanbul and her two friends. It's great – maybe her best book. Elif Şafak is my favourite writer. I'm also reading a book about the government. It's OK.

DON, NEW ZEALAND

I don't read books and stories very much. I usually read the news or read magazines. I sometimes read books about business or politics, but I'm not reading anything at the moment.

DARREN, UK

I had a lot of problems at school and after school. I'm now in prison. I can't read very well, but I'm having lessons. My teacher is very good. I sometimes read and listen to stories at the same time. It helps me. At the moment, I'm reading and listening to *Animal Farm* by George Orwell. It's a really good story. I really like it.

a jumper

a shirt

a T-shirt

a top

a skirt

a hat

trainers

socks

trousers

THIS ONE LOOKS GOOD

SPEAKING

1 Work in groups. Discuss the questions.

- Do you like shopping?
- How often do you go shopping? Where do you go?
- How often do you buy things online (on the internet)?
- How often do you buy these things? Do you buy them online or in a shop?

| clothes for me | food for the week | shoes |
| clothes for the family | presents for my friends and family | |

VOCABULARY Buying clothes

2 ▶ 125 Listen and repeat the words.

12	the de**sign**	**jeans**
25% (**twe**nty-five per**cent**) **off**	a **dress**	**long**
	extra **large**	**looks good**
38	**feels com**fortable	**small**
blue	**green**	a **T-shirt**
brown	**half price**	**white**
a **coat**	a **jacket**	**ye**llow

3 Put the words and phrases from Exercise 2 in the right list.

| Colour | Size | Clothes | Reason to buy |
| black | large | shoes | cheap |

4 Add one more word to each list. Then in groups, compare the words you added.

5 How many of the words from Exercise 2 can you see in photos a and b?

6 For you, are these very important or not very important when you buy clothes:

- the price?
- how they look?
- how they feel?
- the designer or shop?

V For more colours, see page 139.

LISTENING

7 ▶ 126 Listen to three conversations in a shop. Match two of them with photos a and b.

a

b

8 ▶ 126 Listen again. Which conversation (1, 2 or 3) are these sentences from? Write the number.

a What do you think of the blue and red one? _____

b They look nice, but they feel a bit small. _____

c I'm not sure about the colour. _____

d Do you have these in 44? _____

e How much is it? _____

f I'm just looking. _____

GRAMMAR

this/these, one/ones

Singular	Plural
Can I try **this** (one)?	Can I try **these** (ones)?
This looks good.	**These** look good.
This top **is** nice.	**These** shoes **are** nice.
The blue **one** looks good.	The red **ones** are best.
I prefer the green **one**.	I prefer the brown **ones**.

9 **Look at the Grammar box. Choose the correct word(s) in 1–8.**

1 A: What do you think of *this / these* jeans?

  B: They're a bit big.

2 A: *This / These* feels a bit small. What size is it?

  B: Medium. Try this *one / ones*. It's a large.

3 A: What do you think of this *shirt / shirts*?

  B: I don't like the colour. I prefer the green *this / one*.

4 A: What do you think?

  B: They're really comfortable. I prefer *this / these* ones. The other *these / ones* didn't feel good.

5 A: I like this T-shirt. What do you think?

  B: It's OK, but I prefer *the blue one / this blue*.

6 A: What do you think of these *shoe / shoes*? They're half price!

  B: I don't really like them. I don't like the design.

7 A: Are there any toilets?

  B: There's one on *this / one* floor for women and the men's *one / ones* is on the top floor.

8 A: Do you sell children's clothes here?

  B: Not in *this / these* shop, but the *one / ones* in Soroya Street sells them.

For more practice, see Exercise 1 on page 128.

DEVELOPING CONVERSATIONS

Opinions

Asking what people think.

What do you think (of the top)?

Saying what you think.

😊 It's **really** nice. **I really like** the colour.

😐 It's OK, **but I'm not sure about** the design.
It's OK, **but** it's **a bit** small.

☹ **I don't really like** it. I don't like the colour.

10 **Complete the sentences with bold words from the box. Use one word in each space.**

1 A: What do you _____ of these jeans?

  B: They're OK, but they're a _____ big.

2 A: What do you think _____ this shirt?

  B: It's nice. I really like the colour.

3 A: What do you think?

  B: I don't _____ like it. Sorry! I prefer the red one.

4 A: What do you think?

  B: It's OK. I like the design, but I'm not _____ about the colour. Do they have it in blue?

11 **Work in pairs. Discuss what you think of the clothes on page 66.**

12 **Change partners. You are in a shop. Use your ideas from Exercise 11 to have conversations like these.**

Student A	Student B
What do you think (of this/these)?	[Answer] How much is it / are they?
[Say a price]	That's good / OK / a bit expensive.
What do you think of the (size/design/colour)?	[Answer.] Try it/them and see.

13 **Say which clothes from page 66 you are going to buy.**

PRONUNCIATION AND REVIEW

14 ▶ **127** **Listen to the sentences. They are fast. Write the missing word or words.**

1 Do you like _____?

2 Did you watch _____ last night?

3 I'm _____ a lot at the moment.

4 It's a really good Japanese _____.

5 What are you _____?

6 What do you think of _____?

7 They are my favourite _____.

8 What do you normally _____?

15 **Work in pairs. Say the sentences from Exercise 14 but change one word.**

16 **Do the Conversation practice on page 63 again.**

17 **Work in pairs. In one minute say:**

• country adjectives   • colours   • clothes

For more revision and pronunciation, see Exercises 1–3 on page 128.

3

IN THIS UNIT YOU LEARN HOW TO:

- talk about what people are doing
- explain why someone isn't there
- talk about houses and rooms
- ask about things you can't find
- talk about working at home

WORDS FOR UNIT 8

1 **Look at the words and photos.**

1	**car**pets	8	**leave** my **keys** in the **park**
2	it's not **wor**king	9	**chairs**
3	**draw** a **pic**ture	10	**lost**
4	**wear gla**sses	11	**leave** the **di**shes in the **sink**
5	**law**	12	I can't re**mem**ber
6	they **look si**milar	13	an old **fac**tory
7	**look** in the **fridge**	14	work **hard**

5

2 ▶ **128** **Listen and repeat the words.**

3 **Work in pairs. Don't look at the words.**

Student A: say the number.

Student B: say the words.

Friendly, white with one brown spot.
Answers to Harvey. Call 744-555-0129.
REWARD if found and returned.

8

9

10

14

WHERE IS EVERYONE?

VOCABULARY Collocations

Collocations are words that usually go together. In English, *take* goes together with *the bus*, *a photo* or *a break*. In your language, maybe you can use the same verb with these three nouns, or maybe you can't. Different languages often have different collocations.

1 Match the verbs in the box with the words and phrases 1–7.

get   make   meet   study   ~~take~~   travel   work

1 __take__ an exam / __take__ a friend to the airport / __take__ a coat with me

2 _____ hard / _____ in a factory / _____ at home.

3 _____ Law at university / _____ hard / _____ for an exam

4 _____ to Japan / _____ a long way / _____ a lot for work

5 _____ a lot of money / _____ a list / _____ something to eat

6 _____ a client / _____ someone / _____ in a café

7 _____ a coffee / a new job / something to eat

2 ▶ **129** Listen to the seven sentences. Tick (✓) the collocations you hear from Exercise 1.

3 Work in pairs. Make one more collocation with each verb in the box from Exercise 1.

4 Use collocations from Exercise 1 to make true sentences:

a about you.   b about friends.   c about your family.

5 Work in groups. Say your sentences.

I studied Law at Warsaw University. I finished in 2012.

My friend Almir travels to lots of countries. He plays in a band.

My mum's a nurse. She works hard.

LISTENING

6 ▶ **130** Listen to three conversations. Match who they talk about in conversations 1–3 with pictures a–c.

Conversation 1: Picture _____

Conversation 2: Picture _____

Conversation 3: Picture _____

7  **130** Listen again. Tick (✓) the sentences that are true. Change the sentences that are not.

Conversation 1

a They are waiting to start a meeting. ✓

b Jaime is getting a coffee and Ulla is visiting a client.
   ✗ Ulla is talking to a client

c Katya's going to be late for the meeting.

d Katya's not feeling well today.

Conversation 2

a Emma is studying Chinese at university.

b She is going to take some exams.

Conversation 3

a The father is in Dubai.

b He travels a lot for work.

8 ▶ **130** Check your answers. Listen again and read on page 157.

GRAMMAR

Present continuous: all forms
Questions
What's he studying?   *What **are** you reading?*
Is it raining?   ***Are** they waiting?*
Positive
She's working at home today.   *I'm going.*
He's travelling to Dubai today.   *They're coming.*
Negative
Her son's not feeling well.   *The machine's not working.*

9 Complete the conversations. Use the right form of the verbs in brackets.

1 A: _____*Is*_____ Nick ___*working*___ at home today? (work)

   B: No, he's not. He _____ a client in Moscow. (meet)

2 A: How's the weather there? Is it bad?

   B: Well, it _____, but it's very cold. (not / rain)

3 A: What _____ your sister _____ in Greece? (do)

   B: She _____ at a university there. She travels a lot! (teach)

4 A: _____ they _____ for lunch now? (go)

   B: Yes, but I _____ here. I need to finish this. (stay)

5 A: We can start. Ilia _____. (not / come)

   B: Oh, OK. Why?

   A: He _____ well. (not / feel)

6 A: Why _____ she _____ the bus today? She normally drives. (take)

   B: Her car has a problem.

10 ▶ **131** Listen to the sentences. They are fast then slow.

1 What's she studying?

2 What are you doing here?

3 I'm meeting a customer.

4 They're studying hard at the moment.

5 He's not working today.

6 She's not feeling well.

11 ▶ **131** Work in pairs. Practise the sentences.

G For more practice, see Exercises 1–3 on page 129.

12 Work in pairs. Practise the conversation.

A: OK. Are we ready?

B: Yes. Sure.

A: Wait a minute. Where's Ken?

B: Oh, he's not coming today. He's taking his son to the airport.

A: Ah, OK.

13 ▶ **132** Listen to the conversation. Which words are different?

14 Work in pairs. Have similar conversations. Make changes each time.

DEVELOPING CONVERSATIONS

Sending messages
A: *I'm going to call her later.*
B: *Oh, OK. **Say hello/hi.***
A: *Her son's not feeling well.*
B: *Oh, really? **Say I'm sorry.***
A: *This is from my mother.*
B: *Really? **Say thank you.***

15 Read the sentences. Choose the best message to send.

1 This money is for you – from my brother.

2 Her father is in hospital at the moment.

3 I'm going to meet James tonight.

4 My son made a cake for us.

5 I'm going to visit my parents this weekend.

6 He lost his job and he can't get a new one.

16 Work in pairs. Take turns to say the sentences in Exercise 15 and send messages.

CONVERSATION PRACTICE

17 Write the names of five friends or people in your family on a piece of paper. Give it to your partner.

18 Have conversations that start like this:

Student A	Student B

How's X?
[Answer]

What's he/she doing at the moment?
[Answer]

Ask more questions to continue.

▶ **133** For more practice, listen to another example.

I CAN'T FIND MY KEYS

REVIEW AND SPEAKING

1   Work in pairs. Choose two.

* Test each other on the words on pages 69 and 70.

* Say three more words that go with each of the verbs from page 70.

  meet my brother, meet some friends ...

* Have conversations. Start with this question. Continue it in six different ways.

  Where's Su? Is she coming with us now?

  A: *No. She's doing some work.*

  B: *Yes. She's just having a shower.*

VOCABULARY In the house

2   Which of these things can you see in the photos?

a **bed**	a **chair**	a **fridge**	a **sho**wer	a **so**fa
a **car**pet	a **cup**board	a **shelf**	a **sink**	a **ta**ble

3   ▶ **134** Listen and repeat the names of the rooms and furniture.

4   Work in pairs. Say one more thing in each room.

5   Work in pairs. Ask and answer what you think of the rooms and furniture in the photos.

A: *What do you think of the kitchen?*

B: *It's nice / It's OK. It's a bit ...*

A: *What do you think of the sofa?*

B: *I like / don't like the design. It looks ...*

6   Change partner. Discuss the questions.

* Which room in the photos do you like best? Why?

* Are any of the rooms in your home similar to these?

* What's your favourite room in *your* home? Why?

7   ▶ **135** Listen to four conversations. Complete the table.

	I can't find...	Which room?	Where in room?
1	my glasses	bathroom	
2			carpet
3	keys		
4			

8   ▶ **135** Listen again. Complete the sentences with the prepositions.

1   I saw them _____ the bathroom – _____ the sink.

2   Maybe it's _____ the shelf _____ the living room. I saw it there.

3   Oh, look. It's there. _____ the carpet _____ the bed.

4   Oh, look. There they are. _____ the sofa.

5   Maybe I left it _____ the kitchen.

6   Yes, it was _____ the table.

72

a **ki**tchen

a **bath**room

a **bed**room

a **li**ving room

9 **Work in pairs. Answer the questions.**

- Do you know the present form of the verbs in red from Exercise 8?
- Where do you usually put these things when you're not using them? Use a dictionary if you need to.

bag	keys	passport	shoes
coat	money and cards	phone	

DEVELOPING CONVERSATIONS

Maybe

We use *maybe* when we're not sure.

Maybe *it's on the shelf in the living room.*

Maybe *I left it in my bedroom.*

10 **Look at the questions. Change any words in red to make questions to ask your partner.**

1 Where did you last use your phone?

2 When did you last see your parents?

3 How far is your work from here?

4 How long does it normally take to make your dinner?

5 Where's Peter today?

6 How often do you go swimming?

11 **Work in pairs. Ask and answer the questions.**

A: *Where did you last use your phone?*

B: *I can't remember. Maybe on the bus.*

LISTENING

12 ▶ **136** **Listen to Ella and Lucian. Choose the correct word or phrase.**

1 He's looking for his *keys / glasses / phone.*

2 Maybe he left something *in a restaurant / in the kitchen / in a taxi.*

3 He's going to *visit / email / phone.*

13 ▶ **137** **Listen to the first part of Lucian's conversation with the restaurant. Put the questions (a–e) in the order you hear them (1–5).**

a Can you wait one minute? _____

b And what time were you here? _____

c How can I help you? _____

d Where did you sit? Can you remember? _____

e What colour are they? _____

14 ▶ **137** **Listen again. Write the answers to the questions from Exercise 13.**

15 ▶ **138** **Listen to the second part of the conversation. Answer the questions.**

1 Do they find them? Where?

2 What's the last problem?

16 **Write true sentences about things you lost.**

I lost my phone once. I left it on the table in a café.

I lost my passport once. I don't know how. Maybe I left it in the hotel room.

17 **Work in pairs. Talk about the things you lost. Ask and answer another question. Use one of these:**

- Did you find it?
- What did you do?
- Was it expensive?

GRAMMAR

18 **Complete the information in the Grammar box.**

Personal pronouns

Subject pronoun	Object pronoun
I left my bag on the bus.	Can you help _____?
You're late.	Can I talk to _____.
It's in the bathroom.	When did you last have _____?
_____'s nice.	I really like **him**.
_____ lives here.	I didn't see **her** there.
_____ went to the park.	He took **us** there.
They're on the table.	When did you last have _____?

19 **Choose the correct words.**

1 I can't find my ticket. Maybe I left *him / it* in the bathroom.

2 A: Hi. I'm here to get my phone.

  B: Can you see the young woman in the office? Talk to *him / her*. She has it.

3 My name's Juan Martínez. When you come to the shop, ask for *her / me*.

4 A: I can't find my new trainers.

  B: Well, where did you last have *it / them*?

5 I wasn't here yesterday. David was. He's there. You need to ask *him / her*.

6 Hello. How can I help *you / them*?

G For more practice, see Exercises 1 and 2 on page 130.

SPEAKING

20 **Work in pairs. Student A: you work in a hotel. Student B: you left something there. Take turns. Have conversations like this:**

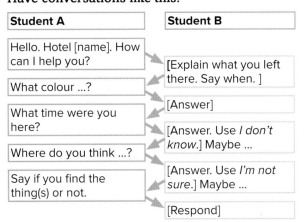

Student A	Student B
Hello. Hotel [name]. How can I help you?	
	[Explain what you left there. Say when.]
What colour ...?	
	[Answer]
What time were you here?	
	[Answer. Use *I don't know.*] Maybe ...
Where do you think ...?	
	[Answer. Use *I'm not sure.*] Maybe ...
Say if you find the thing(s) or not.	
	[Respond]

WORKING AT HOME

SPEAKING

1 **Work in pairs. Look at the photos of homeworkers. Discuss the questions.**

- Where are the people? Where are they from?
- What are they doing?
- What are their jobs?

She's in the living room. I think she's American or maybe she's British.

READING

2 **Work in pairs. Read about homeworkers together. Try to complete the text with these words and phrases.**

45%	the bathroom	the living room	travel
10%	good	make clothes	
bad	listening to music	teachers	

3 **▶ 139 Listen and check your answers.**

4 **Look at the words in red. Guess what they mean. Check in a dictionary.**

5 **Complete the sentences with the words in red from the text.**

1 I want a new flat ____________ we have two children now and we need another room.

2 7% of people don't have jobs at the moment and the number is ____________.

3 We have our own ____________. It's www.eltoutcomes.com.

4 I have a lot of clothes, but I don't have ____________ for them. I only have one cupboard in my bedroom.

5 There are 29 ____________ people in Saudi Arabia and almost ____________ the people are 25 years old or under.

6 **Work in pairs. Don't look at the text. What can you remember about these numbers?**

39 million	13%	25%
45%	13 million	36%

7 **Read again and check.**

8 **What things in the text do you think are similar or different in your country?**

▶ 139

HOMEWORKERS

Work is changing. Lots of people travel to an office or factory every day, but more people now work at home – and the number of homeworkers is growing fast. There are maybe 39 million in India and around 4.5 million in the UK. In Argentina, [1]____________ of people work at home one day a week or more.

There are two kinds of homeworkers. Some people make things. Most homeworkers in India and Cambodia [2]____________. Other people work for a company, but sometimes work at home and use the internet or phone. In Europe, there is a law that anyone can work at home for half a day a week. And homeworking is [3]____________ for companies. Stanford University studied a Chinese company called Ctrip. The homeworkers at Ctrip did 13% more work!

Other people, called freelancers, do work for lots of different clients and companies. These people are often [4]____________, website designers, or project managers. There are around 13 million freelancers in Mexico.

Most people like working at home because they don't need to [5]____________ to work, and it's good for family life, and because they can work when and how they like. 25% of UK home workers like [6]____________ when they work.

Some people think working at home is [7]____________ because you don't see anyone all day. Also, sometimes people don't have space in their home – they need to work in a café. In the UK, only 26% of home workers have an office. 36% do their work in [8]____________, 13% work in the kitchen, [9]____________ work in bed – and a few work in [10]____________!

VOCABULARY Verbs and people

9 Look at how we often make the word for a person or job. Complete the table.

Verb	Person / Job
clean	cleaner
dance	dancer
design	designer
drive	driver
manage	_____
play	_____
teach	_____
work	_____
write	_____

10 Complete 1–6 with the person and the correct form of the verb from Exercise 9.

1 My father is a ___*teacher*___ at a university. He ___*teaches*___ Business and Law.

2 My sister _____ basketball in a professional team. She is a very good _____.

3 My mum is a _____. She _____ for different magazines.

4 My brother _____ very fast. I don't like it. He is a bad _____.

5 My friend, Ashok, is _____ a website for me at the moment. He's a professional web _____.

6 My brother is a _____ in a car company. He's _____ a big project at the moment.

11 Work in pairs. Choose six words from the box. Tell your partner about someone you know who is a good/bad driver, etc. Try to say why they are good or bad.

cleaner	driver	reader	teacher
dancer	[football] player	runner	worker
designer	manager	singer	writer

READING AND SPEAKING

12 Work in pairs. Student A: read the text on this page. Student B: read the text in File 2 on page 144. Answer these questions about the person in your text.

1 What's his/her name?

2 Where does he/she live?

3 What does he/she do?

4 Where does he/she work?

5 Does he/she like it?

6 Does he/she have an office?

7 How's his/her work at the moment?

13 Work in pairs. Tell each other about your text. Use your answers to Exercise 12.

14 Work in groups. Discuss the questions.

- Do you know anyone who works at home? What do they do? Do they like it?
- Would you like to work at home? Why? / Why not?

WRITING

15 Use the questions in Exercise 12 to write a short text about someone you know. Write a sentence for each question.

PRONUNCIATION AND REVIEW

16 ▶ **140** Listen to the sentences. They are fast. Complete the sentences with two words.

1 I'm working _____ _____ this week.

2 She's travelling _____ _____ today.

3 He's in the kitchen _____ _____.

4 She's talking _____ _____.

5 I can't find _____ _____.

6 When did you last _____ _____?

7 They make a lot _____ _____.

8 He's a very _____ _____.

17 Work in pairs. Say the sentences but change the two words.

18 Work in pairs. In one minute say:

- rooms
- furniture
- jobs

G For more revision and pronunciation, see Exercises 1 and 2 on page 130.

Agata

I'm from Krakow in Poland, but ten years ago I moved to Berlin in Germany. I draw pictures for children's books. I normally work in the kitchen at home, but my husband sometimes works there, too. He's a designer. Our flat is very small. When he works at home, I go to a café and work there. It's nice.

I really like my job. I don't make a lot of money, but I have a lot of free time – and I love children.

Every Friday, I go to my son's school and tell stories to the children. It helps my work.

At the moment, I'm writing my own book and drawing all the pictures. My husband and I are going to make the book and sell it. Maybe we can make some more money and move to a new flat!

VIDEO 4

BIKE RIDING IN
UTAH

1 Work in pairs. Look at the photo. Discuss the questions:

- Do you like the photo?
- Do you think it is a good place for a holiday?
- Can you do what they're doing in the photo? Why? / Why not?

2 📹4 Watch the video. Which sentence is true for you?

1 It looks fun. I want to do this one day.

2 It looks fun, but I can't do this.

3 The place looks great, but I don't like this kind of trip.

4 It's not for me. I don't like the place, the activity – or the weather!

3 Work in pairs. Tell your partner what you think of the video.

4 Work in pairs. Put these sentences from the video in the correct order.

a We fly!

b We have a coffee.

c We're going home.

d But then suddenly – rain.

e Pretty amazing place to wake up.

f We take photos. It's beautiful.

g And the sun comes out again.

h The next day we wake up with the sun.

i We push our bikes up the mountain. Three hundred metres.

5 Decide what the words in red mean. Then check in a dictionary.

6 Match the verbs (1–6) with the words and phrases (a–f) to make phrases from the video.

1 go   a ready for the journey
2 get   b fast
3 get up   c home
4 talk about   d with the sun
5 ride down   e early
6 wake up   f what we're going to do

7 📹4 Watch the video again to check your answers.

SPEAKING

8 Which do you prefer:

- walking, cycling or driving?
- going fast or slow?
- getting up early or late?
- the city or the countryside?
- a hot place or a cold place?
- camping or a hotel?
- talking about the past or the future?

REVIEW 4

1 Choose the correct word(s).

1 I love *watch / watching* football.

2 These jeans *is / are* very small.

3 The ticket machine *don't work / isn't working* at the moment.

4 I don't like the yellow one. The white one *look / looks* better.

5 I don't like *this / these* shoes. I prefer the brown *one / ones*.

6 I can't find my keys. Can you see *they / them / it* anywhere?

7 I'm not talking to you. I'm talking to *he / him / his*.

8 He *work / is working / working* at home today.

9 *Do you read / You are reading / Are you reading* anything good at the moment?

10 What *he's studying / he studying / is he studying* at university?

2 Complete the sentences with one word in each space.

1 My boss _____ working at home today.

2 _____ she coming to the meeting today?

3 Can I try on _____ jeans, please?

4 I have a car, but I don't like _____. There's a lot of traffic.

5 These shoes _____ nice. They feel very comfortable.

6 He went home. He's _____ feeling well.

7 She's nice. I really like _____.

8 I _____ reading a great book at the moment.

3 Correct the mistake in each sentence.

1 Do it raining outside?

2 My husband don't like doing exercise.

3 I love your shoes. Where did you buy they?

4 What you are watching?

5 She's meet a client in Athens today.

6 I need some glasses. Can I try this ones, please?

7 This chicken very nice.

8 He's very nice. I really like he.

4 ▶ 141 Listen and complete the sentences.

1 I don't like the red tops. I prefer _____ blue _____.

2 _____ your father _____ in Peru?

3 I _____ _____ a great series at _____ _____.

4 My friends _____ _____ _____ to the gym, but I _____ _____.

5 When _____ you last _____ _____.? Maybe you _____ _____ at home.

5 ▶ 141 Work in pairs. Compare your answers. Listen again to check.

6 Match the verbs in the box with the correct groups of words (1–8).

go	make	study	travel
leave	meet	take	wear

1 _____ a T-shirt / glasses

2 _____ a lot for work / a long way

3 _____ a friend for dinner / a client

4 _____ my bag on the bed / the dishes in the sink

5 _____ an exam / a friend to the airport

6 _____ dancing / running

7 _____ for an exam / French at university

8 _____ a cake / a lot of money

7 Put the words into three groups: in the house, buying clothes or free-time activities.

carpet	extra large	jumper	shelf
concert	fridge	kitchen	story
cupboard	half price	programme	writer
design	jeans	series	

8 Complete the missing words. You have the first two letters.

1 I lo_____ my bag last night. Maybe I left it on the bus.

2 You can sleep on the so_____ in the living room tonight.

3 My brother is a website de_____. He makes a lot of money.

4 I like reading about po_____. I'm reading a book about the government at the moment.

5 My favourite football te_____ is Juventus.

6 My favourite basketball pl_____ is LeBron James from the Los Angeles Lakers.

7 I'm going to take an exam next week. I need to study ha_____

8 Look in the fr_____. The milk is in there.

9 It doesn't feel very comfortable. Can I try the ex_____ large one?

10 Can I tr_____ on this jacket?

9 Complete the text with these words.

concerts	draw	music	read
cook	free	programmes	sing

In my ¹_____ time, I listen to a lot of ²_____, I go to a lot of ³_____ and I ⁴_____ in a band. We're called Chill. I like watching TV too. I love ⁵_____ about travel and different countries. I ⁶_____ a lot – magazines, short stories and books. I ⁷_____ pictures of my friends and places I visit. Oh, and I ⁸_____ a lot. I make very good cakes!

9 HEALTHY AND HAPPY

DANGER

2

3

IN THIS UNIT YOU LEARN HOW TO:

- talk about health and problems
- ask people if they are better
- talk about what's important in a country or society
- talk about small and large quantities
- talk about how you know people
- ask about places people have been to

WORDS FOR UNIT 9

1   Look at the words and photos.

1	a **road** in the **coun**tryside	8	the **World Cup**
2	a **sheep** with two **lambs**	9	a lot of **snow**
3	in the **ar**my	10	it's not **safe**
4	it **hurts**	11	get some **fresh air**
5	**stu**dy to**ge**ther	12	a **war** mus**eum**
6	edu**ca**tion	13	have an ope**ra**tion
7	it **broke** its **leg**	14	at a **con**ference

2   ▶ **142** Listen and repeat the words.

3   Work in pairs. Don't look at the words.

Student A: say the number.

Student B: say the words.

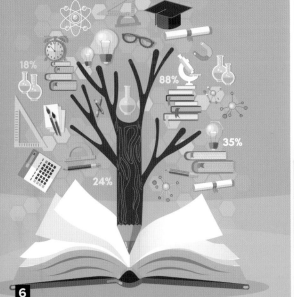

6

7

8

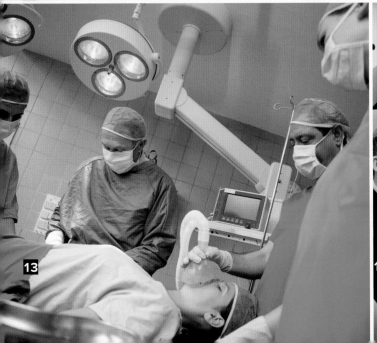

13

14

I HURT MY BACK

SPEAKING

1 ▶ 143 Listen to the conversation.

A: What happened to your arm?

B: I broke it on holiday!

A: Oh no! When was that?

B: Three weeks ago.

2 Work in pairs. Practise the conversation.

GRAMMAR

Time phrases for the past

When was that?

A few days **ago**.	**Last** night.	**On** Monday.	**Today**.
A few weeks **ago**.	**Last** week.	**On** Tuesday.	**Yesterday**.
A few months **ago**.	**Last** Friday.	**On** Sunday.	**This** morning.
Ten minutes **ago**.	**Last** month.		**This** afternoon.
Two weeks **ago**.	**Last** year.		
Ten years **ago**.			

I hurt my back **a few** week**s ago**.

I went on holiday to Vietnam **last** year.

ago = before now   *a few* = 3, 4 or more

3 ▶ 144 Listen to the time phrases. They are fast then slow.

last night   a few days ago

last week   a few weeks ago

4 Work in pairs. Practise the time phrases.

5 Complete the sentences with a time phrase to make them true for you. Then tell a partner.

I broke my mobile phone _____.

I went on holiday _____.

I didn't go to my English class _____.

Ⓖ For more practice, see Exercises 1 and 2 on page 131.

VOCABULARY

Bad health and accidents

6 Match the pictures (a–h) with the sentences (1–8).

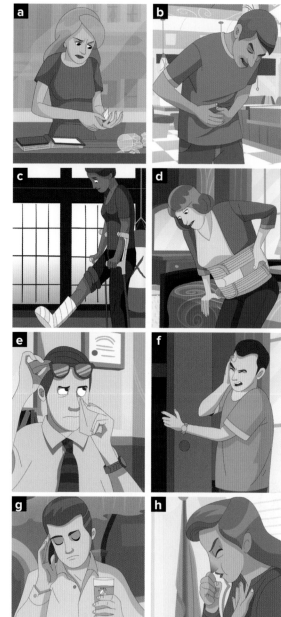

1 I **cut** my **hand**.

2 I **broke** my **leg**.

3 I had a very **bad cold**.

4 I had a **head**ache.

5 I felt **sick**.

6 I **hit** my **head**.

7 I **hurt** my **back**.

8 I had **some**thing in my **eye**.

7 ▶ 145 Listen and repeat sentences 1–8 from Exercise 6.

8 Use the words from Exercise 6 to make two lists:

1 the present forms of the verbs. Add one more verb about bad health or accidents.

2 the names of five parts of the body. Add one more.

9 Work in pairs. Close your books. Test each other.

1 Student A: point to a part of the body.

Student B: say the word.

2 Student B: say a verb in the present tense.

Student A say the verb in the past.

SPEAKING

10 Practise the conversation in Exercise 1. Replace the words in red.

> ### Talking about parts of the body
> *my* eye   *his* head   *your* leg
>
> *What's wrong with **your leg**?*
>
> *It hurt my **eyes**.*
>
> *He cut his **head**.*

11 Work in groups. Tell people problems or accidents you had. Say when you had the problem.

LISTENING

12 ▶ 146 Listen to four conversations. Tick (✓) the problems in Exercise 6 you hear.

13 ▶ 146 Listen again. When did each problem happen?

DEVELOPING CONVERSATIONS

>
> ### Are you feeling better?
> *Are you feeling better? / Is it OK now?*
> ✓ ✓   *(Yes.) Much better, thanks.*
> ✓   *A bit better.*
> ✗   *Not really.*

14 Work in pairs. Take turns to say sentences 1–4. Your partner asks *Are you feeling better?* Answer with the word in brackets.

1 I had a really bad headache. (bit)

2 I had a really bad cold. (much)

3 I was really tired. (much)

4 I really hurt my back. (not)

CONVERSATION PRACTICE

15 Take turns to have conversations like this.

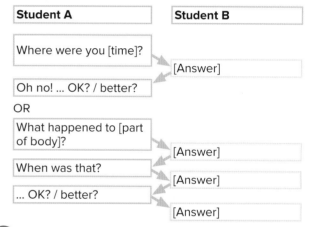

Student A	Student B
Where were you [time]?	
	[Answer]
Oh no! ... OK? / better?	
OR	
What happened to [part of body]?	
	[Answer]
When was that?	
	[Answer]
... OK? / better?	
	[Answer]

▶ 147 For more practice, listen to two more examples.

Siriraj Hospital opened 120 years ago. It is now Thailand's most important hospital.

IT'S A BEAUTIFUL ENVIRONMENT

REVIEW AND SPEAKING

1 Work in pairs. Choose one.

- Say something you did: last week, two months ago and a few years ago. Your partner asks one question about it.
- Tell a partner about something you broke, cut or hurt. Your partner asks one question about it.

VOCABULARY Country and society

2 Match the sentences (1–5) with the groups of words (a–e).

1 Education here is great.
2 The health system here is very bad.
3 The environment is very good.
4 The weather here is OK.
5 Crime is very bad.

a rain   sun   snow
b teachers   schools   university
c safe   police   army
d the air   the water   the countryside
e hospitals   doctors   an operation

3 ▶ 148 Listen and repeat these words.

countryside	environment	**hos**pital	uni**ver**sity
edu**ca**tion	**health sys**tem	operation	**wea**ther

4 Tick (✓) the new words from Exercise 2 you didn't know before.

5 Why is somewhere good to live? Put the words in red from Exercise 2 in order of how important you think they are.

1 most important
2 very important
3 important
4 less important
5 least important

6 Compare in groups. Do you have the same order? What other things are important?

7 Choose one or two words from a–e in Exercise 2 to say something about the sentences 1–5 in Exercise 2.

1 *Education here is great. The **teachers** are very good. A lot of people go to **university**.*

GRAMMAR

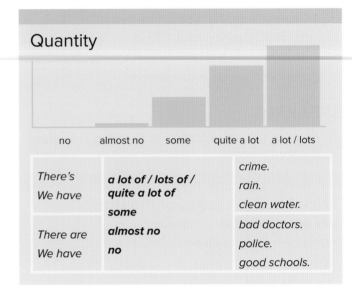

Quantity

no	almost no	some	quite a lot	a lot / lots

There's We have	*a lot of / lots of /* *quite a lot of* *some*	crime. rain. clean water.
There are We have	*almost no* *no*	bad doctors. police. good schools.

8 Complete the sentences with *is*, *are* or *have*.

1 There _____ problems in our hospitals.
2 There _____ crime in the countryside.
3 We _____ snow where I live.
4 There _____ police on the streets here.
5 There _____ beautiful countryside near here.
6 There _____ women in the government.
7 We _____ holidays in our country.
8 I _____ free time at the moment.

9 Add a quantity word or phrase to the sentences in Exercise 8. Make them true for you or your country.

*There are **quite a lot of** problems in our hospitals.*
*There's **almost no** crime in the countryside.*

G For more practice, see Exercises 1–3 on page 131.

READING

10 Do you think your country is a good place to live? Why? / Why not?

11 Read about Iceland. Match each title with the right paragraph (1–7).

Sport   Education   A safe country   Food
The health system   The weather   A great environment

ICELAND: POSSIBLY THE BEST COUNTRY IN THE WORLD

Iceland is a small island in the north of Europe. People are very happy and it's the best country – or almost the best – for lots of things.

1 _____ **(First in the world)**

There is almost no crime. The police don't need guns. Iceland has no army and it never has wars.

2 _____ **(Second in the world)**

Iceland has beautiful countryside. There are a lot of mountains, volcanoes and lakes. It has very clean water and fresh air. 97% of people say the water is very good.

3 _____ **(Number 15 in the world)**

It doesn't cost anything to go to the doctor or a hospital. It's easy to see a doctor, but sometimes you need to wait for an operation. On average, people live until they are 83.

4 _____ **(Number 31 in the world)**

Some people say that students are worse now. They do worse in exams, but 99% of people in Iceland can read. Children stay in the same school between 6 and 16 years old and most people continue studying until they are 20 or 21. 60% of people go to university.

5 _____ **(Number 22 in the world)**

People in Iceland love football. In 2010 their football team was number 110 in the world but it's much better now. In 2018, the team was in the World Cup in Russia.

6 _____

It isn't very hot in Iceland. In December, it's usually about -3 degrees and you only see the sun for about 17 minutes a day. In summer, it is usually about 15 degrees and the day is 22 hours long! On average, it rains or snows three or four times a week.

7 _____

Food is very fresh. Icelanders eat a lot of fish and vegetables. They have the best lamb in the world and a favourite dish is sheep's head.

12 Say what the numbers from the text mean. Read again and check.

97%	22	83	17 minutes	60%	three or four

13 Look at the words in red from the text. Guess what they mean. Check in a dictionary.

Better and *worse*

The football team is much **better** now. = 'more good'

Students are **worse**. = 'more bad'

14 Talk about Iceland and where you live. Say what you think is better or worse in your country.

I think our football team is better.

15 Look at the question below. Write four similar questions. Use a dictionary if you need to.

What do you think of education (in Russia / here)?

16 Work in groups. Ask and answer your questions.

A: *What do you think of education here?*

B: *It's better now. There are lots of good schools.*

WRITING

17 Write some sentences about your country or area. Use ideas from the Reading text. Change them to make them true for your country.

LIVING ABROAD

SPEAKING

1 **Work in pairs. Discuss the questions.**
- Do you know anyone who lives abroad (in another country)?
- Do you think it's easy or difficult to live in another country? Why?

LISTENING

2 ▶ **150** **Listen to the first part of a conversation between the people in the picture. Choose the correct word or phrase in 1–5.**

1 An is Lena's *boss / friend*.
2 An and Lena *go to the same school / work together*.
3 Kasper and Lena's *mothers / brothers* are friends.
4 Kasper is *Polish / British*.
5 An is from *Vietnam / Poland*.

VOCABULARY Meeting and moving

3 **Look at sentences a–j. Check you understand all the words. Find six answers to question 1 and four answers to question 2.**

1 How do you know each other?   *a,* _____

2 Why are you here?   _____

a We met when we were on holiday in Greece.
b For work. My company moved its office here.
c We worked together. He was my boss in my last job.
d We met at a conference. We both work in Health.
e To study. I'm doing a Master's here.
f I'm here on business. I'm meeting a client.
g We were in the army together.
h We were at university together. We did the same course.
i She was a friend of a friend.
j For love! My husband is from Colombia – and the weather here is better!

4 **Cover the sentences. Complete the phrases with one word.**

We met ...   I'm here ...

_____ a conference.   _____ love.
_____ university.   _____ work.
_____ holiday.   _____ business.
_____ the army.   _____ study.

5 **Tell your partner about two people you know who moved to a new place. Say why they moved.**

My friend Dan moved for work.

6 **Think of four different ways you met people you know. Write a list of the four people.**

7 Work in pairs. Give the list of names to your partner. Ask and answer questions.

A: *How do you know Alfie?*

B: *We went to school together. He's my best friend. How do you know Donna?*

LISTENING

8 Work in pairs. Read the second part of the conversation between Kasper, An and Lena. Try to complete it with the phrases in the box.

came to	lot of	quite a	years ago
better	my hand	staying with	
long time	's not working	think of	

K: So, An. Have you been here before?

A: Yes. A few ¹_____.

K: OK. To study English?

A: No. I ²_____ see my sister.

K: Does she live here?

A: Yes. I'm ³_____ her now.

K: Oh, OK. What does she do?

A: She ⁴_____ at the moment. She had a baby last year.

K: Oh, great. What did she ⁵_____ the British health service?

A: I'm not sure. Good, I think. Her baby's very well.

K: That's good. There are a ⁶_____ problems with the health system at the moment.

A: Really?

K: Yes. It's difficult. You sometimes wait a ⁷_____ to see a doctor.

A: Oh.

L: Kasper, tell her what happened to you.

K: I broke ⁸_____ last month and I waited in the hospital for four hours!

A: Oh four hours. It's a lot. Are hospitals ⁹_____ in Poland?

L: I don't know.

K: I've never been to a hospital there!

A: How often do you to go Poland?

K: ¹⁰_____ lot. My mum lives there now.

A: OK.

K: She went back two years ago. Have you been to Poland?

A: No. Maybe next year with Lena!

9 ▶ **151** Listen and check.

10 ▶ **151** Listen to and read the second part of the conversation again. Tick (✓) the sentences that are right. Change the sentences that are wrong.

An has a brother. ✗ *An has a sister.*

An's sister lives in Britain. ✓

1 An had a baby last year.

2 An thinks the British health system is bad.

3 Kasper hurt his hand a few weeks ago.

4 Kasper's mum lived in Britain before, but now lives in Poland.

DEVELOPING CONVERSATIONS

Have you been ...?

A: **Have you been here before**?

B: Yes. Two years ago.

A: **Have you been to** Poland?

B: No, never.

11 Complete the question with the names of four countries and four cities.

1 Have you been to *Brazil?* Have you been to *Berlin?*

12 Work in pairs. Ask your questions.

SPEAKING

13 ▶ **152** Listen to the third part of the conversation between An and Kasper. Write Kasper's answers.

Question	Kasper	Your partner
Why did you go?		
When was that?		
Where did you go?	Hanoi	
What did you think of it?		
How long were you there?		

14 Work in pairs. Have similar conversations.

- Start with one of your *Have you been to...?* questions from Exercise 11.

- Ask and answer the questions in Exercise 13. Complete the table with your partner's answers.

PRONUNCIATION AND REVIEW

15 ▶ **153** Listen to the sounds and the four words. Which word has a different sound?

1	/æ/	hand	arm	accident	back
2	/ɜː/	hurt	worse	first	course
3	/ɒ/	move	boss	job	problem
4	/əʊ/	road	broke	women	snow
5	/e/	leg	health	head	great
6	/ɪ/	air	hit	system	business
7	/aɪ/	eye	quite	friend	crime
8	/eɪ/	safe	war	wait	education

16 Practise saying the three words with the *same* sound from Exercise 15.

17 Choose one word from each group of words. Use the word to say a sentence about you or your country.

G For more revision and pronunciation, see Exercises 1–5 on page 131.

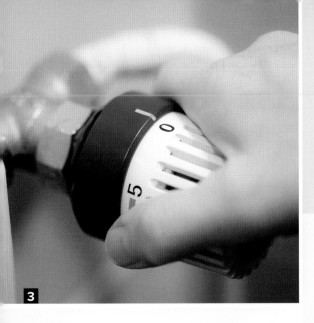

3

6

IN THIS UNIT YOU LEARN HOW TO:

- talk about the weather
- tell people about future plans and predictions
- say what's happening near you
- make plans with other people
- talk about some simple news stories
- ask questions about the news

WORDS FOR UNIT 10

1 Look at the words and photos.

1 an **elec**tion	8 have **fun** (at the **fair**)
2 stay **warm** by the **fire**	9 he **won** the **match**
3 **turn off** the **hea**ting	10 **win**ter in the **city**
4 a **heart**	11 **some**one **died**
5 the **coun**tryside's very **dry**	12 **build** a **sta**dium
6 it's very **win**dy	13 an **ac**cident
7 **turn on** the **air** con**di**tioning	14 **What's** the **score**?

2 ▶ 154 Listen and repeat the words.

3 Work in pairs. Don't look at the words.

Student A: say the number.

Student B: say the words.

10

13

14

BONUS
POSS
PERIOD

HOME   VISITOR

Unit 10 News 87

IT'S GOING TO STAY LIKE THIS

SPEAKING

1 ▶ **155** Work in pairs. Listen to a short conversation.

A: Is it raining now?

B: Yes. It's horrible!

A: Is it going to stay like this?

B: I think so. They say it's going to rain for the next three days.

A: Oh no!

B: What's the problem? Do you have plans?

A: No, but my friends are going camping! They're going to the mountains.

B: Oh! They're going to get very wet!

A: I know!

(stay/be/look) **like** = similar to

Is it going to stay **like** *this?*

It's **like** *my country.*

I look **like** *my dad.*

---

2 Work in pairs. Practise the conversation in Exercise 1.

VOCABULARY Summer and winter

We can talk about the weather with *it + be* + adjective or *it + verb*.

It's **horrible**.   *Is it* **raining** *now?*

It's **cold**.   *It* **snows** *a lot here.*

---

3 Choose the correct word(s).

1 We don't have air conditioning in our house. It's not usually very hot here in the *summer / winter*.

2 It's really cold in the winter. It's sometimes *38 degrees (38 °C) / minus 30 (-30 °C)*.

3 It's really hot here at the moment. It was *38 degrees / minus 30* yesterday. I don't like it.

4 It's warm and sunny today, but it's going to *change / stay like this* tomorrow. It's going to rain.

5 We don't have much rain here. The countryside is very *wet / dry*.

6 It's really cold. I'm going to turn on the *heating / air-con*.

7 The house doesn't have heating. There's only *a fire / a sink* in the living room.

8 Be careful on your bike. It's very *windy / sunny* today.

4 Make two lists of words for *Summer* and *Winter*. Choose any words from Exercise 3.

5 Work in pairs. Compare your lists. Do you have the same? Can you add two words to each list?

6 Complete the sentences with these words.

is	rains	raining	is	was	rained

1 It _____ all day yesterday.

2 It _____ very hot today.

3 Is it _____ now? Do I need to take a coat?

4 It _____ so cold last week.

5 It _____ not usually like this. It normally _____ a lot in April.

V For more months of the year, see page 139.

7 Work in pairs. Ask questions about: a) where you are now and b) another place you know.

- How's the weather now? Is it usually like this?
- How was the weather yesterday?
- How is the weather in January? And in July?
- What time of year and weather do you like best?

GRAMMAR

Future: *am/are/is going*

Plan: **My friends are going** camping. **They're going** to the mountains.

Prediction: **It's going** to rain. **They're going** to get wet.

I	'm am	going	swimming	later.
You We They	're are		home to Berlin	tomorrow. next week. at the weekend.
It He She	's is		to stay like this to win to be here	on Friday.

8 Complete the conversations with the correct form of the verb *be*.

1 A: It's nice and warm today.

B: I know. Do you have any plans for this evening?

A: I _____ going to my friends' house. They _____ going to have a barbecue.

2 A: What are you doing at the weekend?

B: Ricardo _____ going to be in town, so we _____ going to have dinner together.

A: That's nice.

3 A: It _____ going to snow next week.

B: Oh good. My son _____ going skiing next week. He _____ going with the school.

A: Really? Where _____ they going?

4 A: We _____ going to play football later. Do you want to play?

B: I don't think so. It's so hot.

A: I think it _____ going to be OK this evening. Better than now.

9 Write sentences about these things.

- the weather tomorrow, next weekend and next week.
- plans for tomorrow, next week and the summer.
- a plan that a person in your family has.

10 Work in pairs. A: say one of your sentences. B: comment or ask a question. Take turns.

A: *It's going to be sunny tomorrow.*

B: *I know. It's going to be 20 degrees.*

A: *My son's going to Peru in the summer.*

B: *Why's he going there?*

A: *Business.*

Ⓖ For more practice, see Exercises 1–4 on page 132.

LISTENING

11 ▶ **156** Listen to four conversations. In each conversation, is the weather going to change?

12 ▶ **156** Listen again and complete the table.

	Weather now	Weather tomorrow	Plans
1	hot	_____	go to the island stay inside
2	cold	_____	_____ special
3	_____	_____ warm	have a barbecue
4	_____	cold rain	go shopping do some jobs

13 Work in groups. Talk about places you have been to that were very wet, cold, windy or hot.

DEVELOPING CONVERSATIONS

I think so / I don't think so

A: *Is it going to rain?*   A: *Is it going to snow?*

B: **I think so.**   B: **I don't think so.**

NOT: ~~I think yes~~ or ~~I think no~~

14 Look at the questions. Make questions to ask people in your class. Change the words in red.

1 Is it going to be nice tomorrow?

2 Is it going to rain later?

3 Are you going to the cinema this evening?

4 Is Petra married?

5 Does Rosario have any brothers or sisters?

6 Does Kenji live near here?

15 Work in pairs. Ask your questions from Exercise 14. Use *I think so* or *I don't think so*.

CONVERSATION PRACTICE

16 Work in pairs. Have conversations like this.

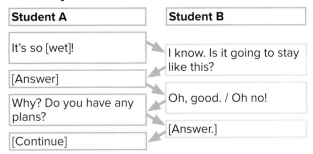

Student A	Student B
It's so [wet]!	I know. Is it going to stay like this?
[Answer]	Oh, good. / Oh no!
Why? Do you have any plans?	[Answer.]
[Continue]	

17 Change partner. Have another conversation, but change how the weather is now.

▶ **157** For more practice, listen to another example.

A FESTIVAL

REVIEW AND SPEAKING

1 Talk about the weather where you live. Say how the weather:

- was last week.
- is going to be next week.
- is normally at this time of year.

2 Talk about your plans for the summer or winter holidays.

VOCABULARY Entertainment

3 Describe the six photos (a–f) with some of the red words in 1–10.

1 There's a good play at the Grand Theatre at the moment.
2 There's a jazz band playing in the main square.
3 There's a circus next to the football stadium.
4 There's a big festival near here.
5 There's a fair in the park.
6 There's a good exhibition at the festival. They're showing some interesting photos.
7 There's a classical concert. It's free.
8 There's a comedy show in a club in town.
9 There's a big match tonight. Inter are playing Juve.
10 They're showing that new film about Picasso at the cinema.

4 ▶ 158 Listen and repeat these words.

circus	comedy	exhibition
classical	concert	festival

5 Work in groups. Discuss the questions.

- Which activities from Exercise 3 are fun for you? Which are boring?
- What fun things are there where you live?

READING

6 Work in pairs. Are there any music festivals in your country? Think of one. How many of these questions can you answer?

1 Where is it?
2 When is the festival?
3 How long is the festival?
4 What kind of music do they play?
5 Can you only see music?
6 How much does the festival cost?

7 Read the article about the Pohoda festival. Answer the questions from Exercise 6 about the text.

▶ 159

A YEAR OF FUN IN ONE WEEKEND!

The Pohoda festival happens in the second weekend of July in Trenčín, Slovakia. Trenčín is in beautiful countryside. It's next to the river Váh and near the Carpathian mountains. The festival started in 1997. In the first year, it was in Trenčín's football stadium. It lasted one day and there were eight bands.

Now, the festival is at an old army airport near the city. It lasts two days and there are over 160 concerts with all kinds of music from all over the world. But it's not only music that you can see: there are plays; there are art exhibitions; they show films; you can listen to writers reading from their books; you can go to discussions about politics. Children can learn circus skills or they can do dancing or play games. There are also yoga and exercise classes.

Almost 30,000 people visit the festival each day. Most people camp. There is a special area for families. The weather is normally hot and sunny at the festival. If it rains, everyone can go inside and stay dry. And there are lots of showers, toilets and wash rooms, so people can stay clean. It costs around $100 per ticket, but it's free for children (under 12), when they are with an adult.

Who is going to be at the festival this year? Go to the Pohoda website to see the list of bands and other artists!

over = more than   under = less than

8   Read again. Are these sentences true (T) or false (F)?

1   The festival started in the stadium, but moved.

2   Only bands from Slovakia play at the festival.

3   It's quite a small festival.

4   It rains a lot at the festival.

5   The festival is good for families.

9   Look at the words in red. Guess what they mean. Check in a dictionary.

10 Work in pairs. Discuss the questions.

- What things at the Pohoda festival do you like doing and seeing?
- Would you like to go to the Pohoda Festival? Why? / Why not?

WRITING

11 Write about a festival in your country. Answer the questions from Exercise 6. Say if you think the festival is good or not.

DEVELOPING CONVERSATIONS

12 ▶ 160 Listen to a conversation between two people at the festival. Tick (✓) the things they talk about.

a concert   an exhibition   a play

a class   a discussion   a film

Deciding what to do
Suggesting an idea
A: **How about** a play?
✓: B: OK. / Yeah, great.
✗: B: **I don't really like** plays.
    I'd prefer a film.
Deciding when and where to meet
I'll meet you after that.

13 Work in pairs. Complete the conversation with the phrases from the box.

A: What do you want to see today?

B: ¹_____ Jessie Ware? She's playing tonight.

A: ²_____. I like her music.

B: What else?

A: How about a play? There's one in the theatre tent this afternoon.

B: I don't really like plays. I'd prefer a film. They're showing *Jaws*.

A: ³_____. What do you want to do now?

B: ⁴_____ a yoga class? There's one in fifteen minutes.

A: No. ⁵_____ the politics discussion.

B: Really? ⁶_____ politics.

A: Well, you go to the yoga and I'll meet you after that. We can get something to eat.

B: OK. Where?

A: ⁷_____ here at twelve .

B: OK.

14 ▶ 160 Listen again and check.

15 Work in pairs. Practise the conversation.

SPEAKING

16 Work in pairs. Make a list of three fun things that are happening this weekend where you live. Say when and where they are happening. Use the ideas from Exercise 3.

17 Change partners. With your new partner decide what you want to do together.

DID YOU SEE THE NEWS?

SPEAKING

1 **Which sentences are true for you? Compare in pairs.**

- I always follow the news. It's important.
- I sometimes watch the news, but not very often.
- A lot of the news isn't true.
- I like news about sport.
- I like news about famous people.
- The news is sad.
- The news makes me angry.
- The news is interesting.

VOCABULARY National and international news

2 **Check you understand the words in red. Choose the best question to ask.**

1 A: Princess Sophia is going to get married.

   B: How old was she? / When?

2 A: President Smith died yesterday. He had a heart attack.

   B: How did he die? / How old was he?

3 A: Barbara Francisco had her baby.

   B: Is it a boy or a girl? / Who did that?

4 A: There was a really big fire in a shopping centre near here.

   B: How did it start? / How much was it?

5 A: There was an election in Germany yesterday.

   B: Who scored? / Who won?

6 A: There was a big accident on the motorway. About ten cars!

   B: Did anyone die? / What was the score?

7 A: They're going to build a new airport.

   B: Why? / How much did it cost?

8 A: Arsenal lost 3–0 to Zenit, St Petersburg.

   B: Who won? / Who scored?

9 A: The government is going to spend more money on education.

   B: How many people were there? / How much?

10 A: Toyota is going to close its factory here.

   B: How much? / How many people work there?

3 ▶ **161** **Listen and check.**

4 **Which of the news stories in Exercise 2 are about the future?**

5 **Choose five stories from Exercise 2. Write an answer to the question.**

6 **Work in pairs. Take turns to start. If you don't have an answer to the question, say *I don't know.***

A: *Barbara Francisco had her baby.*

B: *Is it a boy or a girl?*

A: *A girl.*

A: *President Smith died yesterday. He had a heart attack.*

B: *How old was he?*

A: *I don't know.*

7 **What do you think of each piece of news in Exercise 2?**

It's terrible. / It's good. / I'm not really interested.

GRAMMAR Past forms review

Regular past forms end in *-ed.*

start — started   change — changed   try — tried

Irregular past forms have no rules!

have — had   go — went   lose — lost

8 Complete the table.

Regular		Irregular	
Present	Past	Present	Past
finish			was/were
decide		get	
open		win	
happen			took
	stopped	see	
play	played	meet	
talk			cut
help	helped		cost
	tried		spent
use			came

9 ▶ **162** Listen and repeat the regular past forms from the table in Exercise 8.

10 Cover the table. Complete the sentences with the past form of the verbs.

1 The government _____ the election, so there's going to be a new president. (lose)

2 They _____ the new airport yesterday. It _____ $3 billion. (open / cost)

3 Mustafa Wady _____ yesterday. He _____ cancer. (die / have)

4 Our president _____ the Chinese president yesterday. They _____ about the environment. (meet / talk)

5 It _____ a lot yesterday and there _____ lots of accidents on the roads. (snow / are)

6 Vettel _____ the Brazilian Grand Prix yesterday. Hamilton _____ second. (win / come)

11 Write two sentences about news at the moment. Use words from Exercise 2 or use a dictionary.

Ⓖ For more practice, see Exercises 1–4 on page 133.

READING AND SPEAKING

12 Work in groups of four. Divide into two pairs.

Pair A: Read the two sentences. Write two questions to ask about each news story.

> THERE WAS A BIG FIRE IN A SCHOOL.

> Lesser's is going to close a factory and several shops.

Pair B: Read the two sentences. Write two questions to ask about each news story.

> BAYERN MUNICH WON THE GERMAN CUP.

> The government is going to spend more money on health services.

13 Give your questions to the other pair.

Pair A: read the stories in File 5 on page 145. Try and find answers to pair B's questions.

Pair B: read the stories in File 11 on page 147. Try and find answers to Pair A's questions.

14 Work in pairs of one A and one B. Have conversations like this:

Student A	Student B
Did you see the news?	
	No. What happened?
[Read your first sentence from Exercise 12]	
	[Ask your first question]
[Answer / Say I don't know]	
	[Ask your second question]
[Answer] / Say I don't know.	

15 Work in groups. Talk about the news stories you wrote about in Exercise 11.

PRONUNCIATION AND REVIEW

16 ▶ **163** Listen to the sounds and the four words. Which word has a different sound?

1 /e/	election	weather	heart	wet
2 /ʌ/	fun	use	won	summer
3 /aɪ/	little	dry	fire	die
4 /ɜː/	turn	learn	circus	score
5 /æ/	about	accident	adult	angry
6 /ɒ/	comedy	close	politics	lost
7 /ɪ/	build	winter	like	skill

17 Practise saying the three words with the *same* sound from Exercise 16.

18 In two minutes write:

• weather words. • entertainment words. • news words.

Ⓖ For more pronunciation, see Exercise 1 on page 133.

VIDEO 5

A SPECIAL SKILL

1   Work in pairs. Look at the photo. Write ten things about the photo, including:
   • things you can see
   • what people are doing

2   ▶️ 5 Watch the video and answer the questions.
   • Who is Stephen Wiltshire?
   • What city is he in?
   • What's special about what he does?

3   Tick (✓) the things you learn in the video.
   1 Stephen is British.
   2 Some of his drawings are four metres long.
   3 Stephen has autism.
   4 He didn't learn to speak until he was nine.
   5 He went to a special school.
   6 He draws from memory.
   7 He has drawings of many cities around the world.
   8 There are exhibitions of his work.
   9 He's good at maths.
   10 He took five days to finish the drawing of Mexico.

4   ▶️ 5 Watch the video again and check.

5   Discuss the questions.
   • What do you think of Stephen's art?
   • Did you know about autism before or hear any stories about it?
   • Are there special schools for people like Stephen in your country? Are they good?

SPEAKING

6   What skills do you have? Write a list. Use the ideas in the box or use a dictionary if you need to.

I'm good at I'm quite good at I'm really good at	drawing. writing. cooking. making things. talking to people. listening to people. languages. sport. computer games. maths.

7   Tell your partner the things you are good at. How many skills do you and your partner both have?

REVIEW 5

1 Choose the correct word(s).

1 I met her ten years *ago* / *before*.

2 I went to a concert *in* / *on* Friday.

3 We had almost *not* / *no* rain last year.

4 There are quite *lots of* / *a lot of* good schools in my town.

5 What's wrong with *the* / *your* / *you* back?

6 It's hot today, but *it doesn't stay* / *it's not going to stay* / *it's not staying* like this.

7 *We don't go* / *We're not going* / *We're not go* home this week.

8 It *was* / *were* / *did* very cold last week. It snowed a lot.

2 Complete the text with the past simple of the verbs.

I ¹_____ (have) a really good weekend. On Friday night, I ²_____ (meet) some friends and we ³_____ (go) to a concert. It ⁴_____ (start) at ten and ⁵_____ (finish) at four. I ⁶_____ (take) a taxi home. It ⁷_____ (cost) a lot of money and I ⁸_____ (be) very tired on Saturday! On Sunday, I ⁹_____ (play) football and my team ¹⁰_____ (win).

3 Complete the sentences with one word in each space.

1 I saw her in the street fifteen minutes _____.

2 She started her new job a _____ days ago.

3 He's not here at the moment. He felt sick _____ morning and he went home about an hour ago.

4 We went to Sweden on holiday _____ year. It was great.

5 Look at the sky. It's going _____ rain later.

6 I'm _____ swimming after class today. There's a pool near here.

4 Write full sentences. Use the words in brackets.

1 _____ tonight. (It / snow)

2 _____ in my city. (There / lot / problems)

3 _____ next week. (I / not / be / here)

4 _____ in my area. (There / almost / bad schools)

5 _____ tomorrow. Sorry! (You / lose / the match)

5 ▶ 164 Listen and complete the sentences.

1 He _____ his leg a _____.

2 I _____ to my friends' house _____.

3 I didn't _____ to my yoga class _____.

4 There _____ problems in our hospitals.

5 It _____ at the weekend.

6 ▶ 164 Work in pairs. Compare your answers. Listen again to check.

7 Match the verbs in the box with the correct groups of words (1–8).

break	do	have	turn on
build	get	lose	work

1 _____ in education / together

2 _____ a new stadium / more roads

3 _____ a Master's / a French course

4 _____ married / very wet

5 _____ a baby / something in my eye

6 _____ an election / a match

7 _____ the heating / the air conditioning

8 _____ my arm / my leg

8 Put the words into three groups: health and accidents, society or entertainment.

air	crime	festival
break	cut	headache
circus	education	hurt
classical music	environment	sick
comedy	exhibition	university

9 Complete the missing words. You have the first two letters.

1 It's very hot today. It's about 35 de_____ outside.

2 On av_____, men make more money than women.

3 Education was bad in the past, but I think it's much be_____ now.

4 Liverpool won. Mo Salah sc_____ three times.

5 The festival is in July. It usually la_____ four days.

6 It's always very cold in winter. It's mi_____ 26 now.

7 There's a lot of crime. It's not very sa_____.

8 He died last year. He had a heart at_____.

9 I'm not feeling well. I have a very bad co_____.

10 Complete the sentences with the missing prepositions.

1 We met _____ a conference in Malta.

2 It's a good exhibition. They're showing paintings _____ local artists.

3 They need to spend more money _____ education.

4 We met when we were _____ holiday in Corfu.

5 We met twenty years ago. We were _____ the army together.

6 We met ten years ago. We were _____ university together.

7 He's a friend _____ a friend.

8 I moved here _____ work. My company opened a new office here.

11 LIFE AND HISTORY

IN THIS UNIT YOU LEARN HOW TO:

- talk about celebrations and events
- invite people and reply
- talk about dates and when things happen
- talk about your life
- take part in a guided tour
- ask questions about people and places

WORDS FOR UNIT 11

1 **fight** each **ot**her	8 a **lu**cky **cat**
2 get a de**gree**	9 a **child** with his **grand**mother
3 **ce**lebrate the **fourth** of July	10 **grow ve**getables
4 be **born**	11 get **ang**ry because the
5 the **mi**ddle of the **road**	**prin**ter's not **wor**king
6 **walk** along the **ci**ty **wall**	12 the **king** and **queen**
7 **What's** the **date** to**day**?	13 **birds** on the **rocks**
	14 move **house**

2 ▶ 165 Listen and repeat the words.

3 Work in pairs. Don't look at the words.

Student A: say the number.

Student B: say the words.

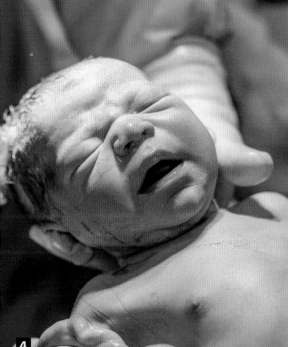

CELEBRATE

Bristol, in the UK, celebrates the 150th anniversary of the building of the Clifton Suspension Bridge

SPEAKING

1 **Check you understand the words in red. Then discuss the questions.**

Your birthday celebrates the day you were born.

An anniversary celebrates the day something important happened, for example when people got married or a country became independent.

- Do you celebrate your birthday? What do you normally do?
- Do you celebrate any anniversaries? Which ones?
- Do you do anything for other people's birthdays or anniversaries?
- What important anniversaries are there in your country? Are there public holidays to celebrate them? What do you do?
- Have you been to a party recently? What did it celebrate?

VOCABULARY Months

2 **Work in pairs. Can you complete the names of the months?**

Jan_____   May_____   Sep_____
Feb_____   Jun_____   Oct_____
Mar_____   Jul_____   Nov_____
Apr_____   Aug_____   Dec_____

3 ▶ **166** **Listen and repeat the months.**

4 **Match phrases 1–4 with phrases a–d that have a similar meaning.**

1 in **May**
2 at the be**gin**ning of **May**
3 in the **mi**ddle of **May**
4 at the **end** of **May**

a in the **se**cond or **third** week of **May**
b **du**ring **May**.
c in the **last** week of **May**
d in the **first** week of **May**

5 ▶ **167** **Listen and repeat the phrases from Exercise 4.**

6 **Complete 1–8 to make true sentences. Use months and phrases from Exercises 2 and 4. Change the words in red, if you need to.**

1 My birthday is _____.
2 My parents' anniversary is _____.
3 My brother's birthday is _____.
4 The next public holiday is _____.
5 I'm going to Spain on holiday _____.
6 I went to see a friend in Moscow in _____.
7 I had a great time _____.
8 Last year was a good year. I _____ in July.

7 **Work in pairs. Tell a partner your sentences. Are any the same?**

Dates

For most dates we add 'th' to the number:
4th (the fourth), 10th (the tenth), 15th (the fifteenth), etc.

1, 2, and 3 are irregular:
1st (the first), 2nd (the second), 3rd (the third)

 **For more on dates, see page 139.**

LISTENING

8 ▶ **168** Listen to four conversations. In which conversation is someone going to have a party?

9 ▶ **168** Choose the correct information. Listen again and check.

Conversation 1

a It's the *16th / 17th / 18th* today.

b It's the woman's *brother's / sister's / son's* birthday on Friday.

Conversation 2

a Their boss wants to meet on the *4th / 5th / 6th*.

b It's *a public holiday / her boyfriend's birthday / her anniversary*.

Conversation 3

a The man is going to be at a conference on a *Friday / Saturday / Monday*.

b The woman got married *6 / 10 / 25* years ago.

Conversation 4

a The conference is to celebrate the school's *5th / 10th / 20th* anniversary.

b It's on *Saturday 3rd / Saturday 13th / Saturday 23rd*.

GRAMMAR

10 Read the information in the box. Complete the questions from the conversations in Exercise 8 with the correct form of *be*, *do* or *can*.

Questions review

We use a form of *be*, *do*, or *can* in different questions. Remember the word order.

Question word	be, do, etc.	person	verb phrase
1 *How old*	*is*	she?	
2 *Where*	_____	*you*	*going?*
3	_____	*she*	*doing anything to celebrate?*
4	_____	*you*	*want to come?*
5	_____	*you*	*tell him it's a public holiday?*
6	_____	*we*	*meet on the 6th?*

11 ▶ **169** Listen and check.

12 Make questions. Put the words in order and add the correct form of *be*, *do* or *can*.

1 A: My birthday's next week.

B: going to be / how old / you / ?

How old are you going to be?

2 A: My parents' anniversary is on July 17th.

B: they / doing anything / ?

3 A: It was my son's birthday last weekend.

B: you / get him / what?

4 A: It was a public holiday yesterday.

B: go anywhere / you?

5 A: help me with my bags / you / ?

B: Sure.

6 A: I'm going to Spain on holiday.

B: going with / who / you / ?

7 A: Last year was a terrible year.

B: terrible / why / it / ?

8 A: I'm having a party on Sunday.   / come / you / ?

B: Of course! I'd love to.

13 Practise the conversations in Exercise 12. Take turns to start. Continue them.

1 A: *My birthday's next week.*

B: *How old are you going to be?*

A: *I don't want to say!*

14 Work in groups. Take turns to say true sentences from Exercise 6 and ask questions.

 **G** For more practice, see Exercises 1–3 on page 134.

DEVELOPING CONVERSATIONS

Invitations

Invite:	*Do you want to come ...? Can you come ...?*
Yes:	*Sure. / I'd love to.*
Maybe:	*What day? / What date? / I need to check (my diary / with my boss).*
No:	*Sorry, I can't.*
Reason:	*I'm going away. / I'm working. / I have a meeting.*

15 Complete the two conversations with one word in each space.

a A: We are going to plan our visit to Rome next week. ¹_____ you come?

B: Maybe. What ²_____?

A: Tuesday morning?

B: I think so, but I need to ³_____ my diary. Can I call you later?

A: OK.

b A: It's our anniversary in January and we're having a party. Do ¹_____ want to ²_____?

B: I'd ³_____ to. What ⁴_____?

A: The 27th.

B: Oh, sorry, I ⁵_____. I'm ⁶_____ to be away.

CONVERSATION PRACTICE

16 Prepare for the conversation.

• Write three things you are going to invite people to. Choose:

a barbecue   a party   a weekend away
a conference   a meeting

• Decide the day/date and the reason for the event.

17 Have conversations like the ones in Exercise 15 with other people in the class. Give true answers.

 170 For more practice, listen to two more examples.

PERSONAL HISTORY

REVIEW AND SPEAKING

1 **Work in pairs. Choose two.**
   - Test each other on the words on page 97.
   - Do the conversation practice on page 99 again.
   - Tell your partner about two parties or special events you've been to in the last year.

VOCABULARY Life events

2 **Complete each group of collocations with the verbs in the boxes.**

become	die	~~live~~	lose	start	was born

1 __*live*__ on the streets / __*live*__ in a nice area / __*live*__ with his mum

2 _____ in Bogota / _____ in the 1960s / _____ near here

3 _____ a teacher / _____ rich / _____ interested in art

4 _____ a business / _____ a new life / _____ teaching

5 _____ in an accident / _____ in her sleep / _____ of a heart attack

6 _____ your job / _____ your home / _____ money

do	finish	get	go	have	move

7 _____ problems with the police / _____ an online shop / _____ a baby

8 _____ to prison / _____ to university / _____ into the army

9 _____ school / _____ to university / _____ working

10 _____ well at school / _____ a Master's / _____ a degree

11 _____ married / _____ divorced / _____ a job in a big company

12 _____ house / _____ to the countryside / _____ to the States

3 **Choose eight words or phrases from Exercise 2 that you don't know or don't remember very well.**

4 **Work in groups. Ask each other about the new words from Exercise 2.**

   A: *What does **prison** mean?*

   B: *I don't know.*

   C: *It's więzienie in Polish.*

   D: *Like this. After a crime, you go to prison.*

5 **Write six sentences about people you know using the collocations.**

   My brother is going to become a teacher. He's at university now.

   My friend Manu did a Masters a few years ago.

READING

6 **Check you understand sentences a–d. Then read about the businessman in the photo on page 101. Complete paragraphs 1–4 with sentences a–d.**

   a When he was in prison, he started to change.

   b There are now over a hundred similar magazines around the world.

   c John Bird started a company called *The Big Issue*.

   d John knows about being homeless.

7 ▶ **171** **Read and listen to check.**

8 **Find six collocations in Exercise 2 that are true about John Bird.**

9 **Read the text again to check.**

10 **Discuss the questions.**
   - Are there homeless people in your town?
   - Do they have any help from the government or other people?
   - Do you think *The Big Issue* is a good idea?
   - Who are the most famous business people in your country? What do they do? Did any of them come from a poor family?

A CHANGED LIFE: JOHN BIRD

1 _____. *The Big Issue* is a magazine that people sell in the streets. The sellers are often homeless (they don't have anywhere to live). They can buy magazines for £1.25 and sell them for £2.50. Doing this work can pay for somewhere to live, so they can start a new life.

2 _____. He was born in a very poor area of London. When he was five, his family lost their home. They lived on the streets for a short time. He then lived in a special home for children. He didn't see his parents much. He had problems at school. He was angry and he didn't learn a lot. After school, he wanted to go into the army, but he couldn't read. He also had problems with the police and he went to prison several times for different crimes.

3 _____. He learned to read and he studied. He became interested in politics. After he left prison, he went to art school and learned about printing. In the 1980s, he started a small printing business. The company did well. In 1991, he decided to use his skills to help homeless people – *The Big Issue* was born!

4 _____. For example, there's *The Big Issue* in Korea, *Aurora de Rua* in Recife, Brazil and *Calle* in Bogotá, Colombia. *The Big Issue* in the UK now also has an online shop and a kind of bank to help other similar businesses.

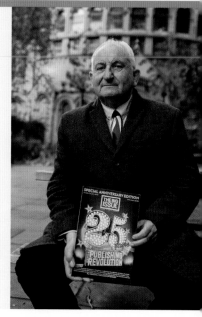

We usually use *could* as the past form of *can*.

He **couldn't** read until he was nine.

He **could** read when he was three.

11 Can you remember when these things happened in John Bird's life? Answer the questions.

1 When did his family lose their home?

2 When did he think about going into the army?

3 When did he go to art school?

4 When did he start his printing business?

5 When did he start *The Big Issue*?

12 Check the answers to Exercise 11 in the Grammar box.

GRAMMAR

Explaining when: time phrases

We can add a phrase with *when*, *after* or *in* to show when something happens.

His family lost their home <u>when he was five</u>.

He wanted to go into the army <u>after school</u>.

He went to art school <u>after he left prison</u>.

He started a small printing business <u>in the 1980s</u>.

He started The Big Issue <u>in 1991</u>.

13 Choose the best word to complete the sentences.

1 I finished university *in / when* 2011.

2 *After / In* the wedding, we went on holiday to Phuket.

3 *After / When* I was a child, I couldn't swim very well.

4 My parents got divorced *in / when* I was fifteen.

5 I was twelve *after / when* my baby sister was born.

6 We got married *after / in* the year 2000.

7 I couldn't find a job *after / when* university.

8 *After / In* I lost my job in the bank, I decided to start a business.

14 ▶ **172** Listen to six phrases starting *When I was*. They are fast then slow. Complete each phrase.

1 when I was _a child_   4 when I was _____

2 when I was _____   5 when I was _____

3 when I was _____   6 when I was _____

15 Complete six of the sentences with a time phrase. Make the sentences true. Change the words in red, if you need to.

1 I finished school _____.

2 I finished university _____.

3 I got my first job _____.

4 I became a doctor _____.

5 I got my first car _____.

6 I met my wife _____.

7 I moved to my flat _____.

8 I became interested in politics _____.

9 I started a business _____.

10 I had my first baby _____.

G For more practice, see Exercises 1 and 2 on page 134.

SPEAKING

16 Work in pairs. Take turns to say a sentence from Exercise 15. Ask and answer one question about it.

A: *I finished school when I was seventeen.*

B: *What did you do after that?*

A: *I got a job.*

A: *I got my first car in 2015.*

B: *What kind of car was it?*

A: *A small Fiat.*

WRITING

17 Write a short history of your life or of someone you know. Write six important things that happened and when they happened.

The walls of Suwon Hwaseong, a fortress in Korea

Pyramids and tombs in Tikal, Guatemala

A temple in Petra, Jordan

ANCIENT HISTORY

SPEAKING

1 Discuss the questions.
   - Do you like visiting old places like the ones in the photos? Why? / Why not?
   - Do you have any similar buildings in your country? Where? Have you been there?

VOCABULARY History

2 Read the facts about history and places round the world. Look at the words in red. Guess what they mean.

   1 The Great Pyramids of Egypt are over 140 metres high. The Eiffel Tower is 324 metres high.

   2 Sobhuza the Second was king of Swaziland for over 82 years. After he died, his son Mswati the Third became king in 1986.

   3 In 1793, the French killed their king, Louis the Sixteenth, and they didn't have another king for twenty years.

   4 Kyoto was the capital city of Japan for over 1000 years. The capital changed to Tokyo in 1868.

   5 In the fourteenth and fifteenth centuries, France and England were at war. They fought for over 100 years.

   6 The Chinese started building the Great Wall over 2000 years ago to protect their country.

   7 The walls of the Coliseum in Rome aren't damaged from war and fighting. The damage is from earthquakes.

   8 In 1992 there was a big fire in Windsor Castle, a home of the Queen of England. It cost almost forty million pounds to repair the buildings.

3 Work in pairs. Explain what the words mean. Use your own language, draw or show the meaning, like Exercise 4 on page 100.

4 How many facts in Exercise 2 did you know?

READING

5 Read the short history of Suwon Hwaseong. Answer the questions.

   1 Who did they build the fortress for?
   2 When did they build it?
   3 Why didn't King Jeongjo like Seoul?
   4 Why did they build schools and houses in it?
   5 Why did the government spend money on the fortress?

A VERY SHORT HISTORY OF SUWON HWASEONG

Suwon Hwaseong is a big fortress in Korea. It is thirty kilometres from the capital city, Seoul. The fortress was built for King Jeongjo in the 1790s after his father died. The king didn't like Seoul because his father was killed there, so he took his father's tomb to Suwon. He wanted to protect the tomb, so they built the fortress around it. But they also built schools and houses inside the walls, because King Jeongjo wanted to make Suwon the new capital city. People started living in Suwon, but it never became the capital.

In the 1950s, there was a war in Korea. Some parts of the fortress were damaged, so the government spent a lot of money after the war to repair the walls and buildings. After that, Suwon Hwaseong became a UNESCO World Heritage Site.

a tomb = place where you put a person's body after they die

GRAMMAR

Explaining why: *because* and *so*

Because and *so* show why something happens or happened.

We use *because* before explaining why (= the cause)
The king didn't like Seoul **because** his father was killed there.
They also built schools there **because** King Jeongjo wanted to make Suwon the new capital city.

We use *so* after explaining why (= the result)
The king didn't like Seoul, **so** he took his father's tomb to Suwon.
The fortress was damaged, **so** the government spent a lot of money to repair it.

Notice the comma (,) before *so*.

6 Complete each pair of sentences. Use *because* in one sentence and *so* in the other. Add the comma (,) before *so*.

1 a I'm studying English _____ I don't have much free time.

   b I'm studying English _____ I didn't do well in my English exam at school.

2 a I want to become a doctor _____ both my parents are doctors!

   b I want to become a doctor _____ I'm studying a lot of science at school.

3 a My parents got divorced _____ I live with my mother now.

   b My parents got divorced _____ they had money problems.

4 a He is in prison _____ he killed someone.

   b He is in prison _____ he can't vote in the election.

7 Write answers to these questions with *because*. Use a dictionary if you need to. Then tell your partner your answers.

- Why are you studying English?
- Why did you choose this school/teacher?
- Why do you (not) like where you live?
- Why do you like (or not like) your job? Why did you choose it?

G For more practice, see Exercises 1 and 2 on page 134.

LISTENING

8 ▶ **173** Listen to some tourists asking a guide questions. Use the numbers in the box to answer *eight* of the questions.

| 1 | 2 | 5.7 | 6 or 4 |
| 47 | 130 | 800 | 1997 |

1 Why didn't Suwon become the capital? _____.

2 How old was the king when he died? _____.

3 How did he die? _____.

4 How long did it take to build the fortress? _____ years.

5 How long are the walls? _____ kilometres.

6 And how high are they? _____ metres.

7 How much did they spend? _____ million dollars.

8 How big is the area inside the fortress? _____ hectares.

9 How many people live here now? _____ million.

10 When did it become a UNESCO site? _____.

9 Compare your answers. Can you remember the answers to the other two questions?

READING AND SPEAKING

10 Work in groups of four. Divide into two pairs. Write questions about the UNESCO sites in the photos on page 102. Look at Exercise 8 for help, or use a dictionary.

Pair A: write five questions to ask about Tikal.

Pair B: write five questions to ask about Petra.

11 Give your questions to the other pair.

Pair A: read about Petra in File 9 on page 147. Try and find answers to pair B's questions. Write one more interesting fact.

Pair B: read about Tikal in File 8 on page 146. Try and find answers to Pair A's questions. Write one more interesting fact.

12 Work in your groups again. Don't look at the text. Ask and answer the questions about each place. Then tell each other the other interesting fact you learned.

13 Have you been on a guided tour? Where? Was it good? What did you learn?

PRONUNCIATION AND REVIEW

14 ▶ **174** Listen to the sounds and the four words. Which word has a different sound?

1	/ɪ/	queen	king	built	business
2	/uː/	June	move	put	choose
3	/ʌ/	luck	become	sure	public
4	/ɜː/	world	bird	history	university
5	/ɔː/	August	poor	fought	rock
6	/aɪ/	high	May	die	inside
7	/əʊ/	born	October	grow	November
8	/i/	angry	July	century	army

15 Practise saying the three words with the *same* sound in Exercise 14.

16 In two minutes write:

- months
- collocations about life events

G For more revision and pronunciation, see Exercises 1–3 on page 135.

12 THANK YOU AND GOODBYE

1

2

4

5

6

9

8

SALE! SALE! SALE!

11

12

3

7

13

IN THIS UNIT YOU LEARN HOW TO:

- tell someone a problem
- offer solutions and say thank you
- explain purpose
- talk about gifts
- tell people what to do
- say goodbye

WORDS FOR UNIT 12

1   Look at the words and photos.

1 a lot of **empty seats**	8 **hurry** to the **shops**
2 the **the**atre's **full**	9 **miss** the **train**
3 carry **hea**vy **bags** of **sho**pping	10 the **seat's bro**ken
4 I **hope** it's OK	11 they **lend books**
5 **help** her to **stand**	12 put a **pain**ting on the **wall**
6 **throw** it in the **bin**	13 some **lo**vely **flo**wers
7 the **sun's** very **strong**	14 the **wa**ter's **low**

2   ▶ **175** Listen and repeat the words.

3   Work in pairs. Don't look at the words.

Student A: say the number.

Student B: say the words.

10

14

I'LL DO IT FOR YOU

SPEAKING

B

1 **Work in groups. Discuss the questions. Use a dictionary if you need to.**

   • How much do you help family / friends / people you don't know? Give an example.

   • How do you offer to help at home / at work / in class / in the street? Give an example.

   I helped my dad to build a wall in his garden.

   I helped my friend Noe to move house.

   I helped an old man I met on the train. I carried his bag.

LISTENING

2 **Look at the pictures (a–c). Discuss the questions.**

   • Where are the people?

   • What problem do you think there is?

   • How can the other person help?

3 ▶ **176** **Listen to three conversations and match 1–3 with pictures a–c.**

   Conversation 1 _B_

   Conversation 2 _C_

   Conversation 3 _A_

B

4 **Match the problem (1–3) with the solution (a–c).**

   1 It's coming out very slowly.
   2 I'm a bit lost.
   3 It's very full.

   a I'll take you there.
   b I'll stand.
   c I'll send someone to look at it.

5 ▶ **176** **Listen again and check.**

GRAMMAR

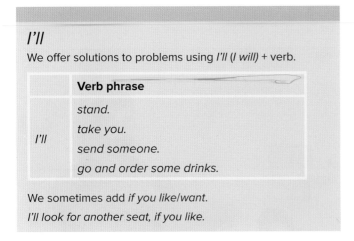

I'll

We offer solutions to problems using *I'll* (*I will*) + verb.

	Verb phrase
I'll	*stand.*
	take you.
	send someone.
	go and order some drinks.

We sometimes add *if you like/want.*

I'll look for another seat, if you like.

6 Complete the offers. Use *I'll* and one of these verbs.

check	go	take	wait

1 A: I'm quite hungry.
   B: ~~go~~ _____ and get something. What do you want?
2 A: I'm late for a meeting.
   B: ~~take~~ _____ you in the car, if you want.
3 A: Sorry, there's no space in the lift.
   B: It's OK. ~~wait~~ _____ for the next one.
4 A: What time do the buses go into town?
   B: I'm not sure. ~~check~~ _____ on the internet.

7 ▶ **177** Listen and repeat the offers from Exercise 6.

8 Think of a *different* solution to each of the situations in Exercise 6.

9 Work in pairs. Have short conversations.
   Student A: say the problem.
   Student B: offer a solution. Take turns.

VOCABULARY Offering solutions

10 Complete the problems with these words.

broken	heavy	low	working
full	lost	strong	wrong

1 There's something ~~wrong~~ _____ with my computer.
2 I'm a bit ~~lost~~ _____. How do I get out of here?
3 This coffee's not very ~~strong~~ _____.
4 It's very ~~full~~ _____. Where can we sit?
5 You sat on my glasses! They're ~~broken~~ _____
6 The battery's very ~~low~~ _____.
7 My card's not ~~working~~ _____. I can't pay for the meal!
8 How are we getting home? The shopping's quite ~~heavy~~ _____

11 Work in pairs. Check you understand the words in red. Match the solutions (a–h) with the problems (1–8) from Exercise 10.
   a I'll ask them to make another one. 3
   b I'll look for a seat. 4

---

c Do you want to use my charger? 6
d Do you want to use this one? 1
e Don't worry. I'll carry it. 8
f I'll show you. 2
g I'll lend you some money, if you like. 7
h I'll repair them. I'll take them to a shop. 5

G For more practice, see Exercises 1 and 2 on page 135.

12 ▶ **178** Listen to the pairs of words. Do they have the same sound or different?

1 broken	low
2 heavy	seat
3 strong	lost
4 carry	charger
5 lend	repair
6 full	computer

13 ▶ **178** Listen again and repeat the words.

DEVELOPING CONVERSATIONS

Checking and thanking

If someone offers to help, we often check that it's OK.

Offer:	A: *I'll stand.*	A: *I'll take you, if you like.*
Check:	B: **Are you sure?**	B: *Really?* **Are you sure?**
Yes:	A: *Yeah.* **It's fine.**	A: **Yeah, it's fine.** *I'm going that way.*
Thanks:	B: *OK.* **Thanks.**	B: *Oh.* **That's great**. *Thanks.*

14 Put the conversation in the correct order (1–5).
   a Are you sure? I can wait a bit.
   b OK. That's great. Thanks.
   c I'll make something now.
   d I'm quite hungry.
   e It's fine. I need to eat, too.

15 Work in pairs. Practise the conversation from Exercise 14.

CONVERSATION PRACTICE

16 Look at the problems in Exercise 10 again. Try to remember them.

17 Work in pairs. Close your books and have conversations like this. Take turns to start.

Student A	Student B
Say a problem from Exercise 10.	
	Offer a solution.
Check or just say thanks.	

18 Think of another problem and write your own short conversation.

▶ **179** For more practice, listen to two more examples.

WHAT A LOVELY GIFT!

REVIEW AND SPEAKING

1 **Work in pairs. Choose two.**

- How many of the problems can you remember from page 107?

- Tell your partner about three problems you have or had using words on page 107.

  The battery on my tablet is very low now.

  I got lost when I was on holiday in Bulgaria.

- Write five things you often offer to do. Then have short conversations starting like this:

  A: *I'll _____.*

  B: *Are you sure?*

READING

2 **Work in groups. Discuss the questions.**

- Do you like buying and giving gifts? Why? / Why not?

- Who did you last give a gift to? What was the gift?

3 **Read a short blog about buying gifts. Are these sentences true (T) or false (F)?**

1 The writer's dad gave him a present when he was nine.

2 He liked his dad's gift.

3 The writer gives ideas about how to choose a good gift.

4 He thinks it's important to always give a gift for birthdays, etc.

4 **Work in pairs. Complete the sentences with one of the words in red from the text. There are two you don't need.**

1 I don't usually eat anything at breakfast – I _____ have a coffee.

2 I _____ go to bed. I need to get up early tomorrow morning.

3 This isn't very _____. I'm going to throw it in the bin.

4 Our neighbours are an old _____. I sometimes help them with their shopping.

5 I have a lot of _____ in the car. Can you help me carry it into the house? Some of the boxes are quite heavy.

5 **Discuss the questions.**

- Do you ever throw presents in the bin or give them to someone else?

- Do you think the writer's questions are good or not? Do you think about them when you buy a present?

Happy Birthday, son! It's just what I always wanted!

▶ 180

HOW TO ...
GIVE BETTER GIFTS

For my ninth birthday, my dad bought me a full set of Dallas Cowboys football stuff (ball, shirt, boots, helmet, etc.). I'm sure some boys would love a present like that, but I was not one of those boys! I was not interested in football – and I was *definitely* not interested in playing it. I was small and I preferred cooking and dancing and art. I understood then that not everyone is good at buying gifts. We often buy things people don't really want. What happens to these bad gifts? We put them in a cupboard and forget about them – or we throw them in the bin! To give better gifts you should ask these questions.

- Who is the gift for? – how old are they? What do they like doing?

- What is the gift for? – is it for a couple getting married, or to thank someone?

- What are they going to do with it? Is it useful?

- Where are they going to put it?

- Do they really want it? Or is it just something *you* want?

You should also ask 'Do I really need to give a gift?' A lot of people are happy with just a thank you or some other nice words. They don't want anything else.

GRAMMAR

6 Look at these two patterns. Complete the rule.

Explaining purpose: *for* or *to*

*He gave me a football **for my birthday**.*
*Is it **to thank** someone?*

*I bought some flowers **for the kitchen**.*
*I bought her some flowers **to say sorry**.*

*Do you have anything **for a cold**?*
*Do you want something **to eat**?*

*There's nothing **for children** here.*
*There's nowhere **to sit**.*

We explain the purpose of something using _____ + noun or _____ + verb.

7 Complete the questions with *for* or *to*.

1 Do you ever buy flowers _____ say sorry?

2 Do you want anything _____ your birthday?

3 Do you need anything _____ your house?

4 Is there anywhere good near here _____ take my children?

5 Do you know anywhere _____ repair a phone?

6 Where's a good place _____ a party near here?

7 Where's the best place _____ go _____ lunch?

8 Think of answers to the questions in Exercise 7.

9 Work in pairs. Ask and answer the questions.

G For more practice, see Exercises 1–3 on page 136.

SPEAKING

10 Work in groups. Discuss the questions.

- Do you think the things below are good gifts? Who for and what for?
- Would you like any of these gifts? Why? / Why not?

> a computer game
> a T-shirt with 'I ♥ New York' printed on it.
> a special local food
> a book of photos of family or friends
> a plastic toy
> a box of chocolates or sweets
> some money
> a big book about your city with lovely photos
> some flowers
> something home-made (for example, a cake)
> a dress or shirt
> a piece of art (a painting or sculpture)

WRITING

11 Write four sentences about things you want and things people gave you. Use these ideas. Change the words in red. Use a dictionary if you need to.

I want to get a new table for my garden.

I need to get a visa to visit Russia.

My girlfriend bought me a ticket for the Grand Prix for my birthday.

My brother bought me a nice box to keep my jewellery in.

12 Tell other people in the class some of your sentences.

- Who wants the same things?
- Who had the best presents?

Offering gifts at the Guelaguetza festival in Oaxaca, Mexico

SAYING GOODBYE IS HARD TO DO

SPEAKING

1 Work in groups. How do you say goodbye? What do you say and do? Is it the same in all these situations?

- when you leave home in the morning
- at the end of a class or meeting
- at the end of an evening out with friends
- after staying at someone's home
- after meeting someone for the first time
- when a friend or one of your family is going away for a long time

VOCABULARY Leaving and saying goodbye

2 Complete the conversations with these words.

a call	forgot	journey	miss
enjoyed	hope	kind	order
everything	hurry	lovely	

1 A: Thanks for having me. I really _____ staying here.
   B: We loved having you. Come again some time.

2 A: It's getting late. It's twelve!
   B: Do you want me to _____ a taxi?
   A: Yes, please.

3 A: Bye, then.
   B: Bye. Give me _____ when you're home.
   A: OK.

4 A: It was _____ to meet you!
   B: Yes. Great to meet you, too. I _____ we see each other again soon.
   A: I hope so, too. Stay in contact. You have my email.

5 A: Here. I made you a sandwich for the _____.
   B: Oh, thanks. That's very _____ of you.
   A: That's OK.

6 A: You're back already! That was quick!
   B: Yes, I _____ my book. I left it on the table.
   A: Oh yes. Do you have _____ now?
   B: I think so. Bye, again!

7 A: I need to go or I'm going to _____ my train.
   B: What time does it leave?
   A: 10.20.
   B: Oh right, yes. You need to _____. Take care!

3 Work in pairs. Compare your answers. Guess the meaning of the words in red.

4 Discuss the questions.

- Can you remember a time when you missed a train or plane? When? Why?
- Do you often need to hurry?
- Do you often forget things? What do you forget?
- How do you stay in contact with friends?

GRAMMAR

5 ▶ **181** Listen to the goodbye conversation between Wilton (W) and Janet (J) (see Unit 3, page 30). Choose the word(s) you hear.

J: The taxi's here. Do you have ¹*all / everything*?

W: I think so.

J: Well, it's been great.

W: Yes. Thanks for ²*have / having* me. I really enjoyed it.

J: Us too. Give us ³*a call / a phone* when you're home.

W: I will.

J: OK. See you. Stay in ⁴*email / contact*.

W: I will. I hope to come ⁵*back / here* one day.

J: I ⁶*think / hope* so, too.

W: And you could come and visit me!

J: We'd love to. OK. Have a good ⁷*visit / journey*.

W: Thanks.

J: Be safe – and don't ⁸*forget / remember* to call us.

W: I won't. Thanks again for everything. And ⁹*say / tell* goodbye to your sons.

J: I will. Bye!

W: Bye.

J: Bye.

6 Practise the conversation in pairs.

7 Read the Grammar box. Find two more examples of imperatives in Exercise 5.

Telling people to do things: imperatives

Positive

You can tell people to do things using a **verb with no subject**.

A: **Give** us a call when you're home.

B: **I will**.

You can promise to do something by saying **I will**.

Negative

A: **Don't forget** to call us.

B: **I won't**.

You can promise *not* to do something by saying **I won't**.

You can also reply to imperatives with **OK**.

---

8 Choose the correct form.

1 *Has / Have* a safe journey.

2 *Don't be / Not be* late!

3 *Are / Be* good!

4 *Don't say / Say* hi to your wife.

5 *Ask / Don't ask* him now. He's busy.

6 *Don't hurry / Hurry* up. We're going to miss the train.

7 *Don't send / Send* me a text when you're there.

8 *Don't go / Go* to the toilet now if you need to. But *be / don't be* quick!

9 *Don't work / Work* too hard. *Don't get / Get* some rest.

10 It's not important. *Don't worry / Worry*. Just *forget / don't forget* it!

9 ▶ **182** Listen and repeat five negative imperatives.

10 Take turns saying a sentence from Exercise 8. Reply with *I will*, *I won't* or *OK*.

 For more practice, see Exercises 1 and 2 on page 136.

LISTENING AND SPEAKING

11 ▶ **183** Listen to two conversations where people say goodbye. Decide who is speaking in each conversation (a or b).

1 a two friends
   b a brother and sister

2 a a parent and child
   b two business people

12 ▶ **183** Work in pairs. Are the sentences (1–9) about Conversation 1 or Conversation 2? Write the number. Listen again and check.

1 It's in the afternoon.

2 It's at night.

3 They talk about going out in two weeks.

4 Someone is going to take a plane.

5 Someone orders a taxi.

6 Someone is going to miss a meeting.

7 Someone says thanks.

8 Someone walks home.

9 Someone is going to send some documents.

13 Look at the situations in Exercise 1. Choose three. You are going to have conversations to say goodbye. Think about:

• what A (the person leaving) is going to say

• what B (the person staying) is going to say

• some phrases and imperatives from this lesson to use in each situation.

14 Work in pairs. Choose two situations each from Exercise 13. Practise saying goodbye in four different conversations. Take turns being A and B.

PRONUNCIATION AND REVIEW

15 Find the four pairs of words with the same sound.

carry	lend	miss	order
send	stand	walk	give

16 ▶ **184** Listen to the four pairs of words and check your answers.

17 ▶ **185** Listen to the verbs in phrases. Write the full phrase you hear.

18 Work in pairs. Can you make two more phrases with each verb? Use a dictionary if you need to.

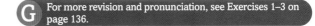 For more revision and pronunciation, see Exercises 1–3 on page 136.

VIDEO 6

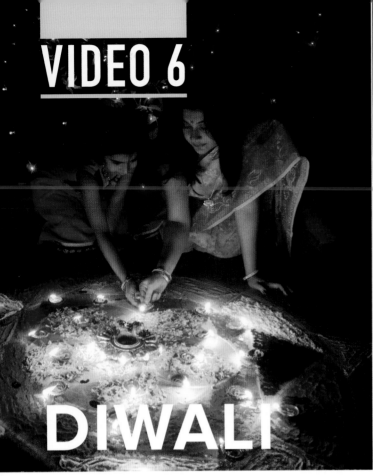

DIWALI

1 Look at the photos of the festival of Diwali. Do you know anything about this festival? Which of the sentences do you think are true?

1 It happens in September.

2 It celebrates light and hope.

3 People draw flowers with sand.

4 People don't make food.

5 There are a lot of fireworks.

2 ◼◤ 6 Watch the video. Which two sentences from Exercise 1 are false?

3 Work in pairs. Read the sentences. Choose the correct ending (a or b).

1 People go to the market early

  a to buy fresh bread.

  b to buy flowers.

2 People draw flowers in sand

  a because the children enjoy doing it.

  b to say visitors are welcome.

3 People often make sweets

  a for their neighbours.

  b to take to the temple.

4 Shops are busy

  a because people often get extra money for Diwali.

  b because people usually buy new clothes for Diwali.

5 Many cities have a firework show on

  a the first night.

  b the last night.

4 ◼◤ 6 Watch the video again and check.

5 Complete the sentences about festivals with the correct form of these verbs.

celebrate	happen	make	take
enjoy	last	put	visit

1 The festival _____ in February.

2 The festival _____ three days.

3 The festival _____ the beginning of a new year.

4 People often _____ flowers and nice things in their homes.

5 People _____ a special fish dish on the main day.

6 People _____ friends and _____ them gifts.

7 Most people _____ the festival a lot, but some people don't like it.

SPEAKING

6 Work in groups. Answer the questions.

• Which of these things do you like / not like about festivals?

buying gifts	cooking
eating sweets and cake	fireworks
neighbours visiting your house	travelling home

• What is your favourite festival? What do you usually do during the festival?

• Do you know any festivals in other countries? When do they happen? What do they celebrate?

• When is the last time you got together with all your family? What did you do?

REVIEW 6

1 Choose the correct word(s).

1 Are you hungry? *I* / *I'll* make you a sandwich.

2 The wall was damaged during the war *so* / *because* they needed to repair it.

3 Do they have any food *to* / *for* vegetarians?

4 Give *we* / *us* a call when you get home.

5 I became a teacher *so* / *because* I didn't want to work in an office.

6 Do you want *come* / *coming* / *to come* with us?

7 It's a very good place *for* / *to* / *for to* take kids. They love it.

8 Sleep well – and *not* / *don't* / *don't to* worry about the problems at work.

2 Complete the questions with these words.

are	did	does	was
can	do	is	were

1 Why _____ you studying English?

2 _____ you call me later? I want to know you're OK.

3 Are you tired? _____ you want to sit here?

4 How old _____ he when he died?

5 What _____ your brother do? Is he a doctor?

6 How old _____ your grandmother now?

7 You didn't come to class last week. Where _____ you?

8 How long _____ it take to build?

3 Write questions. Use the words in brackets.

1 A: _____? (old / you)

   B: I'm 39 now. Nearly 40.

2 A: We're having a party tonight.
   _____? (you / want / come)

   B: Oh, I'd love to. Thank you for inviting me.

3 A: It's my birthday next week.

   B: _____? (old / you / be)?

   A: Twenty-one.

4 A: _____? (when / become / a doctor)

   B: When I was 27. After I left university.

5 A: _____? (like / job)

   B: Yes, I do. I love it.

4 ▶ 186 Listen and complete the sentences.

1 I'm studying English _____ a good job.

2 Where _____ going and _____ there?

3 I'm studying English _____ it _____ my job.

4 _____ some sleep – and _____ call me tomorrow.

5 _____ a minute. _____ on the internet.

5 ▶ 186 Work in pairs. Compare your answers. Listen again to check.

6 Match the verbs in the box with the correct groups of words (1–8).

become	do	have	move
celebrate	go	live	start

1 _____ to university / into the army

2 _____ interested in art / an important city

3 _____ well at school / the same thing

4 _____ our wedding anniversary / my birthday

5 _____ problems at school / an online shop

6 _____ a new life / teaching

7 _____ with my mother and father / in a nice area

8 _____ house / to the countryside

7 Put the words into three groups: life events, history or leaving and saying goodbye.

become a doctor	lovely to meet you
born in the 1980s	miss my train
call a taxi	protect the country
die in his sleep	repair the castle
finish school	a sandwich for the journey
forget my bag	start a business
king and queen	the fifteenth century

8 Write the dates in words (1–4), then write the names of the months (5–8).

1 the 1st   _____

2 the 4th   _____

3 the 15th   _____

4 the 22nd   _____

5 the second month of the year   _____

6 the eighth month of the year   _____

7 the ninth month of the year   _____

8 the eleventh month of the year   _____

9 Complete the sentences with these adjectives.

broken	full	lost	strong
empty	heavy	low	wrong

1 Can you help me carry this? It's very _____.

2 I don't want to use my phone at the moment. The battery is very _____.

3 Don't sit on that chair. It's _____.

4 Can you help me? There's something _____ with my computer.

5 There's nowhere to sit here. It's very _____. Can we go somewhere else?

6 Excuse me. Is this the right way to the station? I'm a bit _____.

7 I didn't sleep very well. I need a _____ coffee.

8 The restaurant wasn't very busy last night. There were lots of _____ seats.

GRAMMAR REFERENCE

1 BE

'M, 'S, 'RE

Pronouns

I

you

he

she

it

we

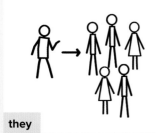
they

they

Exercise 1
▶ 187 Listen and repeat.

be

am
I'm Andrew. (= I am)

are
You're Naomi, right? (= You are)
We're from Saudi Arabia. (= We are)
They're from China. (= They are)

is	
She's a doctor. (= She is)	**He's** my boss. (= He is)
It's good. (= It is)	**This is** my brother.
That's right. (= That is)	
My daughter's 6. (= My daughter is)	

Exercise 2
▶ 188 Listen and write the missing word.

1 _____'m Juan. Nice to meet you.
2 _____ is my teacher, Lena.
3 _____'s my sister.
4 _____'re in the same class.
5 _____'s nice.
6 Who are _____?
7 What's _____?
8 _____ son is three today.

Exercise 3
Write the sentences with the *'m, 're, 's* forms.

1 I am from Berlin. *I'm from Berlin.*
2 He is from London. _____
3 My name is Cathy. _____
4 We are friends. _____
5 They are in my class. _____
6 You are in class 6. _____
7 She is my teacher_____
8 That is right. _____

	Stella. Javier.	**name**
I'm	OK. good.	**adjective**
	a teacher. her father.	**person/job**
	from London. in the class.	**place**

Exercise 4
Write four sentences about you and four sentences about another person. Use a dictionary if you need to.

I'm _____
I'm _____
I'm _____
I'm _____
My _____'s _____.
My _____'s _____.
My _____'s _____.
My _____'s _____.

QUESTIONS WITH *BE*

am	
I'm sorry.	What class **am I** in?

are	
You're right.	How **are you**?
We're in class 1.	Where **are we**?
They're very nice.	Where **are they** from?

is	
He's nice.	How old **is he**?
She's a teacher.	Who **is she**?
It's ten o'clock.	How much **is it**?
This is my book.	Who **is this**?
Your son's nice.	How old **is your son**?

Exercise 1

Complete the sentences with *are*, *is* **or** *'s*.

1 A: Where_____ he from?
   B: Kuwait.
2 A: How old _____ you?
   B: Twenty.
3 A: What_____ your name?
   B: Maria.
4 A: How long _____ the class?
   B: Three hours.
5 A: How old _____ your brother?
   B: Seventeen.
   A: _____ he here?
   B: No, he's at school.
6 A: Where_____ your father from, Reo?
   B: Aizuwakamatsu.
   A: _____ it a big place?
   B: No. It_____ very small.

Exercise 2

Put the words in the correct order to make questions.

1 you / where / are / from *Where are you from?*
2 much / how / are / they
3 he / is / who
4 how / are / old / you
5 their / what / names / are
6 you / how / are
7 what / is / time / bus / the

Exercise 3

Match the answers with the questions from Exercise 2.

a Khalid and Fatima.
b Dubai.
c $25.50.
d Twenty-one.
e My husband.
f Eleven o'clock.
g Good, thanks.

Yes/No questions and short answers

Am I OK here?	Yes, you **are**.	No, you**'re not**.
Are you OK?	Yes, I **am**.	No, I**'m not**.
Are we in the right class?	Yes, you **are**.	No, you**'re not**.
Are they from Tokyo?	Yes, they **are**.	No, they**'re not**.
Is he 16?	Yes, he **is**.	No, he**'s not**.
Is your son at school?	Yes, he **is**.	No, he**'s not**.
Is she your teacher?	Yes, she **is**.	No, she**'s not**.
Is it expensive?	Yes, it **is**.	No, it**'s not**.
Is this your book?	Yes, it **is**.	No, it**'s not**.

Exercise 4

Write a short answer to these questions.

1 Are you Olivia? (✓) *Yes, I am.*
2 Is your name Omar? (✗) *No, it's not.*
3 Am I late? (✓)
4 Are we in this class? (✓)
5 Are you OK? (✗)
6 Is he sixteen? (✓)
7 Is she your wife? (✗)
8 Is it right? (✗)
9 Are they your mother and father? (✓)
10 Is this your bag? (✓)

HIS, HER, OUR, THEIR

Possessive adjectives and *'s*

| **my** cat | **your** cat | **his** cat |
| **her** cat | **our** cat | **their** cat |

Sheila's cat Henry's cat Peter and John's cat

Exercise 1

A Complete the sentences with *my*, *your*, etc. or *[name]'s*.

1 *His* name is Karim. 2 *Karen's* husband is a teacher.

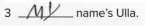

3 __MY__ name's Ulla. 4 __our__ address is 15 New Road.

5 Where's __their__ new flat? 6 When's __his__ party?

7 What's __his__ name? 8 Is __his__ new baby a boy or a girl?

9 What's _____ name?   10 What's _____ phone number?

B ▶ **189** Listen and check.

Exercise 2

Choose the correct word(s).

1 *I* / *My* am from Oman.
2 *I* / *My* name is Fadi.
3 How old are *you* / *your*?
4 Is *you* / *your* class good?
5 Where's *he* / *him* from?
6 What time is *they* / *their* party?
7 How long is *we* / *our* class?
8 Who are *they* / *their*?
9 Here's *I* / *my* phone number. *It's* / *He's* 07490028.
10 *I* / *My* son's at university. *She's* / *He's* 21.
11 This is Maria. *She* / *Her* is in *we* / *our* English class.
12 *He* / *Her* husband is *I* / *my* boss.

NOT

I'm **not** from Moscow.	It's large – **not** small.
You're **not** 18.	It's 20 euros – **not** 30.
We're **not** from here.	He's 20 – **not** 16!
They're **not** new.	I'm from Manchester – **not** London.
It's **not** a black tea.	
He's **not** my husband.	
She's **not** a doctor.	

Exercise 1

Tick (✓) the correct sentence.

1 a My name's not Chelsea. ✓
  b Not my name's Chelsea.
2 a It's a large coffee – small not.
  b It's a large coffee – not small.
3 a I is not from New York.
  b I'm not from New York.
4 a How old you are?
  b How old are you?
5 a Where is she from?
  b Where she's from?
6 a I'm no Leo.
  b Are you Leo?
7 a He's her brother. Her name's Pedro.
  b He's her brother. His name's Pedro.
8 a They is not from here.
  b They're not from here.

PRONUNCIATION

Exercise 1

A ▶ **190** Listen and complete the questions. They're fast.

1 Who _____?
2 Where _____?
3 Where _____ from?
4 How much _____?
5 What day _____?
6 What _____?
7 How old _____?
8 What time _____?
9 How much _____?
10 How _____?
11 How old _____?
12 Where _____?
13 Who _____?
14 How long _____?

B ▶ **191** Listen again and check. They're slow.

2 LIVE, WORK, EAT

PRESENT SIMPLE

Verbs: *(to)* *live, know, like, have, take, work*

I	**live** near here.
You	**know** the city.
We	**like** it here.
They	**work** here.
My mother and father	**have** a nice house.
He	**lives** near here.
She	**knows** the city.
My brother	**likes** it here.
My friend Karen	**has** a nice flat.
It	**takes** 10 minutes.
The bus	

Exercise 1

Choose the correct word.

1 I *live* / *lives* in a flat.
2 My mother and father *live* / *lives* near me.
3 My friend Ali *have* / *has* a nice flat.
4 You *know* / *knows* the park. He *live* / *lives* near there.
5 I *know* / *knows* your sister. She *work* / *works* in the university, right?
6 We *walk* / *walks* to school. It *take* / *takes* an hour.
7 My wife *like* / *likes* Moscow, but I *like* / *likes* St Petersburg.
8 My family *live* / *lives* in a small village. We *know* / *knows* everyone in the village!

PRESENT SIMPLE QUESTIONS: *DO YOU ...?*

Where		live?
Who	**do you**	live with?
What time		go to work?
	Do you	live near here?
		know it?
		like it?

Exercise 1

A Write *do you* in the right places in the conversation. There are one or two in each part 1–5.

        do you

1 A: Where ˄ live?
   B: In Beppu. know it?

2 A: No. Where is it?
   B: It's a small city in the south of Japan.
   A: like it?

3 B: Yes. It's a nice place. Where live?
   A: Birmingham. know it?
   B: Yes. My friend lives there!

4 A: What's his name?
   B: Bryan.
   A: know his family name?

5 B: No. Sorry. like Birmingham?
   A: Yes, it's OK.

B ▶ **192** Listen and check.

be or do?

Be	Other verbs
Where **are you** from?	Where **do you** live?
How **are you**?	What **do you** do?
Are you OK?	**Do you** have a sister?
Are you married?	**Do you** know it?

Exercise 2

Complete the questions with *are* or *do*.

1 Where _____ you from?
2 What _____ you do?
3 How old _____ your children?
4 Who _____ you?
5 Where _____ you live? Is it near?
6 _____ you have a brother?
7 _____ you OK?
8 _____ you know my friend, Sara?
9 Where _____ you work?

Exercise 3

Match the answers (a–i) with the questions in Exercise 2.

a I'm a teacher.
b France.
c Five and seven.
d I'm fine, thanks.
e Yes, he's sixteen.
f Not far. I have a flat in Little Street.
g In an office.
h No. Nice to meet you.
i My name's Alex. I work here.

Exercise 4

Tick (✓) the correct question (a or b).

1 a Do you like it? ✓
  b You like?
2 a Are you live near here?
  b Do you live near here?
3 a Do it far?
  b Is it far?
4 a How are you?
  b How do you?
5 a Where you from?
  b Where are you from?
6 a What do you?
  b What do you do?

PRESENT SIMPLE: *DON'T (DO NOT)*

Negative forms

I **work** 50 hours a week.	I **don't work** here.
I **walk** to work.	I **don't walk** to work.
You **like** the area.	You **don't like** the area.
We **have** a house.	We **don't have** a house.
They **have** a big car.	They **don't have** a car.

Exercise 1

Choose the correct word(s).

1 I *like / don't like* my job. It's good.
2 I *like / don't like* meat. It's bad.
3 I *work / don't work*. I'm at school.
4 I *work / don't work*. I'm retired.
5 I *work / don't work* in a hospital. I'm a nurse.
6 I *have / don't have* a paid job. I'm at home with my son. He's two.
7 I *have / don't have* children. One daughter and one son.
8 I *have / don't have* a car. I take the bus.

Yes/No questions and short answers

Questions			Short answers	
			+	–
Do	I you they Jia and Fan	**have** time for a coffee? **live** here? **like** fish? **work**?	Yes, you **do**. Yes, I **do**. Yes, they **do**. Yes, they **do**.	No, you **don't**. No, I **don't**. No, they **don't**. No, they **don't**.

Exercise 2

Write a short answer.

1 Do we have something to eat? (–)
  No, we don't.
2 Do you know her sister? (–)
3 Do you live near Bob? (+)
4 Do they like London? (+)
5 Do you have a car? (–)
6 Do we have time for a coffee? (+)
7 Do your children live with you? (–)

PLURAL / NO PLURAL

Plurals

Regular	
singular	**plural (+ -s)**
a daughter	two daughters
a nurse	five nurses
a flat	a lot of flats
a boy	some boys
a bus	two buses
a city	some cities

Irregular	
singular	**plural (no -s)**
child	children
person	people
man	men
woman	women

Exercise 1

Write the correct word in each sentence.

1 **job / jobs**

    a I have a good _____. I like it.

    b My brother works a lot. He has three _____.

2 **son / sons**

    a I have three _____ and a daughter.

    b My _____ is a nurse.

3 **teacher / teachers**

    a I'm a _____ in a university.

    b It's a big school with eighty _____.

4 **person / people**

    a Sixty _____ work at my company.

    b She's a nice _____.

5 **flat / flats**

    a We have two _____. One in the city and one in a village.

    b Our _____ is near here.

6 **woman / women**

    a All the English teachers in my school are _____!

    b Francisca is a great _____. She's a good friend.

No Plural

money	The money **is** good.
work	I do **a lot of** work.
meat	The meat **is** nice.
time	I don't have time.

Exercise 2

Tick (✓) the correct sentences.

1 a The hours are bad. ✓

    b The hours is bad.

2 a I eat a lot of meats.

    b I eat a lot of meat.

3 a I have some money.

    b I have some moneys.

4 a The people at work is nice.

    b The people at work are nice.

5 a My children is sixteen.

    b My child is sixteen.

6 a I don't like my works.

    b I don't like my work.

7 a Most people in the office are men.

    b Most people in the office are man.

Exercise 3

Write plurals. Two words have no plural.

1 a village / some small _____

2 a block of flats / lots of _____ of flats

3 one green salad / three green _____

4 one brother and one sister / two _____ and three _____

5 fruit / lots of _____

6 a shop / lots of _____

7 a kebab / two _____

8 a job / lots of _____

9 one room / five _____

10 wine / some _____

11 a chicken curry / two chicken _____

LIKE / DON'T LIKE

PLURAL WORDS	NO PLURAL	
I (don't) like them	*I (don't) like it*	
burgers	meat	rice
chips	chicken	bread
oranges	fish	fruit
apples	sugar	cheese
cakes	tea	coffee
pizzas	wine	beer
people	money	work
children		

Exercise 1

Write the correct sentences.

(😃) = *I love it/them*   (🙁) = *I don't like it/them*

(🙂) = *I like it/them*

1 oranges (😃) *I love them.*   6 cheese (🙂)

2 chicken (🙁) *I don't like it.*   7 pizzas (😃)

3 coffee (🙁)   8 wine (🙁)

4 burgers (🙁)   9 work (🙂)

5 chips (🙂)   10 children (😃)

PRONUNCIATION

Exercise 1

A ▶ 193 Listen to these words. They are fast then slow.

1 do you

2 are you

B ▶ 194 Listen and choose the words you hear (a or b).

1	a do you	b are you
2	a do you	b are you
3	a do you	b are you
4	a do you	b are you
5	a do you	b are you
6	a do you	b are you
7	a Are you OK?	b Where do you work?
8	a Where are you from?	b Where do you live?
9	a When are you here?	b When do you work?
10	a Are you from here?	b Do you live here?
11	a Are you friends?	b Do you know him?
12	a How are you?	b How do you get there?

Exercise 2

▶ 195 Listen and write the five questions you hear.

3 LOVE, WANT, NEED

NEGATIVES WITH *BE*

am	
I'm hungry.	I'm **not** hungry.

are	
You're very good.	You're **not** very good.
We're in Spain.	We're **not** in Spain.
They're friends.	They're **not** friends.

is	
He's well.	He's not well.
She's at school.	She's not at school today.
He's married.	He's not married.
It's very big.	It's not very big.
This is my class.	This is not my class.
My son is tired.	My son's not tired.
The room's cold.	The room's not cold.

Exercise 1

Tick (✓) the correct sentence (a or b).

1 a It's not very expensive. ✓
   b Not it's very expensive.
2 a This exercise not is difficult.
   b This exercise is not difficult.
3 a I not Russian.
   b I'm not Russian
4 a We's not married.
   b We're not married.
5 a You're not old!
   b Your not old!
6 a My mum and dad are not here.
   b My mum and dad is not here.

Exercise 2

Complete the sentences with the negative form of *be*.

1 He _____ from America. He's from Canada.
2 You _____ in this class. Sorry.
3 They _____ married.
4 We _____ retired. We work.
5 I _____ Conrad. I'm Constan.
6 I want it – and it _____ very expensive.
7 Sorry. My brother _____ here today.
8 It _____ a big town. It has 12,000 people.
9 Grammar _____ difficult. It's easy.
10 I _____ in this hotel. It's very expensive!

be: contractions

We also sometimes say *be* negatives in these ways:

You **aren't**	= You**'re not**
We **aren't**	= We**'re not**
They **aren't**	= They**'re not**
It **isn't**	= It**'s not**
He **isn't**	= He**'s not**
She **isn't**	= She**'s not**

He **isn't** from America. He's from Canada.
You **aren't** in this class. Sorry.

PRESENT SIMPLE: *DOESN'T*

Negative forms

Person	don't/ doesn't	Verb
He She My brother Andrew	doesn't	live here. work. have any money. like it.
It	doesn't	take long.
I You We They	don't	live here. work. have any money. like it.

don't = do not; **doesn't** = does not

Exercise 1

Make the sentences negative.

1 I like fish. *I don't like fish.*
2 My son likes meat.
3 It takes a long time.
4 My mum and dad have a big house.
5 My friend Mikel has a very good job.
6 She lives near here.
7 We like this city.
8 I have money.

PRESENT SIMPLE QUESTIONS: *DOES*

Question word	does	person	verb
What		he	**do**?
Where		she	**work**?
Who	does	Ali	**live** with?
How long		it	**take**?
What time		your wife	**get** home?
		it	**take** a long time?
	Does	he	**live** here?
		your sister	**have** a car?

Exercise 1

Add *do*, *don't*, *does* or *doesn't* in the correct part of the conversations. You need one or two in each conversation.

1 A: I'm sorry, I know your name.
   I'm sorry, I don't know your name.
   B: Andrea.
2 A: you know this area?
   B: No. I live here.
3 A: What your mother do?
   B: She work now. She's retired.
4 A: Where Maria live?
   B: I know. Ask Simon. He knows her well.
5 A: Where your girlfriend work?
   B: Sorrento.
   A: How long it take to get there?
   B: Twenty or thirty minutes.

be or do?

be + adjective/noun	do + verb
I'm not **hungry**.	I don't **know**.
He's not **English**.	He doesn't **work** now.
Are they **police**?	Do they **have** a car?
Is your father very **old**?	Does your mum **work**?

Exercise 2

Choose the correct word.

1 What *do / is / does* she eat for lunch?
2 What time *are / is / does* your bus?
3 Where *is / does / do* he live?
4 *Does / Is / Do* your boss married?
5 Where *do / does / are* you from?
6 My daughter *don't / isn't / doesn't* eat meat.
7 *Is / Does / Do* your father like his job?
8 She *work / works / is work* in a school.
9 Where *is / are / do* your parents live?
10 *Are / Is / Do* the people in your class nice?

A and ANY

I **don't** have		charger.
I **don't** need	a	pen.
I **don't** want		brush.
		towel.
Do you have		pens?
Do you need	any	towels?
Do you want		other clothes?
		milk?
		money?
		toothpaste?
	anything (else)?	

Exercise 1

Complete the sentences with *a* or *any*.

1 I have _____ flight at seven tomorrow.
2 Do you want _____ rice?
3 I'm sorry. I don't have _____ time this week.
4 It's _____ good restaurant.
5 I don't have _____ friends here.
6 My father is _____ driver and my mother is _____ nurse.
7 Do you have _____ pens?
8 I work in _____ coffee shop. It's _____ nice job.
9 My mother works in _____ hospital.
10 Do you have _____ milk?

> Use *an* before a vowel sound.
> I want **an** ice cream.
> **An** orange juice, please.
> **an** English class

PRONUNCIATION

Exercise 1

A ▶ 196 Listen to the phrases. They are fast then slow.

1 does he
2 does she
3 does it

B ▶ 197 Listen and choose the sentence you hear (a or b).

1 a Where does he work?
   b Where do you work?
2 a What time does the shop open?
   b What time does your class start?
3 a Does your brother have a car?
   b Do you have a car?
4 a Does he live near here?
   b Is it near here?
5 a What does she do?
   b What does it do?
6 a Do you know everyone?
   b Does she know your mum?
7 a Does he like it?
   b Does she like it?
8 a What does he know?
   b What does she know?

Exercise 2

▶ 198 Listen to the sentences. They are fast. Are they negative (–) or positive (+)?

1	___+___	5	_____	9	_____
2	___–___	6	_____	10	_____
3	_____	7	_____	11	_____
4	_____	8	_____	12	_____

4 WHERE AND WHEN?

IS THERE ...? THERE'S ...

> **Is there** a park near here?
> **Is there** a bank near here?
> **There's** one on this road.
> **There's** a shop on the corner.

We use *is there ....?* and *there's* with singular nouns.

Exercise 1

Complete the sentences with *is there* or *there's*.

1 A: I need to get some money. _____ a cash machine near here?
   B: Oh, right. _____ one in the bus station.
2 A: _____ a park near here?
   B: I'm sorry. I don't know the area.
3 A: Do you know a bar called Lisboa?
   B: No. _____ a place down there. I don't know its name.
4 A: _____ a supermarket near here?
   B: No, sorry, but _____ a fruit and vegetable shop on this road.
5 A: _____ a car park near here?
   B: Yes, _____ one next to the supermarket.
6 A: _____ a café near here?
   B: _____ one in the square. Go down there.

PREPOSITIONS AND DIRECTIONS

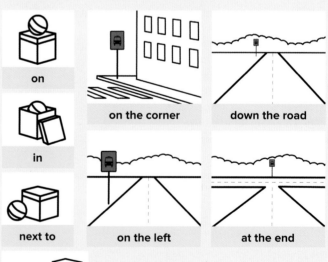

on

on the corner

down the road

in

next to

on the left

at the end

near

Exercise 1

Put the preposition in the correct place.

on

1 There's a small shop the corner of this road. (on)
2 There's a restaurant the hotel. (in)
3 The hotel is the centre. (near)
4 The school is the main square. (in)
5 There's a nice café the school. (next to)
6 It's the next road. (on)
7 There's a swimming pool the park. (in)
8 There's a shop the next corner. (on)
9 There's a small park the end of our street. (at)
10 Is there a toilet the second floor? (on)
11 It's this road. Then take the second the right. (down / on)

Exercise 2

Put the words in the correct order.

1 near / a / here / supermarket / there / is / ?
   Is there a supermarket near here?
2 road / a / hotel / on / this / there's / .
3 a / shop / there's / near / the / train / station / .
4 there / is / a / cash / here / near / machine / ?
5 one / there's / the / corner / on / .
6 near / is / swimming / pool / a / there / here / ?
7 at / there's / of / one / the / end / this / road / .

ADVERBS OF FREQUENCY

With be

The bank **is** <u>always</u> closed on Monday.
It**'s not** <u>normally</u> busy on Thursday.
He**'s** <u>often</u> late.
English **is** <u>sometimes</u> difficult.
I**'m** <u>never</u> late.
Are you <u>normally</u> free on Saturday?

With other verbs

Supermarkets <u>normally</u> **open** at 8 in the morning.
Children **don't** <u>usually</u> **have** classes at the weekend.
I <u>sometimes</u> **have** tea.
We **don't** <u>often</u> **have** coffee.
We <u>never</u> **work** on Friday.
Do you <u>normally</u> **work** late?

Exercise 1

Put the adverb in the correct place in each sentence.

1 I go out on Saturday night. (usually)
   I usually go out on Saturday night.
2 They're late. (always)
3 I work on Saturday. (sometimes)
4 I go to mosque on Friday. (always)
5 I'm free on Wednesday afternoon. (normally)
6 I go swimming. (never)
7 We don't go out at night in the week. (usually)
8 I'm busy at the weekend. (never)
9 He's not here in the afternoon. (usually)
10 They go to the beach on Sunday morning. (sometimes)
11 I don't go to the cinema. (often)

Exercise 2

▶ **199** **Listen to the sentences. They are fast. Add the adverb you hear.**

1 I'm _____ late.
2 We _____ go to church on Sunday.
3 I'm not _____ busy on Thursday.
4 I _____ walk to work.
5 I _____ take the bus.
6 My wife _____ works in the evening.
7 My husband _____ has lunch at home.
8 My brother _____ takes my things.

CAN ...?

We use **can/can't** + verb.

Can I help you?	I **can** help.
	I **can't** help.
Can you help me?	You **can** help.
	You **can't** help.
Can he come tomorrow?	He **can** come.
	He **can't** come.
Can she speak English?	She **can** speak French.
	She **can't** speak English.
Can we do it now?	We **can** do it.
	We **can't** do it.
Can they wait?	They **can** wait.
	They **can't** wait.

Exercise 1

Complete the questions with the correct verb.

change	get	go	help	say	sit	wait	write

1 My English isn't good. Can you _____ it again slowly, please?
2 I have a big problem. Can you _____ me?
3 I don't know this word. Can you _____ it on the board?
4 Can you _____ one minute? I need to finish this.
5 I don't know how to get there. Can I _____ with you?
6 I don't have my book. Can I _____ next to you and share yours?
7 Can you _____ me a coffee? And I think Ben wants a tea.
8 This isn't chicken. It's fish. Can you _____ it, please?

Short answers

We sometimes say *can / can't* in the answers.

Can I open the window?
Of course you **can**.
Yes, you **can**.
Can I open the window?
I'm sorry, you **can't**.
No, you **can't**.

Exercise 2

Complete the sentences with *can* or *can't*.

1 A: _____ you help me?
   B: Sorry, I _____ now. I'm busy.
2 A: It's difficult to hear. _____ you play it again?
   B: Of course I _____.
3 A: I don't feel well. _____ I leave early?
   B: Of course you _____.
4 A: I _____ see the board very well. _____ I sit at the front?
   B: Sorry, you _____. But I _____ turn on the light. Does that help?
   A: Yes, thanks.

Exercise 3

Write sentences with *can* and these words.

1 help me? (you)
   Can you help me?
2 hear you (I / not)
3 cook lots of different things (my mum)
4 speak English (they / not)
5 leave early (we)
6 write it on the board? (you)
7 come in now. (she)
8 help you? (I)
9 share a book? (you three)

PRONUNCIATION

Exercise 1

A ▶ 200 **Listen to the words. They are fast then slow.**

1 can
2 can't

B ▶ 201 **Listen and choose the words you hear. They are fast.**

1 a Sorry, I can.   b Sorry, I can't.
2 a You can.   b You can't.
3 a Can you?   b Can't you?
4 a I can see.   b I can't see.
5 a Can I use your phone?   b Can't I use your phone?
6 a You can sit here.   b You can't sit here.
7 a You can come in.   b You can't come in.
8 a I can play it again.   b I can't play it again.
9 a Can we leave now?   b Can't we leave now?
10 a He can use my tablet.   b He can't use my tablet.
11 a They can help you.   b They can't help you.
12 a Can you turn off the light? b Can't you turn off the light?

5 GOING PLACES

ARE THERE ...? / THERE ARE ...

There are + plural nouns		
There are	fifteen some several a lot of no	shops on this street. nice restaurants in the village. people outside.
There aren't		nice places near here.
Are there	any	cafés near here? people outside?

Remember

People, children, men and *women* are plural!
*There **are** always lots of **people** there.*

With the singular, we use these forms:

There's ... + singular nouns
There's a/no train station in the village. *There isn't a restaurant in the hotel.* *Is there a cinema near here?*

There are no ... = there aren't any ...
There's no ... = there isn't a ...

Exercise 1

Make these sentences plural.

1 There's a man outside. *There are some men outside.*
2 There's no toilet. *There are no toilets.*
3 There's no bar near here.
4 There's a shop on this road.
5 There's a restaurant in the square.
6 There's no cinema in the area.
7 There isn't a hospital in the town.
8 There's one person in the café.
9 There's only one man in our class.

Exercise 2

Read the conversations with a hotel receptionist. Write one word in each space.

Conversation 1

A: Hello. Can I help you?
B: Yes. I want to have a walk. [1]_____ there any nice places near here?
A: There [2]_____ a nice park down the road.
B: How do you get there?
A: It's best to take a bus. It takes ten minutes. There [3]_____ four every hour.
B: Can I buy the ticket on the bus?
A: No. There's [4]_____ machine next to the bus stop.

Conversation 2

A: Hi, I want to go into town. Are there [5]_____ buses going there now?
B: Sorry. You need to drive – or take a taxi.
A: OK. Is there [6]_____ taxi place near here?
B: No, but I can call one.
A: There [7]_____ six people in our group.
B: OK. I can ask for two.
A: Thanks. How much is it normally?
B: Fifteen euros.
A: OK. [8]_____ there a cash machine here?
B: Yes. There [9]_____ one over there. Next to the toilets.
A: Oh yes. Thanks.

Short answers

We sometimes use short answers in replies to *Are there ...?*

***Are** there any good films at the cinema?* *Yes, there **are**.* *No, there **aren't**.*

Exercise 3

Complete the conversations with short answers.

1 A: Are there any good places to eat here?
   B: No, _____. You need to go into the city.
2 A: Is there a hotel near here called the Grand View?
   B: Yes, _____. It's on the main road.
3 A: Is there a supermarket near here?
   B: No, _____, but there's a shop at the end of the road which sells fruit and vegetables and things.

TALKING ABOUT PLANS: *I'M/WE'RE GOING …*

Plan	Where / What	When
I'm going **We're going**	home to a café to the shops	now. this afternoon. at six. tonight. tomorrow. on Saturday. after the class.
	to have lunch to meet my sister to see the game	

Compare with the present simple for habits (*always, usually*, etc.):

I normally go home at five.
I go to mosque on Friday.
I often go to see my grandparents at the weekend.

Exercise 1

Complete with *am/'m, are/'re* or *do*.

1 A: I _____ going to meet Joan later.
   B: Oh, OK. Say hello.
2 A: We _____ going to the shops. _____ you need anything?
   B: Can you buy some milk?
3 A: _____ you know Madrid?
   B: Not really. Why?
   A: I _____ going there at the weekend.
4 A: I _____ going home now.
   B: Really? _____ you OK?
   A: Yes. I _____ fine, but I need to do some work.
5 A: _____ you like football?
   B: Yes.
   A: We _____ going to see the game tonight. _____ you want to come?

Exercise 2

Sentences 1–8 are wrong. They need one more word. Write the correct sentence.

1 I going home at seven.
   I'm going home at seven.
2 We're going to the beach Saturday.
   *We're going to the beach **on** Saturday.*
3 Am going to the cinema tonight.
4 We're to have a coffee.
5 I'm going the park after the class.
6 We going to see the Old Town tomorrow.
7 We're going meet some friends later.
8 We're going to finish six.

Exercise 3

Choose the correct sentence (a or b).

1 a I normally go to the beach on Sundays.
   b I'm normally going to the beach on Sundays.
2 a I go to have lunch later.
   b I'm going to have lunch later.

3 a We're sometimes going to play tennis.
   b We're going to play tennis today.
4 a I go to the cinema a lot.
   b I go to the cinema tonight.
5 a We're going to have a walk now.
   b We have a walk now.

Other forms after *go*

I'm going We're going I need to go Do you want to go	shopping swimming running for lunch for dinner for a walk for a run for a coffee	now. this afternoon. at six. tonight. tomorrow. on Saturday. after the class.

Exercise 4

▶ **202** **Listen and complete.**

1 Do you want to go for a _____?
2 I'm going _____ later.
3 I'm going for a _____. Do you want to come?
4 We're going _____ on Saturday.
5 Do you want to go out for _____ tonight?
6 I need to go for a _____.

ASKING ABOUT PLANS: *GOING* AND *DOING*

	Are you **going**?
What time Where	**are** you **going**?
What	**are** you **doing** after the class? **are** you **doing** tonight?

Compare with the present simple for *want*, *need* and habits.

What time do you need to be there?
Where do you want to go?
What do you do? (= What's your job? / What do you normally do there?)

Exercise 1

Choose the correct word(s).

1 A: What are you *do / doing* tonight?
   B: Nothing special. Why?
2 A: *Do / Are* you want to go for lunch with us?
   B: Sure. Where are you going?
3 A: I'm going to meet a friend later. Do you want to come?
   B: Where *are / do* you going?
4 A: I sometimes need to work late, but I like my job.
   B: What *do you do / are you doing*?
5 A: We're going out later – if you want to come.
   B: Where *do you go / are you going*?
6 A: *What time / Where* are you going to the party tonight?
   B: Ten o'clock.

Other questions

When		?
Why		?
Who	**are you going**	with?
How long		for?

Exercise 2

A Complete the conversations 1–6 with the answers a–e.

a Eight?
b My boyfriend.
c My company has an office there.
d Krakow – it's a city in Poland.
e Two weeks.
f I'm going to the dentist in the morning and I'm going to meet a friend at the airport in the afternoon.

1 A: I'm going to Qatar next week.
   B: Why are you going?
   A: _____
2 A: Do you want to go to the dinner together?
   B: Sure. What time?
   A: _____
3 A: We're going to Costa Rica on holiday.
   B: How long are you going for?
   A: _____
4 A: I'm sorry. I'm not free tomorrow.
   B: What are you doing?
   A: _____
5 A: I'm going to see *An American in Paris* tonight.
   B: Nice! Who are you going with?
   A: _____
6 A: I'm going away for the weekend.
   B: Where are you going?
   A: _____

B ▶ **203** Listen and check.

PRONUNCIATION

Exercise 1

A ▶ **204** Listen to the phrases. They are fast, then slow.

1 there are some   4 there isn't a
2 there's a   5 Are there any
3 there aren't any   6 Is there any

B ▶ **205** Listen and choose the words you hear (a or b).

1 a there are some
   b there's a
2 a there aren't any
   b there isn't a
3 a there's a
   b there isn't a
4 a there are some
   b there aren't any
5 a Are there any
   b Is there a
6 a Are there any good places to visit?
   b Is there a good place to eat?
7 a There aren't any shops near here.
   b There are some shops near here.
8 a There's no parking here.
   b There's some parking here.
9 a Is there a bus to the airport?
   b Are there any buses to the airport?
10 a There are two cash machines there.
   b There's a cash machine there.
11 a There's a shop at the end of the road.
   b There are shops at the end of the road.
12 a There's something in the back of the car.
   b There are some things in the back of the car.

6 AWAY FROM HOME

PAST SIMPLE: COMMON IRREGULAR VERBS

The verb *be* has two past forms – *was* and *were*.
ALL other verbs have only **one** past form.
The most common verbs – *be, have, go, do* – are all **irregular**. Learn them as words.

Person	Present	Past
I *she/he/it*	*am* *is*	*was*
you/we/they	*are*	*were*
I/you/we/they *she/he/it*	*have* *has*	*had*
I/you/we/they *she/he/it*	*do* *does*	*did*
I/you/we/they *she/he/it*	*go* *goes*	*went*

You can find a list of past forms for other verbs in *Outcomes Beginner* on page 138.

Past time words	
last night	yesterday
last Friday	yesterday morning
last week	yesterday afternoon
last year	

Exercise 1

Choose the correct word.

1 I *go / went* to the mountains last weekend.
2 I usually *have / had* lunch at one o'clock, but I don't have time today.
3 I *have / had* a lot of work last night. I *go / went* to bed late.
4 I love basketball. I often *go / went* to see a game.
5 We *are / were* from Brazil. And you?
6 Sorry I'm late. There *is / was* a problem at the airport.
7 A: How was your journey?
   B: It *is / was* fine, but I *am / was* tired now.
8 A: How are your parents?
   B: They *are / were* fine, thanks.
9 A: What do you do?
   B: Well, I *am / was* retired now, but I *am / was* a nurse.
10 A: What did you do yesterday?
   B: Not much. I *do / did* some work and I *go / went* to the gym.

Exercise 2

Complete the two sentences with the correct form of the verbs. One sentence is present, one sentence is past.

1 **be**
   a We ___*were*___ at home all day yesterday.
   b My mum and dad ___*are*___ from Morocco.
2 **go**
   a I usually _____ to my father's village at the weekend.
   b My wife _____ to Rome last week for business.
3 **do**
   a We _____ some shopping yesterday.
   b I usually _____ all my homework.

4 **have**
   a I _____ a very nice lunch with my family last Sunday.
   b My brother _____ a good job. The money's very good.

5 **be**
   a How _____ your hotel?
   b How _____ the film last night?

REGULAR PAST SIMPLE ENDINGS

Regular past simple forms end in **-ed**.

Present	Past
love(s)	I **loved** the film.
rain(s)	It **rained** a lot last week.
stay(s)	We **stayed** in a nice hotel.
share(s)	We **shared** a kitchen.
talk(s)	He **talked** a lot.
want(s)	She **wanted** to go out last night.
need(s)	They **needed** to do some work.

You can find a list of past forms for other verbs in *Outcomes Beginner* on page 138.

Exercise 1

Make these sentences past.

1 They talk a lot.
2 I need a coffee.
3 We share a flat.
4 It rains a lot in April.
5 She loves him.
6 I want to go.

Exercise 2

Complete the text with the past form of the verbs.

We ¹___went___ (go) to the north of Spain on holiday. We ²_____ (want) to see the mountains. We ³_____ (stay) in a small hotel in a village called Oubanca. We ⁴_____ (have) a great view from our room. It ⁵_____ (is) really beautiful. We ⁶_____ (walk) in the area every day. It ⁷_____ (rain) one or two times, but the weather ⁸_____ (is) good. We ⁹_____ (love) it. We want to go there again.

PAST SIMPLE NEGATIVES

Past negatives use a past form of *be* or *do*.
Compare the present and the past negatives.

Present	Past
Be	
There **isn't** anyone at the meeting.	There **wasn't** anyone at the meeting.
We **aren't** hungry.	We **weren't** hungry.
All other verbs	
I **don't** know.	I **didn't** know.
We **don't** go out a lot.	We **didn't** go out last night.
He **doesn't** have any money.	He **didn't** have any money.

Exercise 1

Choose the correct form.

1 I didn't like it. It *was / wasn't* very good.
2 The weather wasn't very good. It *rained / didn't rain* a lot.
3 We didn't see a lot. We *had / didn't have* time.
4 We didn't have a lot of money. We *stayed / didn't stay* in a cheap place.
5 I'm really hungry now. I *don't / didn't* have any breakfast this morning.
6 I didn't understand him. I *don't / didn't* speak Russian.

Exercise 2

Complete the sentences with the past simple negative or present simple negative of the verbs.

1 I ___didn't go out___ yesterday. (go out)
2 I _____ last week. (work)
3 I'm going home. I _____ well. (feel)
4 We _____ usually _____ lunch at home. (have)
5 It took a long time to get here. We _____ the way. (know)
6 My mother _____ meat. She's a vegetarian. (eat)

PAST SIMPLE QUESTIONS

To make past questions with a verb use a past form of *do*.
Compare present and past questions.

Present	Past
Do you like it?	**Did you** like it?
What **do you** do?	What **did you** do last night?
Where **do you** live?	Where **did you** live before?
What time **do you** go home?	What time **did you** go home?

Exercise 1

Read the answers and complete the questions in the past simple or present simple.

1 A: What / do?
   B: I work for a technology company.
2 A: What / do last night?
   B: I had dinner with some friends.
3 A: Where / go after the class?
   B: We went shopping.
4 A: have a nice time on holiday?
   B: Yes, it was great, thanks.
5 A: Where / your parents live?
   B: With me! But they also have a house in a village near here.
6 A: What time / get up this morning?
   B: Five o'clock! That's why I'm so tired now!

Past simple questions with *be*

Present	Past
Where **are** you from?	Where **were** you yesterday?
How**'s** the hotel?	How **was** the hotel?
Is he OK?	**Was** he OK?
Are they happy?	**Were** they happy?

Exercise 2

Complete the questions with the correct past simple form of *be*.

1 Where _____ you last week?
2 How _____ the party yesterday?
3 _____ there a lot of people there?
4 Why _____ they late?
5 How much _____ the tickets?
6 _____ it difficult to get there?

Exercise 3

Match the answers with the questions in Exercise 1.

a Great. The music was great and we danced a lot.
b There was a problem at the airport. Their flight was delayed.
c I was on holiday.
d They were free!
e No. We got a taxi from the airport.
f Not really. Fifteen or twenty.

Exercise 4

Read the answers and write full questions in the past simple.

1 A: What / do in St Petersburg?
   B: Lots of things. We went to see an opera one night.
2 A: What / see?
   B: Faust.
3 A: Good?
   B: Yes, it was.
4 A: Where / be?
   B: The Mariinsky Theatre.
5 A: How long / the opera?
   B: About three hours.
6 A: Sleep?
   B: No, I didn't! I saw all of it!

Short answers

We sometimes use short answers in replies.

A: **Did** you go out last night?	A: **Was** it a good tour?
B: Yes, I **did**.	B: Yes, it **was**.
B: No, I **didn't**.	B: No, it **wasn't**.

REVISION

Exercise 1

Look at the example. Find five more sentences that are wrong. Correct them.

1 Did you went to the museum? ✗ *Did you go to the museum?*
2 I went to see my brother in hospital yesterday. ✓
3 The hotel didn't had a nice restaurant.
4 There is a big problem at work last week.
5 Did you eat on the plane?
6 We go to the beach yesterday afternoon.
7 What you do yesterday evening?
8 We stayed in lots of nice places in Romania.
9 I not see you yesterday. Where were you?
10 How was your day?

PRONUNCIATION

Exercise 2

▶ **206** **Listen to the sound of the regular past forms.**

1 /d/ loved, rained, stayed, shared
2 /t/ talked
3 /ɪd/ wanted, needed

Exercise 3

▶ **207** **Listen and repeat.**

1 It rained a lot last week.
2 I stayed at home.
3 My brother talked to them.
4 I wanted to sleep.
5 I needed to eat something.
6 I shared a room with my sister.
7 I loved Costa Rica.

Exercise 4

A ▶ **208** **Listen to the words. They are fast, then slow.**

1 do you
2 did you

B ▶ **209** **Listen and choose the words you hear (a or b).**

1 a do you
  b did you
2 a do you
  b did you
3 a do you
  b did you
4 a do you
  b did you
5 a Do you know anyone here?
  b Did you know anyone there?
6 a Do you want a coffee?
  b Did you want a coffee?
7 a What do you do?
  b What did you do last night?
8 a What time do you go to bed?
  b What time did you go to bed?
9 a Do you live here?
  b Did you live there?
10 a Do you have any money?
   b Did you have any money?
11 a Where do you go?
   b Where did you go?
12 a Do you sleep well?
   b Did you sleep well?

7 GOING OUT AND STAYING IN

LIKE + -ING

You can use *like* with a noun (see Unit 2).

I like chicken.   I love it too.
I don't like chips.   I love them.

We can also talk about activities we like or don't like using the pattern *like* + **verb** + *-ing*.

I	**like**	
We	**love**	danc**ing**.
They	**don't like**	play**ing** music.
She/He	**likes**	do**ing** yoga.
My son	**loves**	watch**ing** sport.
Pedro	**doesn't like**	

-ing forms

-ing forms are regular.

verb	-ing form	verb (ends in -e)	-ing form
play	play**ing**	danc**e**	danc**ing**
cook	cook**ing**	liv**e**	liv**ing**
walk	walk**ing**	driv**e**	driv**ing**
read	read**ing**	hav**e**	hav**ing**

Some verbs have double letters when you write the -ing form.
swim – swi**mm**ing   run – ru**nn**ing   travel – trave**ll**ing

Exercise 1

Complete the sentences with the -ing form of the verbs.

1 I don't like _cooking_. I eat out a lot. (cook)
2 I love _____ to music – especially electronic music. (listen)
3 Jo uses the car more than me. I don't like _____. (drive)
4 I like _____ cards. I play poker with some friends every Tuesday evening. (play)
5 My husband doesn't like _____ shopping. I buy all his clothes. (go)
6 I love _____. I went to South America with my girlfriend last year. (travel)
7 My wife and I love _____ live sport. We have tickets to go to the next Olympics. (watch)
8 My brother doesn't like _____ any green food! He eats a lot of meat. (eat)
9 I don't like _____ in a flat, but houses are very expensive here. (live)
10 I wanted a cat, but my parents didn't like _____ animals in our flat. (have)

Questions and answers

Look at how we normally reply to these questions.

Questions			
Do you like	play**ing** games? cook**ing**? read**ing**? it?	**Does he like** **Does she like**	danc**ing**? play**ing** music? do**ing** yoga? watch**ing** sport?

Answers			
++	**Yes.** / **Yes, I do.** *I love it.* / *It's great.*	++	**Yes.** / **Yes, he does.** *He loves it.*
+	**Yeah** – a bit. / **It's OK.**	+	**Yeah** – a bit.
–	**Not really.**	–	**Not really.**
– –	**No.** / **No, I don't.**	– –	**No.** / **No, he doesn't.**

Exercise 2

Write questions and answers about liking activities.

1 you / cook?   ++
   A: *Do you like cooking?*
   B: *Yes. I love it.*
2 your husband / cook?   –
   A: *Does your husband like cooking?*
   B: *Not really.*
3 you / swim?   –
4 you / watch TV?   +
5 your son / play football   – –
6 you / read   ++
7 you / drive   – –
8 your sister / travel   +

Did you like ...?

You can ask about events people went to with *Did you like ...?*

A: **Did you like** the film last night?
B: *Yes. It was great.*
A: How was the dinner? **Did you like** it?
B: *Yeah. It was OK.*

Exercise 3

Complete with one word in each space. Contractions (*don't/didn't* etc.) are one word.

1 A: _____ you like running?
   B: Yes. I often go running in the park.
2 A: _____ you like the tour yesterday?
   B: Yeah, it was OK.
3 A: Do you like _____ to the beach?
   B: Not really. I prefer swimming in a pool.
4 A: Did you go to the cinema yesterday?
   B: Yes, but I _____ like the film. It was very slow.
5 A: Do you do a lot of exercise?
   B: Yes. I walk a lot and I love _____ golf.
6 A: Do you like learning English?
   B: Yes, I _____. I love _____!
7 A: Did you like your presents?
   B: Yes. _____ were great!

PRESENT CONTINUOUS (*I'M* AND *ARE YOU* ...?)

Positive form

The present continuous is the present of *be* + -ing form.

Person	be	-ing form	
I	**'m** **am**	read**ing** a good book watch**ing** Narcos work**ing** hard	*now.* *at the moment.*

You can make a negative like this:
*I'm **not** reading anything at the moment.*

Question form

Question	be + person	-ing form
What	**are you**	listen**ing** to? read**ing**? mak**ing**?
	Are you	read**ing** anything good at the moment?

Exercise 1

A Complete the sentences with '*m/am* or '*re/are*.

1 A: What _____ you doing?
   B: Nothing much. I _____ waiting for a phone call.
2 A: _____ you listening to the radio?
   B: No. You can turn it off.
3 A: Can I turn on the TV?
   B: No. I _____ trying to do some work.
4 A: I _____ making dinner now.
   B: OK. What _____ we having?
   A: Chicken curry.
5 A: Are you on your own? What _____ your friends doing tonight?
   B: They _____ studying. There's an exam tomorrow.
   A: Why _____ you not studying?
   B: I am! I _____ having a break!

B ▶ **210** Listen and check.

Other forms

Here are the other forms of the present continuous.
You study these more in Unit 8.

You/We/They	**are**	com**ing** now.
She/He/It	**is**	work**ing**.

Are	you/we/they	leav**ing** now?
Is	she/he/it	work**ing**?

Exercise 2

A Write questions in the present continuous with these words.

1 you / work / now?
   Are you working now?
2 What / you / look at?
3 What / you / listen to?
4 What / they / do?
5 you / do / anything / now?
6 you / come / with us?

B Write an answer to each question.

Present continuous v present simple

We use **present continuous** for activities around **now** or **at the moment**. Actions in the present continuous **are not complete**.

We use **present simple** for **regular activities** (*always*, *usually*, *every day*, etc).

I'm watching a good series called 'The City' at the moment. (I'm on episode 5 of 13)
I watch a lot of series. *I normally watch* something every night.

Exercise 3

Complete the pairs of sentences with the correct form of the verb. One sentence is present continuous and one sentence is present simple.

listen
1 a My wife _____ to a lot of classical music.
  b What _____ you _____ to? Can I listen to it?

not read
2 a I like reading, but I _____ anything at the moment. I'm very busy.
  b Children _____ a lot these days. They only look at their phones.

work
3 a I _____ this week, but I'm on holiday for the next two weeks.
  b My brother _____ in a bank. He likes it, but I think it's boring.

go out
4 a My friends and I usually _____ on Thursday evenings.
  b _____ you _____ tonight?

do
5 a I _____ English homework for an hour every day, if I can.
  b I _____ a course next week for my job.

eat
6 a What _____ you _____? It looks horrible!
  b What _____ you normally _____ at breakfast?

THIS/THESE, ONE/ONES

Singular	Plural
Can I try **this** (one)?	Can I try **these** (ones)?
This doesn't look good.	**These don't** look good.
This dress **is** nice.	**These** jeans **are** OK.
The red **one** looks good. I prefer the blue **one**.	The blue **ones** are fine. I prefer these **ones**.

Exercise 1

Decide which sentence is wrong (a or b). Correct it.

1 a This shoes are very comfortable.
  b These jeans are very comfortable.
2 a What do you think of this shirt?
  b What do you think of jacket?
3 a These shirts are OK, but I'm not sure about the colour.
  b The brown coats are OK, but I don't like ones.
4 a This skirt look good.
  b This top doesn't look very good.
5 a I like the design on this T-shirt.
  b I like the design on these bag.
6 a I like this dress, but it's a bit short.
  b This dress is nice, but I prefer the red.

REVISION

Exercise 1

A Complete the conversation with one word in each space.

A: What ¹_____ you think of this dress?
B: It's OK. I prefer the other ²_____.
A: Which one? ³_____ one?
B: Yes. I like the design.
A: Really? I don't like ⁴_____. I'm going to buy this one.
B: OK. It looks nice too.
A: ⁵_____ you buying anything?
B: No, I ⁶_____ just looking. I don't have any money.
A: You do! You don't ⁷_____ spending money!
B: That's right! And I don't like ⁸_____ shopping!

B ▶ **211** Listen and check.

PRONUNCIATION

Exercise 2

A ▶ **212** Listen to the phrases. They are fast, then slow.

1 are you
2 do you
3 did you

B ▶ **213** Listen and choose the words you hear (a or b).

1 a are you
  b do you
2 a do you
  b did you
3 a are you
  b did you
4 a Are you going swimming?
  b Do you go swimming much?
5 a What do you like cooking?
  b What are you cooking?
6 a Where are you staying?
  b Where did you stay?

7 a What are you reading?
  b What do you read?
8 a Why do you like it?
  b Why did you like it?
9 a Do you like going to the cinema?
  b Did you go to the cinema?
10 a Do you like playing tennis?
   b Are you playing tennis later?
11 a When are you going?
   b When did you go?
   c When do you go?
12 a What are you doing?
   b What did you do?
   c What do you do?

Exercise 3

▶ **214** Listen and write the sentences. Two words are given.

1	travelling a	*I like travelling a lot.*
2	listening to	_____
3	the moment	_____
4	anything good	_____
5	think of	_____
6	prefer the	_____

8 HERE AND THERE

PRESENT CONTINUOUS: ALL FORMS

The present continuous is the **present** of *be* + *-ing* form. (See also Units 5 and 7 *am/are* + *-ing*).

Person	be	-ing form
I	'm am	going out.
He She My mum It The work	's is	working hard. staying with us. making dinner. raining outside. taking a long time.
We You They	're are	trying.

Negatives

I	'm not am not	waiting.
He She It	's not is not	feeling well. working. raining
We You They	're not are not	listening.

You can also say *isn't* and *aren't*.

*The cash machine **isn't** working.*
*They **aren't** coming.*

Questions

Is he feel**ing** OK?	What**'s** he do**ing**?
Is she stay**ing** long?	Where**'s** she stay**ing**?
Is it work**ing** now?	What time**'s** she go**ing**?
Are you do**ing** anything now?	What **are** you read**ing**?

Remember

We use **present continuous** for plans and activities around **now** or **at the moment**. Actions in the present continuous **are not complete**. (see Units 5 and 7)

We use **present simple** for **regular activities** (*always, usually, every day*, etc). (see Unit 4)

Exercise 1

Choose the correct form.

1 My car *doesn't / isn't* working at the moment.
2 *Is it / It is* raining outside?
3 My sister *teaching / is teaching* in China at the moment.
4 He's not here. He *takes / is taking* his son to school.
5 *Sue's not / Sue don't* coming with us.
6 What *he does / he's doing / is he doing* in Canada?
7 *He not working / He's not working / He doesn't work* at the moment. He needs a job.
8 Why *is she driving / she is driving / does she drive* there? She usually takes the train.

Exercise 2

Complete the pairs of sentences with the correct form of the verbs. One sentence is present continuous, one sentence is present simple.

1 **rain**
   a: It _____ a lot here.
   b: Take a coat. It _____ outside again.

2 **work**
   a: My boss _____ from home this week.
   b: Usually she _____ four days a week: Monday, Tuesday, Wednesday and Friday.

3 **do**
   a: She _____ a Spanish course at the moment. She wants to go to Argentina.
   b: He _____ a lot of exercise: running, football and yoga.

4 **meet**
   a: I _____ my old school friends every month.
   b: I _____ a client in Manchester today.

5 **travel**
   a: He _____ a lot for work.
   b: We _____ to Singapore today for a business meeting.

6 **stay**
   a: She _____ with her parents for one or two days.
   b: He _____ late at work a lot – sometimes three or four days a week.

Short answers

A: **Is** he feeling OK?
B: Yes, he **is**. / No, he**'s not**.

A: **Is** it working now?
B: Yes, it **is**. / No, it**'s not**.

A: **Is** she staying long?
B: Yes, she **is**. / No, she**'s not**.

A: **Are** you working?
B: Yes, I **am**. / No, I**'m not**.

You can also use **isn't** instead of **'s not**.

No, she/he/it **isn't**.

Exercise 3

A Write a short answer to these questions.

1 Is it raining? (✓) *Yes, it is.*
2 Is he feeling OK? (✗) *No, he's not.*
3 Is your mother working at the moment? ✓
4 Is he living with his parents again? ✓
5 Is your sister staying in Slovakia? ✗
6 Is the shop closing now? ✓
7 Are you going to the beach today? ✗
8 Is the train stopping here? ✓
9 Are you reading this? ✓
10 Is the cash machine working? ✗

B ▶ **215** **Listen and check.**

PERSONAL PRONOUNS

Subject pronouns	Object pronouns
I work in an office in the city centre.	Can you take **me** to the airport?
You're right.	Sorry. I can't help **you**.
He works with my brother.	My brother plays football with **him**.
She teaches at a school near here.	I meet **her** for coffee every Friday.
It's a really good book.	I don't like **it**.
We live in a small village.	She's staying with **us** at the moment.
They are good friends.	How do you know **them**?

Exercise 1

Tick (✓) the correct sentence (a or b).

1 a: My mum and dad moved to Norway. They like it a lot.
  b: My mum and dad moved to Norway. Them like it a lot.
2 a: My son cooked dinner for us last night.
  b: My son cooked dinner for we last night.
3 a: My favourite singer is Tim Buckley. Do you know he?
  b: My favourite singer is Tim Buckley. Do you know him?
4 a: I like your shoes. Where did you buy they?
  b: I like your shoes. Where did you buy them?
5 a: My husband and I work from home. We make good money.
  b: My husband and I work from home. They make good money.

6 a: I like your jacket. Where did you buy them?
  b: I like your jacket. Where did you buy it?
7 a: When did you last see she?
  b: When did you last see her?
8 a: It's cold there. Me need to take a coat.
  b: It's cold there. I need to take a coat.

Exercise 2

Complete the sentences with the missing pronouns.

1 I love American music. _____ is my favourite!
2 My brother lives in Amsterdam. _____ is a student.
3 I like her father, but he doesn't like _____. It's bad!
4 My friends love football, but I don't like _____.
5 My parents are very old. _____ are retired now.
6 I'm going on holiday with my parents, but my sister isn't going to come with _____.
7 I have a brother. _____ live in the same area. It's nice.
8 He has two brothers and three sisters, but he doesn't see _____ a lot.
9 That's my friend Julian and his wife. I know _____ very well, but I don't know _____.
10 This is my wife, Amy. _____ have a daughter, Clara. _____ is three.

REVISION

Exercise 1

Look at the example. Find five more sentences which are wrong. Correct them.

1 Do your sister working now? ✗ *Is your sister working now?*
2 I like them. They helped us. ✓
3 What she's doing in Russia?
4 He's at the gym. He's doing some exercise.
5 I like your jeans. How much did them cost?
6 She's stay in the Hilton Hotel.
7 Who Anna talking to?
8 They helped us. I want to help them.
9 He not is working at the moment.
10 Rose isn't coming. We can start the meeting now.

PRONUNCIATION

Exercise 2

A ▶ **216** **Listen and complete the sentences. They're fast.**

1 *She's cooking something* nice for dinner.
2 _____ Business at university.
3 _____ OK?
4 _____ basketball with some friends in the park.
5 I'm going _____ and they can _____ too.
6 He's in his room. He _____ TV.
7 What _____ at the moment? _____ working?
8 Can you talk _____? She doesn't _____.

B ▶ **217** **Listen again and check. They're slow.**

9 HEALTHY AND HAPPY

TIME PHRASES FOR THE PAST

We use lots of different expressions to explain when things happened.

a few days **ago**	**last** night	**on** Monday
a few weeks **ago**	**last** Friday	**on** Thursday
a few months **ago**	**last** week	**on** Saturday
a few years **ago**	**last** month	**on** Sunday
five minutes **ago**	**last** year	
three hours **ago**		today
four days **ago**		yesterday
two weeks **ago**		this morning
six months **ago**		this afternoon
ten years **ago**		

Note: we can use *today*, *this morning* and *this afternoon* when the event is in the past.

Exercise 1
Complete the sentences. Use one word in each space.

1 I hit my head _____ afternoon. It was bad. I went home.
2 I went to Laos on holiday two years _____.
3 I hurt my back _____ few weeks ago. It feels bad again today.
4 I cut my hand _____ night.
5 I broke my leg a _____ years ago. It happened in Switzerland.
6 I saw him on the train _____ morning.
7 She's coming. I saw her in the lift a few _____ ago.
8 I didn't go to work _____ Monday. I had a bad cold.

Exercise 2
Put the expressions in order from 1 (= near to now) to 8 (= a long time ago).

It's now 7 in the evening on Saturday.

a last year
b this morning
c a few days ago
d this afternoon
e five years ago
f last night
g on Sunday
h last month

QUANTITY

There's We have	a lot of / lots of quite a lot of some	money. snow. clean water.
There are We have	almost no no	women in government. holidays. good universities.

Exercise 1
Rewrite the sentences. Change *We have* to *There's* or *There are*.

1 We have lots of good restaurants in my town.
   There are lots of good restaurants in my town.

2 We have quite a lot of good seafood in this area.
3 We have no women in government.

4 We have some beautiful countryside.
5 We have lots of problems with the health system.
6 We have almost no rain in the summer.
7 We have some crime in the small towns, but not a lot.
8 We have almost no museums in my city.

Exercise 2
Choose the correct word.

1 There *is / are* quite a lot of hotels and restaurants near here.
2 We have some *teacher / teachers* in the villages, but we need more.
3 There *is / are* lots of men in government, but not a lot of *women / woman*.
4 There's almost no clean *water / waters*.
5 There *isn't / aren't* a lot of people in the mountains.
6 They have a lot of very good *meat / meats* in this restaurant.
7 I'm a student. I have a lot of free *time / times*.
8 Some old people have almost no *education / educations*.

Exercise 3
Rewrite the sentences as negatives (–) or questions (?).

1 You have a lot of universities. (?)
2 There's a lot of rain most of the time. (–)
3 There are a lot of police on the streets. (?)
4 We have a lot of football teams in my city. (–)
5 There's a lot of crime. (?)
6 There are a lot of guns here. (–)

REVISION

Exercise 1
Look at the time expressions. Choose the correct form.

1 *They went / They're going* to a great festival a few weeks ago.
2 *She took / She's going to take* an exam tomorrow.
3 *I went / I'm going* out with some friends three days ago.
4 *We visited / We're going to visit* the war museum next week.
5 *He played / He plays / He's going to play* basketball every week on Sunday.
6 *I watched / I'm watching / I'm going to watch* a film at the moment.
7 *She went / She goes / She's going* to the gym every day after work.
8 *He cooked / He's cooking / He's going to cook* a great dinner last night.

Exercise 2
Which five sentences are wrong? Correct them.

1 It happened six or seven years ago.
2 I cut my hand in Monday.
3 There is lots of beautiful mountains near here.
4 There are quite lots of problems here at the moment.
5 The weather was horrible last week.
6 She broke her arm before three weeks.
7 There are some very good players in the team.
8 It's usually hot in my country. We have almost not snow.

PRONUNCIATION

Exercise 3

A ▶ **218** Listen and write the time expressions.
They're fast.

1 We had a lot of snow _____.
2 The last World Cup was _____.
3 I went to a great concert _____.
4 They met in Paris _____.
5 I bought it _____.
6 It rained a lot _____.
7 He cut his head _____.
8 What time did you get home _____?
9 We met at a conference _____.
10 It happened _____.

B ▶ **219** Listen again and check. They're slow.

Exercise 4

▶ **220** Listen. Repeat the time expressions.

Exercise 5

▶ **221** Listen. Complete the sentences.

1 There _____ crime here.
2 We _____ winter in my country.
3 _____ very cheap areas.
4 There _____ noise outside.
5 There _____ volcanoes here.
6 _____ mountains and lakes.
7 _____ grammar in my language.
8 _____ army in Iceland.

10 NEWS

FUTURE: *AM/ARE/IS GOING*

Plans and predictions

Plans (= someone already decided to do this):
I'm going home now.
We're going to Rome for our holiday this summer.
She's going to an exhibition this evening.

Predictions (= what I think is happening in the future)
I'm not going to like it.
You're going to have fun.
The weather is going to be nice.

Exercise 1

A Complete the sentences with *'m/am*, *'re/are* or *'s/is*.
Use contractions where you can.

1 _____ you going to be OK in that top? It's cold today.
2 They said on the news it _____ going to be 38 degrees here today.
3 They _____ going to lose the election.
4 I _____ not going to work for a month this summer. I need a holiday.
5 The house doesn't have heating. You _____ going to be cold in there.
6 _____ the weather going to be OK?
7 Look at the snow! There _____ going to be accidents on this road.
8 I _____ going camping with some friends this weekend.

B ▶ **222** Listen and check.

Exercise 2

Rewrite the sentences as negatives (–) or questions (?).

1 You're going to lose your job. (–)
2 I'm going to travel a lot this summer. (–)
3 You're going to Japan. (?)
4 They're going to drive there. (–)
5 They're going to university next year. (?)
6 We're going to meet Anya tonight. (?)

Exercise 3

Write whole sentences. Use the words in brackets.

1 I / go to bed early tonight
   I'm going to bed early tonight.

2 I / not / have / time this weekend
3 What / you / wear to the party tonight
4 They / get married in June
5 We / travel there by train
6 Where / you / eat tonight

Exercise 4

Match the questions (1–6) with the answers (a–f).

1 What are you doing tonight?
2 Where are you going on holiday?
3 What time are you going to leave?
4 How long are you going to stay?
5 Where are you going to stay?
6 Is the weather going to be OK?

a No. They said it's going to be cold and windy!
b Poland. We're going to the Tatra mountains for a week.
c We're going to a concert.
d Not long. I'm going to fly home next Tuesday.
e We're going to be at the Hilton in the city centre.
f It's an early flight. We're going to get a taxi at 5!

PAST FORMS REVIEW

Regular past forms end in -ed.

start – start**ed**
finish – finish**ed**
play – play**ed**
talk – talk**ed**
help – help**ed**

For verbs that end in -e, just add -d to make the past simple.

like – like**d**
change – change**d**
use – use**d**

Notice these spellings.

try – tri**ed**
stop – stop**ped**

Irregular past forms have no rules. You need to learn the words. See the verb list on page 138.

be – was/were
go – went
have – had
do – did
get – got
win – won
say – said

To make negatives, use *didn't*.

> *I **didn't have** time. Sorry.*
> *You **didn't try***.
> *We **didn't win**. We lost.*
> *They **didn't help**. It was horrible.*

To make questions, use *did*.

> *Why **did** I **do** that?*
> ***Did** you **see** him?*
> *Where **did** we **change** flights?*
> ***Did** they **like** it?*

Exercise 1

Complete the text with the past simple form of the verbs.

I ¹_____ (have) a great holiday. I ²_____ (go) to Croatia for three weeks. I ³_____ (spend) one week in Zagreb. I have friends there and I ⁴_____ (stay) with them. It ⁵_____ (be) very good to see them again. They ⁶_____ (help) me find a cheap hotel in Split. I ⁷_____ (take) the train there. I ⁸_____ (meet) some great people in Split. We ⁹_____ (talk) a lot and they ¹⁰_____ (try) to pay for everything, but I ¹¹_____ (say) no! I ¹²_____ (come) home last Saturday.

Exercise 2

Make the sentences positive.

1 It didn't cost a lot.
2 It didn't take a long time.
3 You didn't try very hard.
4 We didn't spend a lot of money.
5 We didn't win.
6 I didn't meet her.
7 He didn't come to class yesterday.
8 They weren't very happy about it.

Exercise 3

Complete the sentences using the verbs in the box. Two sentences need to be negative.

be	have	open	see	start
die	like	rain	sleep	win

1 They _____ a new airport last May. It's great.
2 I'm tired. I _____ well last night.
3 The Popular Party _____ the election – again!
4 How _____ the fire _____?
   Do they know?
5 A: _____ you _____ Copenhagen?
   B: Yes. It was great.
6 A: _____ you _____ the news this morning?
   B: No. Why?
7 My grandmother _____ last year. She _____ cancer. It was horrible.
8 The weather in Corfu _____ great. It _____ for three weeks!

Exercise 4

Add *wasn't, weren't* and *didn't* in the correct places. Use each word twice in the conversation.

A: You in class last week. What happened?
B: Oh. Sorry. I had a cold and I feel very well. I stayed in bed for three days.
A: Oh no! I'm sorry.
B: It's OK. I'm better now.
A: We very busy. It a very good class. We do a lot of work.
B: No?
A: No. The teacher very well. She said she was tired.
B: Maybe we had the same cold.
A: Maybe.

PRONUNCIATION

Exercise 1

A ▶ 223 Listen to the phrases. They are fast, then slow.

1 you are
2 we are
3 they are
4 there are

B ▶ 224 Listen and choose the words you hear (a or b).

1 a they're   b there are
2 a they're   b there are
3 a you're   b we're
4 a we're   b they're
5 a you're   b there are
6 a You're going to take an exam next week.
   b We're going to take an exam next week.
7 a We're going to have a lot of fun.
   b They're going to have a lot of fun.
8 a They're going shopping later.
   b You're going shopping later.
9 a They're going to win.
   b We're going to win.

11 LIFE AND HISTORY

QUESTIONS REVIEW

To make questions, we use a form of *be, do* or *can*. When we use these verbs to make a question, they are called auxiliary verbs. Remember the word order.

	Question word	be, do, etc.	person noun	verb phrase
Present be	How old	are	you?	
	Where	is	she?	
Present simple	What	do	you	do?
	What time	does	it	finish?
Present continuous	How	are	we	getting there?
	Why	is	she	leaving?
Past be	How	was	the film?	
	Where	were	they?	
Past simple	How long	did	you	stay?
	How far	did	he	walk?
Can	How	can	I	help?
		Can	you	open the window?

Exercise 1

Choose the correct auxiliary.

1 A: I'm going to the cinema later to see the new Bond film.
   B: What time *are / did* you going?
   B: Six. *Do / Can* you want to come?
2 A: I'm sorry. I can't see the screen. *Do / Can* you move a bit?
   B: Oh yeah, sorry. *Are / Is* that better?
   A: Yes, thanks.
3 A: *Do / Did* you have a nice weekend?
   B: Yes. It was great. We went walking in the countryside.
   A: How *did / was* the weather? It rained here.
   B: It rained a bit, but we didn't get very wet.
4 A: *Can / Are* you take us to the airport?
   B: I'm sorry, I can't. I don't have the car.
   A: Oh, don't worry. How much *does / is* a taxi?
5 A: This weather is horrible.
   B: I know. *Is / Was* it going to stay like this?
   A: I think so.
   B: *Are / Does* it normally rain a lot at this time of year?
   A: Yes, but not so much.
6 A: *Can / Are* you leaving now?
   B: Yes. *Are / Do* you coming?
   A: *Do / Can* you wait? I need to go to the toilet.
   B: Sure. I'll meet you outside.

Exercise 2

Put each auxiliary in the correct place in these sentences. Use each word once.

are	do	did	was
can	does	is	were

1 A: What you do yesterday after the class?
   B: I just went home. And you?
2 A: You like playing computer games?
   B: Yeah, a bit. Why?
3 A: We're going to Panama for our holidays. Have you been there?
   B: No. What you going to see there?
4 A: I speak to you?
   B: Sure. What the problem?
5 A: I can get free tickets for the zoo. My girlfriend works there.
   B: What she do?
   A: She works in one of the cafés.
6 A: I went to the school's anniversary.
   B: Oh, yes? it good? there many people there?

There are other auxiliary verbs in *Outcomes Beginner*. You learn more about these in *Outcomes Elementary*.

> **Could** you turn up the heating?
> What time **will** you be back?
> What **would** you like?
> **Have** you been there?

Exercise 3

Correct the mistake in each question.

1 Did you went out last night?
2 Where live you?
3 Are you like swimming?
4 Can you to turn on the light?
5 Where do your friend Paola work?
6 Do you move, please?

EXPLAINING WHEN: TIME PHRASES

We can add a phrase with *when*, *after* or *in* to show when something happens.

> I moved here **when I was five**.
> She went into the army **after university**.
> I started this job **after I left school**.
> He opened the restaurant **in 2008**.

Remember we can also use *ago*. (see Unit 9)

*He opened the restaurant **10 years ago**.*

Exercise 1

Complete the sentences with a past time phrase and the word or phrase in brackets.

1 My dad was born _____*in 1932*_____. (1932)
2 My uncle started a business _____. (he left the army)
3 My sister got married _____. (she was 20)
4 I spent time in Italy _____. (2000s)
5 I met my girlfriend _____. (we were both at school)
6 They got divorced _____. (three years)
7 I normally go straight home _____. (class)
8 We normally kiss three times _____. (we say goodbye)

Exercise 2

Complete the short text with one word in each space.

Nelson Mandela was South Africa's first black President. He was born [1]_____ 1918. He studied Law at university. [2]_____ university, he worked as a lawyer. He became interested in politics and started fighting the white-only government. [3]_____ 1962 he went to prison. [4]_____ he was there, people all over the world said he should be free, but the South African government said no. Finally, it happened [5]_____ 27 years. [6]_____ he left prison, he became the president. He was president for five years. He died [7]_____ December 2013.

EXPLAINING WHY: *BECAUSE* AND *SO*

Because and *so* show why something happens/happened.

> We use *because* to describe the cause of something. We put *because* <u>before</u> explaining why.
> *We visited Machu Picchu **because** we are studying the Incas at university.*

> We use *so* to describe the result of something. We put *so* <u>after</u> explaining why.
> *We are studying the Incas at university, **so** we visited Machu Picchu.*

Notice we need a comma (,) before *so*.

Exercise 1

Choose the best word.

1 There are a lot of famous places to visit *because / , so* we get a lot of tourists.
2 The weather is very bad in February *because / , so* it's not a good time to visit.
3 The castle is closed at the moment *because / , so* they are doing repairs.
4 There was a war here in the 16th century. It started *because / , so* the king died and he didn't have any children.
5 There was a war *because / , so* a lot of people left the country.
6 There is a lot of crime in that area *because / , so* I don't walk round there at night.
7 The health system here is bad *because / , so* the government doesn't spend enough money.
8 I send my children to a private school *because / , so* public education is very bad.

Exercise 2

A Match 1–8 with a–e to make complete sentences.

1 Most people like working at home because
2 Some people think working from home is bad because
3 I didn't feel very well, so
4 I didn't like the hotel because
5 My friend is going to be in town, so
6 The government lost the election, so
7 I was really late because
8 The school was closed when the fire happened, so

a I went to bed early.
b no-one was hurt.
c there's going to be a new president.
d you don't see anyone all day.
e there was a lot of noise outside.
f they don't need to travel to work.
g we're going to have dinner together.
h there was a lot of traffic.

B Choose five sentences from 1–8 in Part A. Write them with a different ending.

REVISION

Exercise 1

Complete the conversations with a pair of words.

are + after	can + after	did + in	is + when
are + so	did + because	~~did + so~~	when + did

1 A: Why ____did____ people stop living in Petra?
　 B: I'm not sure. It's very dry there, ____so____ maybe it was difficult to grow food.
2 A: When _____ Brasília become the capital of Brazil?
　 B: I'm not sure. It was _____ the 1960s, I think.
3 A: Why _____ you move here?
　 B: _____ I got a new job.
4 A: When _____ you going to the shops?
　 B: _____ lunch. Do you need anything?
5 A: _____ that you in the photo?
　 B: Yes. That was probably ten years ago, _____ I had hair!
6 A: What _____ you doing this weekend?
　 B: I have exams next week, _____ I need to study.
7 A: _____ I ask you something about my homework?
　 B: Sure. But _____ the class.
8 A: I broke my foot _____ I was on holiday.
　 B: Oh, no! How _____ you do that?

PRONUNCIATION

Exercise 2

A ▶ 225 Listen to how the letters in red sound together.

1 when I was there
2 when I'm tired
3 when I need it
4 after I left her.
5 in a minute
6 in a few weeks

B ▶ 225 Listen again and repeat the phrases.

Exercise 3

▶ 226 Listen and complete the sentences.

1 _____ help me _____?
2 _____ weather _____.
3 _____ happened _____.
4 _____ the car _____.
5 _____ there _____.
6 _____ angry _____.

12 THANK YOU AND GOODBYE

I'LL

We offer solutions to problems using *I'll* (*I will*) + verb.
We sometimes add a time word or check it's OK using *if you like* or *if you want*.

	Verb
I'll	*help you.* *order a taxi.* *come with you, if you like.* *go and get some food.*

Exercise 1

Complete the offer with *I'll* and a verb.

go and look for	make	stand	take
lend	pay	stay	wash

1 You sit there. _____
2 You don't need to walk. _____ you there.
3 You don't need any money. _____
4 You go. _____ here and wait.
5 You don't need an umbrella. _____ you mine.
6 You wait here and see if he comes back. _____ him.
7 You don't need to bring any food. _____ something.
8 Don't worry about the dirty dishes. _____ them up.

Exercise 2

Add *'ll* in the correct place in the sentences. You need one in each conversation 1–6.

1 A: I don't have room for everyone in my car.
　 B: It's OK. I walk. It's only fifteen minutes.
2 A: I meet you at the restaurant at nine.
　 B: OK. See you there.
3 A: It's OK. I clean everything.
　 B: Are you sure? I can help, if you like.
4 A: I'm going to Switzerland next week.
　 B: Lucky you. I love Switzerland – especially their chocolate.
　 A: Yeah. I bring you some, if you like.
5 A: How much is that?
　 B: It's OK. I buy it.
　 A: I have money.
　 B: It's fine.
6 A: Oh. We don't have any bread.
　 B: I go and get some now.
　 A: It's OK. I'm going to the shops later.

EXPLAINING PURPOSE: *FOR* OR *TO*

We explain the purpose of something using *for* and *to*.

for + noun
*The doctor gave me this **for my headache**.*
*I bought a sofa **for our living room**.*
*It's a game **for children**.*

to + verb
*The doctor gave me something **to feel better**.*
*I bought her some flowers **to say thank you**.*
*Do you want something **to eat**?*

Exercise 1

Complete the two patterns with these phrases.

an appointment	meet Mr Hassan
check out	Sylvia's birthday party
collect a computer	the conference
help you	work and pleasure

I'm here for ...
_____
_____
_____
_____

I'm here to ...
_____
_____
_____
_____

Exercise 2

Choose the best ending and add *for* or *to*.

1 I'm going to the bank ...   _____ a change.
    to get some money.
2 We're going out later ...   _____ dinner.
    _____ watch TV.
3 They gave us flowers ...   _____ our anniversary.
    _____ help.
4 I bought him some chocolates ...   _____ lunch.
    _____ say thanks.
5 The school needs help ...   _____ their birthday.
    _____ buy desks.
6 The government wants money ...   _____ schools.
    _____ say sorry.

Exercise 3

Make questions with these words.

1 we / need anything / make dinner?
    Do we need anything to make dinner?
2 you / have anything / headaches?
3 you / need anyone / help you?
4 you know / anywhere nice / a picnic?
5 there / any nice places / children?
6 who / the best person / ask?
7 what / you / getting her / her birthday?

TELLING PEOPLE TO DO THINGS: IMPERATIVES

You can tell people to do things using the infinitive of the verb (without *to*) and you can tell people not to do something using *don't* + infinitive. This is called an imperative.

Positive
A: **Give** us a call when you're home.
B: *I will.*
Negative
A: **Don't forget** to call us.
B: *I won't.*

You can promise to do something by saying *I will*.
You can promise *not* to do something by saying *I won't*.
You can also reply with *Yes / OK*.

Exercise 1

Complete the sentences with the imperatives of these verbs. You sometimes need a negative.

~~be~~	forget	have	send	tell

1   *Don't be* late
2 _____ him you're sorry.
3 _____ to call him.
4 _____ a safe journey.
5 _____ me an email.

be	have	hurry	say	wait

6 _____ a nice day.
7 _____ quick! We're late already.
8 _____. We have lots of time.
9 _____ for me. I'll be very quick.
10 _____ anything. Nobody else knows.

Exercise 2

Complete with *will* or *won't*.

1 A: Don't forget to bring your book next time.
   B: I _____.
2 A: Say hi to Diego.
   B: We _____.
3 A: Tell me if you need help.
   B: I _____.
4 A: Don't start without me.
   B: OK, we _____.
5 A: Don't wait for us. Go and get a good seat.
   A: OK. We _____. See you later.

REVISION

Exercise 1

A Complete the conversation with these words.

be	don't	for	I'll	say	will
don't	for	have	I'll	to	won't

A: So, Ivan. It was lovely to meet you.
B: You too, Fei.
A: Thanks [1]_____ everything.
B: It was a pleasure.
A: I made you something [2]_____ remember our time together!
B: Oh, what lovely photos! Thanks!
A: That's OK. It's been great.
B: I'm going to put them on the wall in our kitchen.
A: I'm happy you like them.
B: [3]_____ help you put your bags in the taxi.
A: Oh, [4]_____ careful! [5]_____ hurt your back!
B: Wow – they are heavy! What do you have in there?
A: I bought a lot of gifts [6]_____ my family.
B: Yes – a lot! So, Fei. Stay in contact. [7]_____ forget us!
A: I [8]_____.
B: [9]_____ a good journey.
A: I hope so. [10]_____ call you from home.
B: OK. [11]_____ hi to your family.
A: I [12]_____.
B: Bye now.
A: Bye.

B ▶ **227** Listen and check.

PRONUNCIATION

Exercise 2

A ▶ **228** Listen. Notice how you *don't* hear the red letters in these phrases.

1 don't forget
2 don't wait
3 don't be
4 next time
5 can't drive
6 a bit broken
7 not very
8 want to
9 go and get
10 go and see
11 come and visit
12 fish and chips
13 a good journey
14 a good place
15 send someone
16 need to

B ▶ **228** Listen again and repeat.

Exercise 3

▶ **229** Listen and complete the sentences.

1 _____ call them.
2 _____ to drink.
3 _____ look at it.
4 _____ I'll do it later.
5 _____ for lunch?
6 _____ and chips.

REGULAR AND IRREGULAR VERBS

Present	Past simple	-ing form
add	added	adding
ask	asked	asking
be	was	being
become	became	becoming
break	broke	breaking
build	built	building
buy	bought	buying
can	could	–
change	changed	changing
choose	chose	choosing
come	came	coming
continue	continued	continuing
cost	cost	costing
cut	cut	cutting
die	died	dying
do	did	doing
drink	drank	drinking
drive	drove	driving
eat	ate	eating
feel	felt	feeling
find	found	finding
get	got	getting
give	gave	giving
go	went	going
grow	grew	growing
happen	happened	happening
have	had	having
hear	heard	hearing
help	helped	helping
hit	hit	hitting
hold	held	holding
hurt	hurt	hurting
keep	kept	keeping
know	knew	knowing
learn	learned or learnt	learning
leave	left	leaving
lend	lent	lending
like	liked	liking
live	lived	living
look	looked	looking
lose	lost	losing
love	loved	loving
make	made	making
mean	meant	meaning
meet	met	meeting

Present	Past simple	-ing form
move	moved	moving
need	needed	needing
offer	offered	offering
open	opened	opening
pay	paid	paying
play	played	playing
prefer	preferred	preferring
put	put	putting
read	read	reading
remember	remembered	remembering
run	ran	running
see	saw	seeing
sell	sold	selling
send	sent	sending
show	showed	showing
sing	sang	singing
sit	sat	sitting
sleep	slept	sleeping
speak	spoke	speaking
spend	spent	spending
stand	stood	standing
start	started	starting
stay	stayed	staying
stop	stopped	stopping
study	studied	studying
swim	swam	swimming
take	took	taking
talk	talked	talking
teach	taught	teaching
tell	told	telling
think	thought	thinking
throw	threw	throwing
travel	travelled	travelling
try	tried	trying
turn	turned	turning
understand	understood	understanding
use	used	using
wait	waited	waiting
walk	walked	walking
want	wanted	wanting
watch	watched	watching
wear	wore	wearing
win	won	winning
work	worked	working
write	wrote	writing

Red words are in the list of 100 most frequent verbs in English.

VOCABULARY REFERENCE

COUNTRIES AND COUNTRY ADJECTIVES

	Country	Country adjective	Capital
	Argentina	Argentinian	Buenos Aires
	Brazil	Brazilian	Brasília
	Chile	Chilean	Santiago
	China	Chinese	Beijing
	Colombia	Colombian	Bogotá
	France	French	Paris
	Italy	Italian	Rome
	Japan	Japanese	Tokyo
	Mexico	Mexican	Mexico City
	Morocco	Moroccan	Rabat
	Peru	Peruvian	Lima
	Poland	Polish	Warsaw
	Russia	Russian	Moscow
	Saudi Arabia	Saudi	Riyadh
	South Korea	Korean	Seoul
	Spain	Spanish	Madrid
	Thailand	Thai	Bangkok
	The UK	British	London
	The US / The States	American	Washington D.C.
	Vietnam	Vietnamese	Hanoi

COLOURS

- black
- blue
- brown
- green
- grey
- pink
- orange
- purple
- red
- white
- yellow
- dark blue
- light blue

DATES

Months
January
February
March
April
May
June
July
August
September
October
November
December

Monday	Tuesday	Wednesday	Thursday	Friday	Saturday	Sunday
1 the first	2 the second	3 the third	4 the fourth	5 the fifth	6 the sixth	7 the seventh
8 the eighth	9 the ninth	10 the tenth	11 the eleventh	12 the twelfth	13 the thirteenth	14 the fourteenth
15 the fifteenth	16 the sixteenth	17 the seventeenth	18 the eighteenth	19 the nineteenth	20 the twentieth	21 the twenty-first
22 the twenty-second	23 the twenty-third	24 the twenty-fourth	25 the twenty-fifth	26 the twenty-sixth	27 the twenty-seventh	28 the twenty-eighth
29 the twenty-ninth	30 the thirtieth	31 the thirty-first				

YEARS

1850	eighteen fifty	1901	nineteen oh one	1700	seventeen hundred
1800–1899	the 19th Century	2000–2099	the 21st Century	1900	nineteen hundred
1993	nineteen ninety-three	2005	two thousand and five	2000	the year two thousand
1900–1999	the 20th Century	2010	twenty ten		

PRONOUNS

		Person	Thing	Place
		who	**what** **which**	**where**
every / all		**ev**erybody **ev**eryone	**ev**erything	**ev**erywhere
no / none		**no**body **no**-one	**no**thing	**no**where
any		anybody anyone	anything	**any**where
a *or* an (one not specific)		**some**body **some**one	**some**thing	**some**where
the (specific)		he, she, etc. him, her, etc.	it one/ones	
near			this/these	here
far			that/those	there

LETTERS AND SOUNDS

Consonant sounds

Letter(s)	Most common sound → less common		
	/b/	silent	
B b	baby husband brother bad	lamb	
	/k/	/s/	
C c	coffee doctor o'clock cut	city price juice nice	
	/ʧ/	/k/	
Ch ch	lunch teacher children choose	school	

Letter(s)	Most common sound → less common		
	/d/	/t/	
D d	don't drink food student	asked talked	
	/f/	/v/	
F f	father flat fifty wife	of	
	/g/	/ŋ/	/ʤ/
G g	good give big English	long anything listening reading	orange page large village

Letter(s)	Most common sound → less common		
	silent		
gh	right daughter eighty high		
	/h/		
H h	hi have how husband		
	/dʒ/		
J j	job juice Japan		
	/k/	silent	
K k	drink milk take kitchen	know knew	
	/l/	/əl/	
L l	like listen flat village	people single table	
	/m/		
M m	meet I'm milk mum		
	/n/	/ŋ/	
N n	in new not seventy	ring long reading working	
	/p/		
P p	page people repeat map		
	/f/		
Ph ph	photo phone		
	/kw/		
Qu qu	question quite quiet square		

Letter(s)	Most common sound → less common		
	/r/		
R r	right red drink sorry		
	/s/	/z/	/ʃ/
S s	seven listen class cakes	is was plays	discussion
	/ʃ/		
Sh sh	she shop fresh English		
	/t/	/ʃ/	silent
T t	time tea twenty hot	station action national dictionary	listen castle soft drink don't know
	/ð/	/θ/	
Th th	the that's mother with	three thanks sixteenth south	
	/v/		
V v	five have never very		
	/w/	silent	
W w	we with twelve flower	two answer	
	/w/	/h/	
Wh wh	what when why white	who whole	
	/ks/		
X x	six taxi expensive next		
	/j/		
Y y	yes you your yellow		

Vowel sounds

Letter(s)	Most common sound → less common						
	/æ/	/eɪ/	/ə/	/e/	/ɔː/	/ɒ/	/ɑː/
A a	black have that can	same plane station conversation	a again abroad another	any anything many	water always talk	want	can't
	/eɪ/	/eə/	/e/	/ɪ/			
ai	email waiter train wait	pair air fair	again said	mountain			
	/eɪ/	/e/					
ay	day play way	says					
	/ɑː/	/eə/					
ar	are large far	area care					
	/e/	silent	/ɪ/	/iː/	/ə/		
E e	ten help fresh very	five name talked played	English wanted decided chooses	he she people email	the listen		
	/iː/						
ee	three meet week see						
	/iː/	/eɪ/	/e/	/ɪə/			
ea	tea teacher leave please	break great	weather breakfast	idea area			
	/ɜː/	/ə/	/eə/				
er	person were verb	sister answer enter	there where				
	/ɪə/	/ɜːː/	/eə/				
ear	near year	learn early	wear				
	/ɪ/	/aɪ/					
I i	is in six drink	I nine price right					
	/i/	/juː/	/e/				
ie	cities countries companies	view review	friend				
	/ə/						
io(n)	question dictionary station discussion						

Letter(s)	Most common sound → less common				
	/ɒ/	/əʊ/	/ʌ/	/uː/	/ə/
O o	hot not conversation sorry	both don't clothes cold	brother does London son	do to who	 do you to work
	/uː/	/ʊ/	/ɔː/		
oo	food too choose school	good look book	floor		
	/aʊ/	/uː/	/ʌ/	/ə/	/ʊ/
ou	house south about mountain	you group	country	famous continuous	would could
	/əʊ/	/ɔː/			
oa	road coat soap goal	board abroad			
	/ɔɪ/				
oi	point toilet				
	/əʊ/	/aʊ/			
ow	know show window own	how now towel shower			
	/ɔɪ/				
oy	boy toy enjoy				
	/ɔː/	/ə/	/ɜː/		
or	more or for	actor doctor for you	work		
	/ɔː/	/aʊə/	/ɑː/		
our	four your tour	hour	our		
	/ʌ/	/uː/	/ʊ/	/ə/	/ɪ/
U u	number bus husband lunch	student university use	full put	medium	minute
	/ɪ/	/uː/			
ui	build building	juice fruit			
	/aɪ/				
uy	buy				
	/aɪ/	/i/	/ɪ/		
y	my try	very thirty city	system		

INFORMATION FILES

Unit 1 page 9   DEVELOPING CONVERSATIONS

FILE 2

Unit 8 page 75   READING AND SPEAKING

Student B

Higor

I'm a teacher – and I work hard! Three days a week, I teach English and Spanish in a school here in Curitiba, in the south of Brazil. The other three days a week, I sometimes work at home and sometimes in the city. I teach lots of people in big companies. At home, I teach online. It's not difficult. I have a small office and a good computer. I love people and I love my job, but working at home is best. It's quiet. I can relax. I don't need to travel. The traffic here is bad. Sometimes it takes an hour to get to my school. At home, I can use this time to do other things. At the moment, I'm making my own website. It's going to be great.

FILE 3

Unit 1 page 12   VOCABULARY

Student B

Ask the prices. Complete the menu.

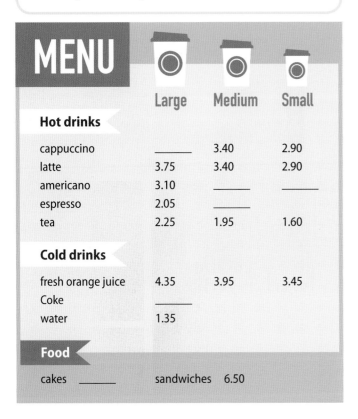

MENU	Large	Medium	Small
Hot drinks			
cappuccino	_____	3.40	2.90
latte	3.75	3.40	2.90
americano	3.10	_____	_____
espresso	2.05	_____	
tea	2.25	1.95	1.60
Cold drinks			
fresh orange juice	4.35	3.95	3.45
Coke	_____		
water	1.35		
Food			
cakes _____	sandwiches 6.50		

FILE 4

Unit 7 page 64   GRAMMAR

Student A

Act one of these activities:

- listening to music
- doing my homework
- looking at Facebook

FILE 5

Unit 10 page 93   READING AND SPEAKING

Pair A

1 Bayern Munich won the German Cup yesterday. They won two-nil (2–0) against Dortmund. Coman scored in the first half and Joshua Kimmich scored the second goal in the 76th minute.

2 The government is going to spend $3 billion more on the health system next year. The money is going to pay for new hospitals and doctors. At the moment people are waiting a long time to have operations. The government is going to spend less on education and the environment.

FILE 6

Unit 4 page 35   GRAMMAR

Student A

FILE 7

Student B

FILE 8

Pair B

TIKAL

Tikal is an ancient Mayan city in the jungle of Guatemala. It became a big city 2,000 years ago after Yax Ehb Xook became its first king, but there were many buildings before then. For eight centuries it was the capital of Mayan culture and, in 750 CE, 60,000–90,000 people lived there. During this time, the Mayans built many temples and pyramids for their religion. They put their kings and queens in these pyramids after they died. Some of the temples are about sixty or seventy metres high. The people of Tikal often fought with other cities and, around the year 800 CE, Tikal lost a big war. After the war, the city became less important. People left the area because it was difficult to grow food and from the tenth century nobody lived there. The city became lost.

People found the city again in the 19th century. Tikal is now part of the Tikal National Park. The park has 360 km² (square kilometres) of jungle. There are hundreds of different kinds of birds and three thousand ancient Mayan buildings. In 1979 the city of Tikal became a UNESCO world heritage site.

jungle = a kind of forest

Unit 11 page 103   READING AND SPEAKING

Pair A

PETRA

The ancient city of Petra is in the desert in Jordan. It became an important city around 2,000 years ago, but there were many buildings before then. It was the capital city for people called the Nabataeans. The Nabataeans travelled a lot to buy and sell things. They became rich and built houses and temples in the rock. Some of these buildings are forty metres high. About 20,000 people lived in the city. In the second century the Roman army came to Petra and the Romans became the government.

For the next three centuries it stayed an important city. In 363 CE there was a big earthquake. The earthquake killed many people and damaged a lot of houses. After the earthquake people continued living in Petra but the city became less important. The Romans stopped using the city. People left the area, maybe because it was difficult to grow food. It's also possible a lot of people died in a flood. By the 8th century nobody lived there. The city became lost.

People found the city again in the 19th century. Petra is now a national park. 700, 000 people visit the area every year. In 1985 Petra became a UNESCO world heritage site. In 1989 it was in one of Steven Spielberg's Indiana Jones films.

earthquake = when the ground moves suddenly

Unit 7 page 64   GRAMMAR

Student B

Act one of these activities:
- reading
- making a cake
- writing some emails

Unit 10 page 93   READING AND SPEAKING

Pair B

1 There was a very big fire in a school in Madrid yesterday. The fire happened in the evening. The school was closed, so no-one was hurt. They say the school is going to be closed for a year. Police think it was an accident.

2 Lesser's is a big clothes company. 10,000 people work for the company in Europe, but now the company is losing money. It's going to close one factory in Romania and thirteen shops in different countries. Maybe 3,000 people are going to lose their jobs.

AUDIO SCRIPTS

▶ TRACK 6

B = Bob, T = Tina, P = Poppy, C = Connor
1 B: Tina is my wife. She's a doctor. This is my daughter, Poppy and he is my son Connor.
2 T: Bob is my husband. He's a teacher in an English school.
3 P: My mother is a doctor and my father is a teacher. Connor is my big brother.
4 C: Poppy's my sister. She's eight. Kevin is my best friend. We're in the same class at school.

▶ TRACK 8

1 A: Who is Maria?
   B: She's my wife.
2 A: Who is he?
   B: Greg. He's our teacher.
3 A: Lara. This is my sister, Katia.
   B: Hi. Nice to meet you.
4 A: You're Ana, right?
   B: No. I'm Zeynep. She's Ana!
   A: Oh! Sorry!
5 A Who are they?
   B: They're my children!
   A: Nice! What are their names?
   B: My son is Cristiano and my daughter is Inés.

▶ TRACK 9

1
A: He's my friend, Peter.
2
A: Who's she?
B: My mother.
3
A: What's her name?
B: Fatima.

▶ TRACK 11

1 ten, twelve, fourteen, sixteen
2 four, eight, twelve, sixteen
3 seven, eleven, thirteen, seventeen
4 one, three, six, ten

▶ TRACK 12

1 ten, twelve, fourteen, sixteen, eighteen
2 four, eight, twelve, sixteen, twenty
3 seven, eleven, thirteen, seventeen, nineteen
4 one, three, six, ten, fifteen

▶ TRACK 14

1 Who is she?
2 Where is it?
3 What time is it?
4 How much is it?
5 How long is it?
6 How old is she?

▶ TRACK 15

1 A: How are you?
   B: Fine, thanks.
2 A: How long is the class?
   B: One hour.
3 A: How old are you?
   B: Thirteen.
4 A: Where are you from?
   B: China.
5 A: Who's she?
   B: My mother.
6 A: How much is lunch?
   B: Sixteen dollars.
7 A: What time is it?
   B: Three o'clock.
8 A: What's your phone number?
   B: 0694 55 781.

▶ TRACK 16

1 Where are you from?
2 How are you?
3 Where is he from?
4 How long is the class?
5 How old are you?
6 What time is the party?
7 How old is your son?
8 Is she nice?
9 Who is he?
10 How much is it?

▶ TRACK 19

1
A: What time is it?
B: Three thirty-five.
2
A: How much is it?
B: It's fifteen seventy.
3
A: What time is the class?
B: Eleven o'clock.
4
A: What time is the coffee break?
B: Twelve fifteen.
5
A: How much is a cappuccino?
B: Four euros eighty.
6
A: What time is lunch?
B: One thirty.
7
A: How much are the sandwiches?
B: Eight ninety-five.
8
A: What time's your bus?
B: Sixteen fifty-two.

▶ TRACK 21

1 a large cappuccino
2 a medium latte
3 a small orange juice
4 a medium tea
5 a large americano
6 How much is a medium cappuccino?
7 How much are sandwiches?
8 How much is a large orange juice?

▶ TRACK 23

A: Yes sir. How are you today?
B: Er, yes, good.
A: What would you like?
B: Er, two coffees – large.
A: Cappuccino? Latte? Americano?
B: Er, one cappuccino and one americano with milk.
A: OK. Americano – with milk. Anything else?
B: Yes. One medium tea.
A: Milk?
B: No. No milk, thanks. And a juice for my daughter.
A: OK. Is that large?
B: No – small.
A: OK. One large cappuccino. One large americano with milk, one medium black tea, one small orange juice. Anything else?
B: And two of those. What's that?
A: Chocolate cake?
B: Yes, please. Two.
A: OK. And two chocolate cakes. That's twenty-two fifteen.
B: Sorry. How much?
A: Twenty-two pounds fifteen pence.
B: Is fifty OK?
A: Yes. Your change. Next.

▶ TRACK 24

A: That's twenty-two fifteen.
B: Sorry. How much?
A: Twenty-two pounds fifteen pence.
B: Is fifty OK?
A: Yes. Your change. Next. Are you OK?
B: Er, it's not right.
A: Sorry. What's the problem?
B: The change. This is seventeen eighty five.
A: Yeah.
B: Seventeen's not right. Twenty-two fifteen and seventeen eighty-five – that's not fifty pounds.
A: Oh yes. You're right. Sorry. Sorry. Here's ten more.
B: OK. Thank you.

▶ TRACKS 25 & 26

1 A: What's the problem?
   B: My tea – it's not right.
2 A: What's the problem?
   B: My coffee. It's not a cappuccino.
3 A: Yes. Sir. Are you OK?
   B: Sorry. It's a small tea – not large.
4 A: Are you OK?
   B: No. It's coffee cake – not chocolate.
5 A: Is everything OK?
   B: No. My tea's not hot.
6 A: What's the problem?
   B: It's not right. It's not 35 euros. It's 29.

▶ TRACKS 27 & 28

1 What's her name?
2 This is my friend, Don.
3 This is my son, John.
4 What time is the class?
5 Where are you from?
6 What's your phone number?

UNIT 2

▶ TRACK 33

My name's Leo.
I'm from Chile.
I live in a city called Temuco.
Temuco is in an area called Araucanía. It's in the south of Chile.
I live in a small house with my daughter and my dog.
It's on Los Leones road.
It's near the university.

▶ TRACKS 34 & 35

1 A: Where do you live?
   B: London.
2 A: Do you live with your brother?
   B: No. I live with a friend.
3 A: Who do you live with?
   B: My husband and my dog!
4 A: Do you like your city?
   B: Yeah. It's OK.
5 A: Do you know my name?
   B: Yes – it's Mohammed.
6 A: Do you have a house or a flat?
   B: A house.

▶ TRACK 36

A: Hi. Sorry. What's your name?
B: Ali. And you?
A: Maria. Nice to meet you.
B: You too.
A: So, Ali. Where do you live?
B: Clayton. It's a small village. Do you know it?
A: No. Is it far?
B: It takes thirty minutes by car. And you? Where do you live?
A: I live on Havana Road. Do you know it?
B: Yes. It's near here, right?
A: Yes. I walk here. It takes fifteen minutes.

▶ TRACK 37

A: Hi. Sorry. What's your name?
B: Otar. And you?
A: Tamar. Nice to meet you.
B: You too. Where do you live?
A: District 7. And you?
B: I live in District 3.
A: I know it. It's near.
B: Yes. I walk here.

▶ TRACK 39

1
A: What do you do?
B: I'm a bus driver.
2
A: What do you do?
B: I'm a teacher in a language school.
3
A: What do you do?
B: I'm a waiter.
4
A: What do you do?
B: I'm a student. I'm at university.
5
A: What do you do?
B: I'm a nurse.
6
A: What do you do?
B: I work in an office.
7
A: What do you do?
B: I don't have a job. I'm retired.
8
A: What do you do?
B: I'm a mum. I don't work for money.

▶ TRACK 40

1 I don't work on Friday and Saturday.
2 I don't know.
3 You don't live near here.
4 I don't like it.
5 We don't have children.
6 They don't live in the centre.
7 I don't walk to class.
8 I don't go to a language school.

▶ TRACK 42

My name's Carlos. I'm from Mexico, but now I live in London. I live in north London and I work in a university in the south. It takes 80 minutes by train. The job's great. I like my students and the money's OK.

▶ TRACK 43

1
My name's Jessica. I'm from Australia, but I'm a nurse here in London. My job's OK, but I don't like the hospital. It's small and I don't live near it. It's an hour by car from my flat. The other nurses are nice, but I don't like some doctors.
2
My name's Rasa. I'm from Lithuania, but now I live and work in Tooting – an area in south London. I work in an office. It's OK. I like the people and the hours are good for me. I work from nine to three and then I go to a language school.
3
My name's Ali. I'm from Turkey. I work for a taxi company. I don't like my job. London traffic is bad. The money is OK but I work a lot – 70 or 80 hours a week. I don't have time with my wife and two daughters.

▶ TRACK 44

A: What do you do?
B: I'm a taxi driver.
A: Do you like it?
B: No.
A: Why not?
B: The hours are bad.

▶ TRACK 47

A: Do you have a table for three?
B: Yes. Would you like a menu in English?
A: Please.
B: Would you like some drinks?
A: Yes. Two orange juices, a Coke and some water.

▶ TRACK 48

B: Are you ready to order?
A: Yes. A kebab with rice for me.
B: And for you?
C: Chicken, please.
B: With rice or chips?
C: Chips, please.
B: And you?
D: Prawns with rice.
B: Anything else? A salad?
C: How much is the tomato salad?
B: Fifteen euros.
C: Oh. It's expensive. No, thanks.

▶ TRACK 49

A: Do you have a table for three?
B: Yes. Would you like a menu in English?
B: Please.
A: Would you like some drinks?
B: Yes. Two orange juices, a Coke and some water.
B: Are you ready to order?
A: Yes. A kebab with rice for me.
B: OK. And you?
C: Chicken, please.
B: With rice or chips?
C: Chips, please.
B: And you?
D: Prawns with rice.
B: Anything else? A salad?
C: How much is the tomato salad?
B: Fifteen euros.
C: Oh. It's expensive. No, thanks.
B: So, that's one kebab and rice, one chicken and chips and one prawns with rice.

▶ TRACKS 50 & 51

1 It's a nice area.
2 It's in the north.
3 She's a teacher in a language school.
4 Where do you live?
5 I like it here.
6 I don't live near here.
7 I don't know it.
8 I don't like it.
9 He's a student at university
10 They have a nice house.

UNIT 3

▶ TRACK 55

1
A: How's your room?
B: It's not very big. How's *your* room?
A: The same. And it's old!
B: Yeah, I know.
2
A: How's the class?
B: It's good, but English is difficult.
A: Yes!
3
A: How's the chicken?
B: It's not very nice.
A: Oh no! I'm sorry.
B: How's the fish?
A: It's great!
B: Good.
4
A: How's the weather?
B: It's cold. It's not good.
A: Oh no! It's normally hot there.

▶ TRACK 56

1 She's not my friend.
2 It's not a big city.
3 We're not married.
4 I'm not very hungry.
5 They're not from here.
6 The rooms are not very expensive.
7 My job's not very good. The money's not great.

▶ TRACK 58

1 A: It's not very expensive.
   B: Oh, good.
2 A: My room is nice and big.
   B: Oh, good.
3 A: It's very cold in my flat.
   B: I'm sorry.
4 A: The weather here is great.
   B: Oh, good.
5 A: I love my English class.
   B: Oh, good.
6 A: The fish is very good.
   B: Oh, good.
7 A: My father's not very well.
   B: I'm sorry.
8 A: I don't like my new job. The hours are very bad.
   B: I'm sorry.

▶ TRACK 59

A: How's your room?
B: Very nice. It's big.
A: Oh, good. How's the restaurant?
B: It's not very good. It's expensive.

▶ TRACK 60

1 take the bus
   take a photo
   take a shower
   take a long time
2 go to the park every day
   go to the doctor
   go on holiday
   go shopping
3 want a coffee
   want a new house
   want to go to China
   want to buy some clothes

▶ TRACK 63

J = Janet, W = Wilton, A = Aled, B = Ben
J: Hello. Are you Wilton?
W: Yes, yes.
J: Hi. Nice to meet you! I'm Janet.
W: Hello. Janet. Nice to meet you too.
J: Come in. Leave your bag there.
W: OK, thanks.
J: Come in. Meet my family.
W: Yes, thank you.
J: So Wilton is a student and he's with us for one month.
A/B: Welcome. Hi.
J: These are my sons Aled and Ben.
W: Ben and ... can you say that again?
A: Aled.
W: Nice to meet you.
A: Yeah, you too. How are you?
W: Good, thanks.
J: You're not tired?
W: No. I'm OK.
B: Where are you from, Wilton?
W: Arequipa.
B: Sorry – where?
W: Arequipa – Peru.

▶ TRACK 64

B: Where are you from, Wilton?
W: Arequipa.
B: Sorry – where?
W: Arequipa – Peru.
B: OK. How long does it take to get here?
W: Sorry. Can you say it again?
B: How long does it take from Peru to here?
W: Oh, er, sixteen hours.
A: OK. A long time! But you're not tired.
W: No. I ... I'm OK.
J: Are you hungry? Do you want anything to eat?
W: Sorry. Can you say that again?
J: Yeah sorry. Are you hungry? ... Do you want any food?
W: Er. No. Thank you. Do you have any tea?
J: Of course. Do you want any milk in it?
W: Sorry?
J: Tea with milk?
W: No – black. Thanks.
J: And you don't want anything else? No food?
W: No, thank you. Er ... do you have a ... for my phone?
J: A charger?

W: Yes. My phone doesn't have … er, *batería.* How do you say it?

A: It's the same – battery!

W: Yes, my phone has no battery and I need a …can you say it?

A: Charger!

W: Yes, I don't have my charger. It's in Peru!

J: Oh, OK. Ben, do you have a charger?

B: What phone is it?

W: This.

B: Oh yes – no problem.

▶ TRACK 65

A: How are you?

B: Sorry? Can you say that again?

A: How are you?

B: Oh, I have … how do you say *tengo hambre*?

A: I'm hungry.

B: Yes. I'm hungry.

A: Do you want a sandwich?

B: Yes, please.

▶ TRACK 66

Sorry? Can you say that again?

How do you say *batería* (in English)?

▶ TRACK 67

1 A: Do you need a dictionary?
   B: No, thanks. I understand the word.

2 A: Do you have any money? I only have euros.
   B: Yes. How much do you need?

3 A: It's very cold here. Do you have any other clothes?
   B: Yes. I have a big coat.

4 A: Do you need a towel?
   B: No, it's OK. I have one.

5 A: Do you want any food?
   B: Yes, please. I'm hungry.

6 A: Do you have any brothers or sisters?
   B: Yes. One brother and three sisters.

▶ TRACKS 68 & 69

1 Do you have a pen?
2 Do you have any brothers or sisters?
3 Do you want to go shopping?
4 I don't have a lot of free time.
5 How's your class?
6 It's not very nice. It's very cold.
7 How's the weather?
8 It's not very expensive.

UNIT 4

▶ TRACKS 72 & 73

1 Is there a café near here?
   Yes. There's one on this road. Down there. On the left.

2 Is there a supermarket near here?
   Yes. There's one next to the train station.

3 Is there a bank near here?
   Yes. There's a Santander bank on this road. Down there. On the right.

4 Is there a hospital near here?
   Sorry. I don't know. I don't live here.

▶ TRACK 74

1

A: Hi. Excuse me. Excuse me!

B: Sorry. Yes.

A: Is there a cash machine near here?

B: A cash machine … er… yeah. There's one down there.

A: How far is it?

B: I don't know – 200 metres? It's next to a small supermarket called Jones.

A: OK – next to the supermarket.

B: Yeah – it's on the left. The other side of the road.

A: Oh, OK! Thanks.

2

A: Excuse me. Do you know a restaurant called Gema near here?

B: Er … I don't know. I don't know the area.

A: Oh.

B: There are some restaurants on this road, but I don't know their names.

A: Oh, OK.

B: Go down this road. I think the first one is a pizza place.

A: Oh yes – pizza! It's a pizza restaurant.

B: Maybe that's it. Down here on the right.

A: OK. Thank you!

3

A: Excuse me. Hello.

B: Yes.

A: Is there a car park near here?

B: A car park … car park. Oh, wait, yes – there's one on London Road. Down here. The second on the right.

A: Sorry, can you say that again?

B: Sorry, yeah. So, down here. The second road. Go right.

A: The second road.

B: Yes. It's a big road called London Road. And on London Road the car park is on the left.

A: OK. Thank you.

▶ TRACK 75

1

A: Is there a swimming pool near here?

B: Yes. There's one on Green Road. It's next to the park.

A: OK, thanks.

2

A: Do you know a church called St Mary's?

B: Yes. It's on Church Road.

A: Is it far?

B: No. It's about ten minutes from here.

▶ TRACK 80

1

T = teacher, S = student

T: James. Are you OK?
S: No. It's difficult. Can you help me?
T: Sure.

2

T: Kevin. Are you OK?
S: Can you close the window? I'm cold.
T: Is everybody else cold?
S: Yes.
T: Oh, OK. Sure.

3

S1 = Student 1, S2 = Student 2

S1: Do you want to go and have a coffee?
S2: Sure. Can you wait a minute? I need to go to the toilet.
S1: OK.
S2: Where is it?
S1: Oh – it's on the second floor. Next to the stairs.

4

S: I'm sorry. I can't come to class on Thursday.
T: OK. Can you do exercises 6 and 7?
S: Sure.
T: And exercise 8.
S: OK.
T: And maybe read page 39.
S: It's a lot!

5

T: Are you OK?
S: We're tired. Can we have a break?
T: Of course. Sorry.
S: Is there a café near here?
T: Yes there's one on this road. On the right.
S: How long do we have?
T: Ten minutes.
S: Can we have drinks in the class?
T: No, sorry. You can't.
S: OK. Can we have five more minutes? We don't have time to drink our coffee.
T: Yes, fine.

▶ TRACKS 81 & 82

1 Do you know a town called Atrani?
2 Is there a hospital near here?
3 Are you free tomorrow night?
4 It's down this road on the right.
5 I normally work late on Mondays.
6 It's at the end of this road on the left.
7 There's one on the third floor.
8 There's one near here. The first road on the right.

▶ TRACK 83

1 Does she have any brothers or sisters?
2 I sometimes go shopping in the market near here.
3 They're not in my class at school.
4 Do you need anything else?
5 There's a car park on the left.

UNIT 5

▶ TRACKS 85 & 87

1

A: I want to buy some new clothes. Are there any good shops near here?
B: Yes. Try an area called Cihangir. I always go shopping there. There are lots of nice places.
A: OK. How do you get there?
B: Oh, you can walk. It's not very far. Maybe ten minutes.
A: Thank you.

2

C: I want to go swimming this afternoon. Where's the best place to go?
D: Well, there's a pool on this road. Or there's a beach about thirty minutes from here.
C: A beach is good. How do you get there?
D: Take the train. The station is two minutes from here. Leave the hotel. Go left. It's there. Trains go every fifteen minutes, so ...
C: Great. Thank you.

3

E: Are there any places to go out in the evening here?
F: Not in the village. People go to the town. There's a cinema in the town and there are some nice places in the main square.
E: OK. How do you get there?
F: Car or taxi. It takes twenty minutes.
E: How much is a taxi?
F: About twenty euros.

4

G: Is there a nice café or restaurant near here? I want to have some lunch.
H: Yes. There are lots of good places. Try Ariel. It's on a street called Szeroka. In Kazimierz.
G: OK. Thank you. How do you get there?
H: Take the bus. Number 16 and number 25 go there. The stop is one minute from here.
G: Great. How long does it take?
H: About ten minutes.

5

I: Hello there. I want to see some interesting art today. Where's a good place to visit?
J: Well, there's a good museum in the centre. It's near the station.
I: OK. Thanks. How do you get there?
J: You can take the bus, but it's best to get a taxi. It takes ten or fifteen minutes. They're not very expensive.
I: OK. Thank you. Can I get a taxi from here?
J: Yes, of course. I can phone and get one for you.

▶ TRACK 88

A: Hello. Can I help you?
B: Yes I want to have a walk. Is there anywhere nice near here?
A: There's a nice park down the road.
B: How do you get there?
A: It's best to take a bus! It takes ten minutes. Or you can walk. It takes twenty minutes.
B: OK. Thanks.

▶ TRACK 91

A = assistant, T = tourist

A: Do you want to buy a ticket?

T: Er... yes.

A: You can use the machine over here. You can pay by cash or card and you don't need to wait.

T: Oh, OK. Is the machine in German?

A: Yes, but I can help you. Come with me.

T: OK.

A: Where are you going?

T: Lausanne.

A: Single or return?

T: Return.

A: For now, right?

T: Yes. And back on Monday.

A: Yes, fine. First class? Second class?

T: Second class is fine.

A: OK. Do you want a receipt?

T: Yes, please.

A: Put your card in here and enter your number.

T: OK.

A: And here are your tickets and receipt.

T: When's the next train?

A: 9.47. From platform eight.

T: Sorry. Which platform?

A: Eight -– at 9.47.

T: OK. Thank you for your help.

A: You're welcome. Have a good day.

▶ TRACK 92

1

A: What are you doing now?

B: I'm going home. I need to study. And you?

A: I'm going to have a coffee. Do you want to come?

B: Sorry, I can't. I don't have time today.

A: OK. See you tomorrow.

2

C: What are we doing now? Do you want to get something to eat?

D: No. I'm going to stay here.

C: Are you going to your room now?

D: Yes. I'm tired. I'm going to bed. It's an early flight tomorrow.

C: That's true. What time are we going?

D: Five. The flight is at 7.15 and it takes thirty minutes to the airport.

C: Right. Well, I need to eat something.

D: OK. I'll meet you here tomorrow morning.

C: Five o'clock?

D: That's right. See you then.

C: Yep. Sleep well.

3

E: What are you doing now?

F: I'm going to meet a friend. Do you want to come?

E: Where are you going?

F: Cheers. It's a place in New Street. Do you know it?

E: No.

F: It's good.

E: OK. Great. How do you get there?

F: Bus.

E: OK. Can I go the toilet first?

F: Sure. I'll meet you outside.

E: I need some money, too.

F: Me too. There's a cash machine next to the bar.

▶ TRACK 94

1 I'm going to meet my brother tonight.

2 We're going to the park this afternoon.

3 We're going to the beach on Sunday.

4 I'm going to have a coffee now.

5 We're going to have a party tomorrow night.

6 I'm going to the pool with some friends tomorrow morning.

▶ TRACK 96

1 I'll meet you at the hotel.

2 I'll meet you at the station.

3 I'll meet you at the bus stop at six.

4 I'll meet you there in ten minutes.

5 I'll meet you here at five o'clock.

▶ TRACKS 97 & 98

1 I'm going to meet a friend.

2 We need to get off at the next stop.

3 When's the next train?

4 Where are you going?

5 What time are you going?

6 We need to change at Red Square.

7 I'll meet you at six.

8 How do you get there?

UNIT 6

▶ TRACK 101

1 I have a problem at work. I need to work late.

2 I can't sleep. There's a lot of noise outside my room.

3 The weather's very bad. There's a lot of rain.

4 The flight is two hours late. We need to wait in the airport.

5 We need help, but there's no-one here.

6 There are a lot of people here. There's nowhere to sit.

7 I'm going to bed early. I'm very tired.

8 We're going the wrong way. This isn't the right train!

▶ TRACK 102

D = Dana, B = Bryan

D: Bryan. Great to see you!

B: Hi, Dana. How are you?

D: Great.

B: Sorry I'm late! There was a problem in London.

D: Don't worry. It was on the airport website.

B: Oh, good.

D: How was the flight?

B: Not very good. The weather was bad.

D: Oh, I'm sorry. Are you tired?

B: Yeah. Where are we going now?

D: To the hotel and then we can have something to eat.

B: Oh, sorry. I had dinner on the plane. I'm not hungry.

D: That's OK. Do you want to stay in the hotel?

B: Is that OK? I did a lot yesterday and I went to bed late.

D: Of course! We can go out tomorrow.

B: Great. Thanks.

▶ TRACK 104

1 Sorry I didn't come to class on Monday.

2 Sorry. I don't have any money.

3 Sorry. I'm very early!

4 Sorry the room isn't very big.

5 Sorry. I don't know the answer.

▶ TRACK 105

A: Hi. How are you?
B: I'm good, thanks. And you?
A: I'm OK. Sorry, I'm late.
B: Don't worry.
A: How was your journey?
B: There was a lot of traffic.
A: I know.
B: How was your day?
A: Not very good. I had a lot of problems.
B: Sorry to hear that.

▶ TRACK 106

1 Good evening. Do you have any rooms for tonight?
2 Hi. We have a booking. My name's Kim Jae-Sung.
3 Can I have your passport, please?
4 Can you write your name and address here? And sign here?
5 Do you need help with your bags?
6 Here's your key. Your room number is 351.
7 What time do we need to check out?
8 I'm sorry there's no lift. The stairs are over there.
9 What time is breakfast in the morning?
10 What's the password for the WiFi?

▶ TRACK 107

A: Hi.
B: Hello, sir. How can I help you?
A: We have a booking. My name's Kim Jae-Sung.
B: OK. Yes. Welcome. Can I have your passport, please?
A: Sure.
B: Do you have a car?
A: No.
B: OK. Can you write your name and address here? And sign here?
A: OK.
B: Here's your key. Your room number is 351. It's on the third floor.
A: Thanks.
B: Do you need help with your bags?
A: Sorry. Can you say that again?
B: Do you need help with your bags?
A: Oh. No. That's OK.
B: The lift is over there.
A: OK. What time is breakfast in the morning?
B: Seven to ten, in the restaurant. It's fifteen dollars.
A: Oh, I didn't pay?
B: No. Sorry. Your booking is not with breakfast.
A: OK. Don't worry.

▶ TRACKS 109 & 110

L = Lucy, D = Dom

Parts 1 and 2

L: Do you need somewhere to sit?
D: Yes. Can I sit here?
L: Of course. Your name's Dom, right? We met yesterday.
D: Yeah, yeah. And you're ... er ... Lucy.
L: That's right. Well, good morning.
D: Yes. Hi. ... How was your breakfast?
L: It was good.
D: What did you have?
L: Just eggs and fruit juice. I wasn't very hungry.
D: OK.

L: And how are you? Did you sleep well?
D: Yes, thanks. You?
L: Fine, but I went to bed late.
D: What time?
L: About three in the morning.
D: Oh. What did you do?
L: I went out with some other people from here.
D: Where did you go?
L: We walked round the Old Town.
D: How was it?
L: Great. They had music in the street. We danced a lot.
D: Great. Was it busy?
L: Yeah. There were lots of people. And you? What did you do last night?
D: Not much. I stayed here.
L: OK.
D: I had dinner and I talked to some people.
L: Yeah, it's great here – people are very nice.
D: Yeah – but I didn't feel very well, so I went to bed early.
L: Oh, I'm sorry. Are you OK now?
D: Yeah, I feel fine.
L: Good.
D: Maybe I was just tired.

▶ TRACKS 111 & 112

Part 3

L: Yeah. So, what are you doing today?
D: I'm going to visit the modern art museum.
L: Oh really? Me too.
D: Oh OK. Well, do you want to go together?
L: Yeah – if that's OK.
D: Of course.
L: When are you going?
D: I'm going to have a shower first. After that?
L: Yes. Fine.
D: OK. Well, I'll meet you here. In ... thirty minutes?
L: OK. What time is it now?
D: Er, 9.25.
L: Great! See you at about ten.

▶ TRACK 114

1 A: I went shopping.
   B: What did you buy?
2 A: I went to work.
   B: Where do you work?
3 A: I went out.
   B: Where did you go?
4 A: I went to my classes at the university.
   B: What do you study?
5 A: I went to the beach.
   B: Did you stay there all day?
6 A: I stayed at home.
   B: What did you do?
7 A: I watched TV.
   B: What did you see?
8 A: I went to the gym.
   B: Do you go every day?

▶ TRACK 115

1 How was your journey?
2 I had a very busy day.
3 We stayed in a hostel.
4 We had a great view of the lake.
5 What's the password for the WiFi?
6 What did you do last night?
7 I met some friends.
8 I went to the gym.

▶ TRACK 116

1 Did you go to the museum yesterday?
2 I'm going to meet some friends this afternoon.
3 There are some good places to eat in Kalamaki.
4 What time did you go to bed last night?
5 We had good weather on Saturday. We went to the beach.

UNIT 7

▶ TRACK 118

cook – cooked
do – did
go – went
listen – listened
read – read
watch – watched

▶ TRACKS 119 & 120

1
A: What did you do last night?
B: Not much. I stayed at home and made dinner.
A: Oh. Do you like cooking?
B: Yes! I love it.
A: Me too. What do you usually cook?
B: Russian food. Sometimes Italian – pasta.
A: OK. Do you have a favourite dish?
B: Not really. I love everything Russian.
A: Right.
2
C: What did you do last night?
D: I watched TV.
C: Do you watch TV a lot?
D: Yes.
C: Me too. What do you like watching?
D: I watch a lot of news programmes. And you?
C: I prefer watching series.
D: OK. Do you have a favourite?
C: I really like *WarGames*.
D: Really? I saw it, but I didn't like it. I prefer *The Crown*.
3
E: What did you do last night?
F: I played basketball with some friends.
E: Do you do a lot of sport?
F: Yeah. I usually play basketball on Tuesdays and I go running sometimes. Do you like sport?
E: Yes, I love it, but I prefer watching it.
F: Do you have a favourite sport?
E: Football.

F: Do you have a favourite team?
E: Madrid!
F: Real Madrid or Atlético?
E: Sorry? Can you say that again?
F: Real Madrid or Atlético Madrid?
E: Real Madrid, of course!
F: I prefer Atlético.

▶ TRACK 121

A: What did you do last night?
B: I went to the cinema.
A: OK. Do you go to the cinema a lot?
B: Yes. I love watching films.
A: Me too. Do you have a favourite film?
B: Not really. But I love Japanese films.
A: I prefer Disney or Pixar.
B: OK. I like their films too.

▶ TRACK 122

1
A: What are you reading?
B: A book called *The Lake*. Do you know it?
A: No. Is it good?
B: Yes, it's OK. Are you reading anything at the moment?
A: No, I'm very busy. I don't have time. Do you read a lot?
B: Maybe one book a month.
A: I think that's a lot!
2
C: What are you listening to?
D: A French band called Superbus. Do you know them?
C: No. Are they good?
D: Yes. They're great. I love them. Do you listen to music a lot?
C: Yes.
D: What do you like?
C: Lots of different things. Pop, Mozart... And you? What do you like?
D: I listen to a lot of Brazilian music.
3
E: What are you watching?
F: Just a video on YouTube.
E: Is it good?
F: Not really.
E: What else do you watch?
F: Films, series. Lots of things. And you?
E: I don't watch a lot.
4
G: What are you doing?
H: I'm doing something for work.
G: Do you work at night a lot?
H: Not really. But I have an important meeting tomorrow.

▶ TRACK 126

1
A: What do you think?
B: They're OK. They feel comfortable but I'm not sure about the design.
A: And the brown ones?
B: They look nice, but they feel a bit small.
A: OK.
B: Do you have these in 44?
A: I don't know. I'll go and look.

2
A: Hello. Can I help you?
B: No, thanks, I'm just looking.
A: OK. No problem.
3
A: What do you think of this one?
B: It looks nice. I like the design.
A: Yeah. I'm not sure about the colour. What do you think of the blue and red one?
B: Yeah. It's nice. How much is it?
A: Fifteen dollars.
B: That's good!
A: What do you think of the size?
B: It looks fine, but try it and see.
A: OK.

▶ TRACK 127

1 Do you like cooking?
2 Did you watch the game last night?
3 I'm working a lot at the moment.
4 It's a really good Japanese film.
5 What are you listening to?
6 What do you think of these?
7 They are my favourite shoes.
8 What do you normally watch?

UNIT 8

▶ TRACK 129

1 I'm going to take some friends to the airport.
2 I'm working at home this week.
3 I'm studying for an exam at the moment.
4 They travelled a long way.
5 She makes a lot of money.
6 I met a client yesterday.
7 I need to get something to eat.

▶ TRACK 130

1
A: Where is everyone? We said three o'clock.
B: They're coming. Look here's Lizzie.
C: Hi.
A: Hi Lizzie. We're waiting for everyone.
C: Yeah. They're coming. Jaime's getting coffee for everyone and Ulla is talking to someone on the phone.
A: OK. Here's Jaime. No coffee?
D: The machine's not working!
B: Oh.
A: And Katya? Is she coming?
B: No, she's working at home.
A: Oh.
B: Her son's not feeling well today.
A: Oh, OK.
B: I'm going to phone her later and tell her about the meeting.
A: Great, thanks. Well say hi. And sorry her son's not feeling well.
B: OK.
D: Hi everyone.
A: Hi Ulla.
E: Sorry I'm a bit late. I needed to talk to a client.
A: That's OK. We can start now.
E: And Katya?
C: She's working at home. Her son's not well.
E: Oh, OK.

2
F: How's your sister? Is she OK?
G: Emma? She's fine. She's at university now in Leeds.
F: Oh, really? What's she studying?
G: French and Spanish.
F: OK. That's good.
G: Yes. She's studying hard for her exams at the moment.
F: Oh, really?
G: Yeah. I'm going to visit her this weekend.
F: Oh, say hello.
3
H: And then she said ... Sorry. Can I answer this?
I: Yes. Sure.
H: Thanks. Hello? Oh, hiya. How are you? OK. Bye. Thanks for calling. Have a good flight. ... Right . Sorry.
I: Who was that?
H: My dad. He's travelling to Dubai today.
I: Really? What's he doing there?
H: Work. He's going there for two weeks.
I: What does he do?
H: He's a designer.
I: That's good. Does he travel a lot?
H: Yes, he does. He went to Spain last month – and he's going to China in the summer.

▶ TRACK 132

A: OK. Are we ready?
B: Yes. Sure.
A: Wait a minute. Where's Kim?
B: Oh, she's not coming today. She's meeting a friend.
A: Ah, OK.

▶ TRACK 133

A: How's your brother Martin?
B: He's fine. Thank you.
A: What's he doing at the moment?
B: Well, he's a doctor now. He started last year. He's working hard.
A: Really? Where did he study?
B: in Bucharest.
A: And where's he working?
B: In a hospital in Madrid.
A: OK. Well, say hello.

▶ TRACK 135

1
A: Are you OK?
B: No. I can't find my glasses.
A: Oh, I saw them in the bathroom. Next to the sink.
B: Ah, great. Thank you.
2
C: What are you looking for?
D: My passport. I can't find it and I'm going to the airport this afternoon.
C: Maybe it's on the shelf in the living room. I saw it there.
D: I took it from there. It was here!
C: Oh, look. It's there. On the carpet. Next to the bed.
3
E: I can't find my keys.
F: Where did you last have them?
E: Here in the living room.
F: OK. Oh, look. There they are. On the sofa.

4
G: Can you wait one minute? I don't have my phone.
H: OK.
G: Maybe I left it in the kitchen.
H: Did you find it?
G: Yes, it was on the table.

▶ TRACK 136

E = Ella, L = Lucian

E: Are you OK?
L: No. I can't find my glasses.
E: Oh no! When did you last have them?
L: I'm not sure. I can't remember.
E: Well, did you have them this morning?
L: No. I don't think so.
E: What did you do last night? Did you go out?
L: Yes, I went for dinner with some friends.
E: Well, maybe you left them in the restaurant.
L: Yes. Maybe. I'm going to phone them and ask.

▶ TRACK 137

W = waiter, L = Lucian

Part 1

W: Hello. Selale Restaurant. How can I help you?
L Hi. I had dinner in your restaurant last night.
W: Yes …
L: And I think I left my glasses there.
W: OK. What colour are they?
L: Blue.
W: And what time were you here?
L: We arrived at eight and finished at maybe ten.
W: OK. Where did you sit? Can you remember?
L: Near the window. We had a big table.
W: OK. I need to ask someone. Can you wait one minute?
L: Sure.

▶ TRACK 138

Part 2

W: Hello?
L: Hi. Did you find them?
W: Yes. They were on the floor.
L: Oh, that's great. Thank you. I'm going to come and get them now.
W: OK. Ask for me – Hakan. I have them here.
L: Sure. … Now, where are my car keys?

▶ TRACK 140

1 I'm working at home this week.
2 She's travelling to Tokyo today.
3 He's in the kitchen making dinner.
4 She's talking to someone.
5 I can't find my keys.
6 When did you last have them?
7 They make a lot of money.
8 He's a very good teacher.

▶ TRACK 141

1 I don't like the red tops. I prefer these blue ones.
2 What's your father doing in Peru?
3 I'm watching a great series at the moment.
4 My friends don't like going to the gym, but I love it.
5 When did you last have them? Maybe you left them at home.

UNIT 9

▶ TRACK 146

1
A: Hi Luca.
B: Hello.
A: Oh no! What happened to your hand?
B: I cut it.
A: When was that?
B: A few days ago.
A: I'm sorry. Is it OK now?
B: Yes. It's much better.
2
C: Where were you last week?
D: I had a cold. I stayed at home.
C: Oh, sorry. Are you feeling better?
D: A bit better, thanks.
3
E: You missed the class on Thursday.
F: Yes, I was in the hospital!
E: Really? Why?
F: My son broke his leg playing football!
E: Oh no. Is he OK?
F: Not really. It hurts a lot. He can't sleep.
E: Oh, I'm sorry.
4
G: Where did you go after the meeting this morning?
H: I had something in my eye. I went to the toilet.
G: I waited but then I went.
H: That's OK. Don't worry.
G: So is your eye OK now?
H: Yes, much better thanks.
G: Good.

▶ TRACK 147

1
A: Where were you this morning?
B: I had a headache. I stayed in bed.
A: Oh no! Are you feeling better?
B: Much better.
2
C: What happened to your head?
D: I hit it on the door and cut it.
C: When was that?
D: A few days ago.
C: Is it OK now?
D: A bit better, but it hurts.

▶ TRACK 150

L = Lena, K = Kasper, A = An

Part 1

L: Kasper!
K: Lena! Great to see you!
L: How are you?
K: Good, good. Long time!
L: Yeah.
A: Hi.
L: Oh, sorry. Kasper. This is my friend An.
K: Hi. Nice to meet you. How do you know Lena?
A: We go to the same English class. And you?
K: My mum and her mum are friends.

A: Oh. OK – are you from Poland?

K: My mum is. I'm British. Where are you from?

A: Vietnam.

▶ TRACK 151

Part 2

K: So, An. Have you been here before?

A: Yes. A few years ago.

K: OK. To study English?

A: No. I came to see my sister.

K: Does she live here?

A: Yes. I'm staying with her now.

K: OK. What does she do?

A: She's not working at the moment. She had a baby last year.

K: Oh, great. What did she think of the British health service?

A: I'm not sure. Good, I think. Her baby's very well.

K: That's good. There are a lot of problems with the health system at the moment.

A: Really?

K: Yes. It's difficult. You sometimes wait a long time to see a doctor.

A: Oh.

L: Kasper, tell her what happened to you.

K: I broke my hand last month and I waited in the hospital for four hours!

A: Oh four hours. It's a lot. Are hospitals better in Poland?

L: I don't know.

K: I've never been to a hospital there!

A: How often do you go to Poland?

K: Quite a lot. My mum lives there now.

A: OK.

K: She went back two years ago. Have you been to Poland?

A: No. Maybe next year with Lena!

▶ TRACK 152

Part 3

A: Have you ever been to Vietnam?

K: Yes!

A: Really? Why did you go?

K: For work.

A: When was that?

K: Four or five years ago.

A: Where did you go?

K: Hanoi.

A: What did you think of it?

K: It was very hot and busy!

A: Yes. There's a lot of traffic. How long were you there?

K: Only two days.

A: Oh. A very short time.

K: Yes – and we were mostly in the office or hotel.

A: Oh no. Maybe next time you can see more.

UNIT 10

▶ TRACK 156

1

A: It's so hot!

B: I know! Is it going to stay like this?

A: Yes. It's going to be 35 degrees tomorrow.

A: Really? I don't like it.

B: I do. We're going to the island tomorrow. Do you have any plans?

A: I'm going to stay inside – and turn on the air conditioning!

2

C: It's so cold!

D: I know. Is it going to stay like this?

C: It's going to be worse! It's going to be minus 10 tomorrow.

D: Really? Is it going to snow?

C: I don't think so. Why? What are you doing tomorrow?

D: Nothing special.

3

E: It's horrible! It's so wet!

F: I know, but they said it's going to be better tomorrow.

E: Really?

F: Yes. It's going to be sunny and 25 degrees!

E: Oh good. We're going to have a barbecue tomorrow maybe.

F: That's nice.

4

G: It's lovely!

H: I know. It's really nice in the sun.

G: Is it going to stay like this?

H: I don't think so. I think it's going to get cold and windy.

G: Really? Is it going to rain?

H: I think so. Do you have any plans for tomorrow?

G: I'm going shopping in the morning. I also need to clean the house and do some other jobs.

▶ TRACK 157

A: It's so nice.

B: I know. Is it going to stay like this?

A: I think so. It's going to be warm and sunny for a few days.

B: Oh, good.

A: Why? Do you have any plans?

B: Yes. I'm going walking at the weekend.

A: Oh really? Where are you going?

B: To the countryside near here.

A: Nice.

B: And you? Do you have any plans?

A: No.

▶ TRACK 160

A: What do you want to see today?

B: How about Jessie Ware? She's playing tonight.

A: Yeah, great. I like her music.

B: What else?

A: How about a play? There's one in the theatre tent this afternoon.

B: I don't really like plays. I'd prefer a film. They're showing *Jaws*.

A: OK. What do you want to do now?

B: How about a yoga class? There's one in fifteen minutes.

A: No. I'd prefer the politics discussion.

B: Really? I don't really like politics.

A: Well, you go to the yoga and I'll meet you after that. We can get something to eat.

B: OK. Where?

A: I'll meet you here at twelve.

B: OK.

▶ TRACK 161

1 A: Princess Sophia is going to get married.

   B: When?

2 A: President Smith died yesterday. He had a heart attack.

   B: How old was he?

3 A: Barbara Francisco had her baby.

   B: Is it a boy or a girl?

4 A: There was a really big fire in a shopping centre near here.
   B: How did it start?

5 A: There was an election in Germany yesterday.
   B: Who won?

6 A: There was a big accident on the motorway. About ten cars!
   B: Did anyone die?

7 A: They're going to build a new airport.
   B: Why?

8 A: Arsenal lost 3–0 to Zenit, St Petersburg.
   B: Who scored?

9 A: The government is going to spend more money on education.
   B: How much?

10 A: Toyota is going to close its factory here.
    B: How many people work there?

▶ TRACK 162

finished

decided

opened

happened

stopped

played

talked

helped

tried

used

▶ TRACK 164

1 He broke his leg a few months ago.
2 I'm going to my friends' house this weekend.
3 I didn't go to my yoga class last Thursday.
4 There are quite a lot of problems in our hospitals.
5 It's not going to rain at the weekend.

UNIT 11

▶ TRACK 166

January

February

March

April

May

June

July

August

September

October

November

December

▶ TRACK 167

1 in May
  during May

2 at the beginning of May
  in the first week of May

3 in the middle of May
  in the second or third week of May

4 at the end of May
  in the last week of May

▶ TRACK 168

1

A: What's the date today?
B: It's the 18th.
A: Really? Already?
B: Yeah. It's my sister's birthday on Friday.
A: Really? How old is she?
B: She's going to be … er 23. Yeah. 23.
A: Is she doing anything to celebrate?
B: I don't think so. She's doing exams at the moment.

2

C: Who was that?
D: Eric. He wants to have a meeting on the fifth of May.
C: Really. Did you tell him it's a public holiday here?
D: Yes, but he still wants to meet. Can you come?
C: Sorry. It's my boyfriend's birthday on the second and we're going away for a long weekend.
D: Lucky you.
C: Can we meet on the sixth?
D: No. Eric's going back to the States that day.
C: Oh.
D: Don't worry. It's not so important. So where are you going? …

3

E: We're having a party in a couple of weeks. Can you come?
F: I'd love to. When is it?
E: Not next Friday. It's the Friday after that. It's the twelfth.
F: Oh no, I can't. I'm really sorry. I'm at a conference that weekend.
E: Really? Are you sure you can't come?
F: I need to check the train times. Maybe I can go to the conference on Saturday morning.
E: OK, great.
F: So what's the party for?
E: Our anniversary.
F: Really? How many years?
E: Six. It's not special, but we have a party every year.
F: That's nice.

4

G: We're holding a conference in September to celebrate the tenth anniversary of our school.
H: Really? That's great.
G: Do you want to come?
H: Sure. What date?
G: The 23rd. It's a Saturday.
H: I think that's OK. I need to check my diary.
G: OK.
H: Can I tell you tomorrow?
G: Of course.

▶ TRACK 169

1 How old is she?
2 Where are you going?
3 Is she doing anything to celebrate?
4 Do you want to come?
5 Did you tell him it's a public holiday?
6 Can we meet on the sixth?

▶ TRACK 170

1

A: I'm having a barbecue in a few weeks. Do you want to come?
B: I'd love to. What date?
A: The 27th. It's a Saturday.
B: OK. Great!

2

B: We want to have a meeting next week. Can you come?

A: What day?

B: Wednesday.

A: Sorry, I can't come. I have another meeting.

B: How about Tuesday?

A: What time?

B: In the morning. Ten o'clock?

A: I think so. I need to check my diary.

▶ TRACK 172

1 when I was a child
2 when I was there
3 when I was ten
4 when I was on holiday
5 when I was at university
6 when I was in the army

▶ TRACK 173

A: So, this is end of the tour, but does anyone have any questions?

B: Yes. Why didn't Suwon become the capital?

A: I think because the king died quite young.

B: How old was he when he died?

A: 47.

B: How did he die?

A: They don't know. People have a lot of different ideas.

B: Like they killed him?

A: Maybe. The politics were difficult then.

B: Politics are always difficult!

A: Yes!

C: How long did it take to build?

A: Two years.

C: How long are the walls?

A: Five point seven kilometres.

B: And how high are they?

A: Well, here they are six metres, but in other parts they are only four metres.

C: You said the government spent money to repair the walls. How much did they spend?

A: In the last twenty years I think it's three trillion won – that's about 800 million dollars.

C: Wow. A lot. How big is the area inside the fort?

A: About 130 hectares.

B: How many people live here now?

A: In the fortress?

B: Yes. There are lots of houses, I think.

A: Good question. I don't know. But there are over one million people in Suwon now.

C: Last question. When did it become a UNESCO site?

A: 1997.

UNIT 12

▶ TRACK 176

1

A: Excuse me.

B: Hi.

A: Sorry, I'm a bit lost. Is this the way to the hospital?

B: Yes. But it's a twenty-minute walk.

A Oh, OK.

B: I'll take you, if you like.

A: Really? Are you sure?

B: Yes. I'm going that way.

A: Oh. That's great. Thanks.

B: No problem.

2

C: Hi.

D: Hello, Madam. How can I help you?

C: Yes. Er, yes. There's, er, something wrong with the shower in my room.

D: Oh I'm very sorry about that. What's the problem?

C: The water's cold and it's coming out very slowly.

D: Oh right. Well, I'll send someone to look at it, now.

C: OK. Thanks.

D: And sorry again for the problem.

C: That's OK.

3

E: It's very full in here.

F: I know. It's a popular place.

E: Look. There's a seat there.

F: But there's only one.

E: That's OK. I'll stand.

F: Are you sure?

E: Yeah. It's fine.

F: I'll look for another seat, if you like.

E: I'm happy to stand. I'll go and order some drinks. What do you want?

F: A cappuccino.

E: OK.

▶ TRACK 177

1 I'll go and get something.
2 I'll take you in the car.
3 I'll wait for the next one.
4 I'll check on the internet.

▶ TRACK 179

1

A: There's something wrong with this computer.

B: Do want to use this one?

A: Are you sure?

B: Yeah. It's fine. I'm not using it now.

A: OK. Thanks.

2

C: I'm a bit lost. How do I get out of here?

D: I'll show you.

C: Oh, thanks.

D: It's this way.

▶ TRACK 181

J = Janet, W = Wilton

J: The taxi's here. Do you have everything?

W: I think so.

J: Well, it's been great.

W: Yes. Thanks for having me. I really enjoyed it.

J: Us too. Give us a call when you're home.

W: I will.

J: OK. See you. Stay in contact.

W: I will. I hope to come back one day.

J: I hope so too.

W: And you could come and visit me!

J: We'd love to. OK. Have a good journey.

W: Thanks.

J: Be safe – and don't forget to call us.

W: I won't. Thanks again for everything. And say goodbye to your sons.
J: I will. Bye!
W: Bye.
J: Bye.

▶ TRACK 182

1 Don't forget to call.
2 Don't be late.
3 Don't ask him now.
4 Don't work too hard.
5 Don't worry.

▶ TRACK 183

1
A: What time is it?
B: 11.45.
A: Really?
B: Yeah. It's getting late.
A: I should go.
B: Yeah.
A: I need to get up early tomorrow.
B: Yeah I'm quite tired too.
A: How are you getting home?
B: Taxi. You?
A: I can walk. It's not far.
B: OK. Are you sure? I'm ordering the taxi now.
A: Yeah it's fine. I prefer to walk.
B: OK. Well, it's been a lovely evening.
A: Yes. I really enjoyed it.
B: We should do it again soon.
A: Yeah. I'm going to see a band the week after next. Do you want to come?
B: Maybe. What date is it?
A: The 19th I think. I need to check. They're a good band.
B: OK. Well, I'll give you a call next week.
A: Yeah. Great.
B: Oh, the taxi's here.
A: That was quick!
B: Yeah. Well, listen. I'll see you soon. Don't work too hard!
A: I won't.
B: See you.
A: Yeah, bye. And say hi to your brother.
B: I will. Bye now.
A: Bye.
2
C: Hey – Look at the time. It's almost four!
D: Oh right. Do I need to go?
C: Your flight's at seven, right?
D: Yeah.
C: Yeah. You should go now. The traffic can be bad later.
D: Sure.
C: There's a taxi place outside. You don't need to order one.
D: OK. Great. So, thanks.
C: No problem.
D: It's been lovely meeting you and I hope to see again soon.
C: Yes. Well, we're going to have another meeting next month.
D: Yes, but I'm not sure I can come.
C: Oh yes. You said.
D: Anyway, it's been good. I'm happy.
C: Yes. I think the project's going well.
D: Good. So, say bye and thanks to everyone.
C: I will.
D: And thanks again to you.

C: OK. Have a good journey back.
D: Thanks.
C: There's a taxi over there. It's 25 euros to the airport.
D: OK – great.
C: Oh and don't forget to send me those documents.
D: I won't. Bye now.
C: See you.

▶ TRACK 184

carry	stand
lend	send
miss	give
walk	order

▶ TRACK 185

carry a bag
stand by the bar
lend me some money
send them an email
miss the bus
give them a gift
order a taxi
walk home

▶ TRACK 186

1 I'm studying English, so I can get a good job.
2 Where are you going and why are you going there?
3 I'm studying English because I need it for my job.
4 Get some sleep – and don't forget to call me tomorrow.
5 Wait a minute. I'll check on the internet.

GRAMMAR REFERENCE

▶ TRACK 188

1 I'm Juan. Nice to meet you.
2 This is my teacher, Lena.
3 She's my sister.
4 We're in the same class.
5 He's nice.
6 Who are they?
7 What's your name?
8 My son is three today.

▶ TRACK 189

1 His name is Karim.
2 Karen's husband is a teacher.
3 My name's Ulla.
4 Our address is 15 New Road.
5 Where's their new flat?
6 When's his party?
7 What's your cat's name?
8 Is Liam's new baby a boy or a girl?
9 What's your name?
10 What's Tomas and Pepa's phone number?

▶ TRACKS 190 & 191

1 Who's he?
2 Where is it?
3 Where are you from?
4 How much is it?
5 What day is it?
6 What's your name?

7 How old is she?
8 What time is it?
9 How much are they?
10 How are you?
11 How old are you?
12 Where is he?
13 Who's she?
14 How long is it?

▶ TRACK 192

A: Where do you live?
B: In Beppu. Do you know it?
A: No. Where is it?
B: It's a small city in the south of Japan.
A: Do you like it?
B: Yes. It's a nice place. Where do you live?
A: Birmingham. Do you know it?
B: Yes. My friend lives there!
A: What's his name?
B: Brian.
A: Do you know his family name?
B: No. Sorry. Do you like Birmingham?
A: Yes, it's OK.

▶ TRACK 194

1 do you
2 are you
3 do you
4 do you
5 are you
6 do you
7 Where do you work?
8 Where are you from?
9 When do you work?
10 Are you from here?
11 Do you know him?
12 How are you?

▶ TRACK 195

1 Where are you from?
2 Do you live here?
3 Are you OK?
4 What do you do?
5 Do you know it?

▶ TRACK 197

1 Where does he work?
2 What time does your class start?
3 Do you have a car?
4 Is it near here?
5 What does she do?
6 Does she know your mum?
7 Does he like it?
8 What does she know?

▶ TRACK 198

1 It's good.
2 It's not very hot.
3 I'm not married.
4 He's not Michel.
5 We're from Rome.
6 She's not from here.
7 This isn't very good.
8 They're very nice people.

9 That's right.
10 My sister's small.
11 My coffee's cold.
12 They aren't very big.

▶ TRACK 199

1 I'm never late.
2 We always go to church on Sunday.
3 I'm not usually busy on Thursday.
4 I normally walk to work.
5 I sometimes take the bus.
6 My wife often works in the evening.
7 My husband usually has lunch at home.
8 My brother sometimes takes my things.

▶ TRACK 201

1 Sorry, I can't.
2 You can.
3 Can you?
4 I can't see.
5 Can I use your phone?
6 You can sit here.
7 You can't come in.
8 I can play it again.
9 Can't we leave now?
10 He can use my tablet.
11 They can't help you.
12 Can you turn off the light?

▶ TRACK 202

1 Do you want to go for a walk?
2 I'm going swimming later.
3 I'm going for a coffee. Do you want to come?
4 We're going shopping on Saturday.
5 Do you want to go out for dinner tonight?
6 I need to go for a run.

▶ TRACK 203

1 A: I'm going to Qatar next week.
   B: Why are you going?
   A: My company has an office there.
2 A: Do you want to go to the dinner together?
   B: Sure. What time?
   A: Eight?
3 A: We're going to Costa Rica on holiday.
   B: How long are going for?
   A: Two weeks.
4 A: I'm sorry. I'm not free tomorrow.
   B: What are you doing?
   A: I'm going to the dentist in the morning and I'm going to meet a friend at the airport in the afternoon.
5 A: I'm going to see *An American in Paris* tonight.
   B: Nice! Who are you going with?
   A: My boyfriend.
6 A: I'm going away for the weekend.
   B: Where are you going?
   A: Krakow – it's a city in Poland.

▶ TRACK 205

1 there are some
2 there aren't any
3 there isn't a
4 there aren't any
5 Is there a

6 Are there any good places to visit?
7 There aren't any shops near here.
8 There's some parking here.
9 Are there any buses to the airport?
10 There are two cash machines there.
11 There's a shop at the end of the road.
12 There are some things in the back of the car.

▶ TRACK 209

1 do you
2 did you
3 did you
4 do you
5 Did you know anyone there?
6 Do you want a coffee?
7 What do you do?
8 What time did you go to bed?
9 Did you live there?
10 Do you have any money?
11 Where did you go?
12 Did you sleep well?

▶ TRACK 210

1 A: What are you doing?
   B: Nothing much. I'm waiting for a phone call.
2 A: Are you listening to the radio?
   B: No. You can turn it off.
3 A: Can I turn on the TV?
   B: No. I'm trying to do some work.
4 A: I'm making dinner now.
   B: OK. What are we having?
   A: Chicken curry.
5 A: Are you on your own? What are your friends doing tonight?
   B: They're studying. There's an exam tomorrow.
   A: Why are you not studying?
   B: I am! I'm having a break!

▶ TRACK 211

A: What do you think of this dress?
B: It's OK. I prefer the other one.
A: Which one? This one?
B: Yes. I like the design.
A: Really? I don't like it. I'm going to buy this one.
B: OK. It looks nice too.
A: Are you buying anything?
B: No, I'm just looking. I don't have any money.
A: You do! You don't like spending money!
B: That's right! And I don't like going shopping!

▶ TRACK 213

1 are you
2 do you
3 did you
4 Are you going swimming?
5 What do you like cooking?
6 Where are you staying?
7 What do you read?
8 Why did you like it?
9 Do you like going to the cinema?
10 Do you like playing tennis?
11 When are you going?
12 What did you do?

▶ TRACK 214

1 I like travelling a lot.
2 I don't like listening to music.
3 I'm reading a good book at the moment.
4 Are you watching anything good at the moment?
5 What do you think of these shoes?
6 I prefer the black ones.

▶ TRACK 215

1 A: Is it raining?
   B: Yes, it is.
2 A: Is he feeling OK?
   B: No, he's not.
3 A: Is your mother working at the moment?
   B: Yes, she is.
4 A: Is he living with his parents again?
   B: Yes, he is.
5 A: Is your sister staying in Slovakia?
   B: No, she's not.
6 A: Is the shop closing now?
   B: Yes, it is.
7 A: Are you going to the beach today?
   B: No, I'm not.
8 A: Is the train stopping here?
   B: Yes, it is.
9 A: Are you reading this?
   B: Yes, I am.
10 A: Is the cash machine working?
   B: No, it isn't.

▶ TRACKS 216 & 217

1 She's cooking something nice for dinner.
2 He's studying Business at university.
3 Are you feeling OK?
4 He's playing basketball with some friends in the park.
5 I'm going with them and they can take you too.
6 He's in his room. He's watching TV.
7 What's she doing at the moment? Is she working?
8 Can you talk to her? She doesn't listen to me.

▶ TRACKS 218 & 219

1 We had a lot of snow last month.
2 The last World Cup was three years ago.
3 I went to a great concert on Thursday.
4 They met in Paris forty years ago.
5 I bought it a few days ago.
6 It rained a lot this morning.
7 He cut his head this afternoon.
8 What time did you get home last night?
9 We met at a conference nine or ten years ago.
10 It happened four or five years ago.

▶ TRACK 220

1 last month
2 three years ago
3 on Thursday
4 forty years ago
5 a few days ago
6 this morning
7 this afternoon
8 last night
9 nine or ten years ago
10 four or five years ago

▶ TRACK 221

1 There's almost no crime here.
2 We have no winter in my country.
3 There are some very cheap areas.
4 There's a lot of noise outside.
5 There are quite a lot of volcanoes here.
6 There are lots of mountains and lakes.
7 There's almost no grammar in my language.
8 There's no army in Iceland.

▶ TRACK 222

1 Are you going to be OK in that top? It's cold today.
2 They said on the news it's going to be 38 degrees here today.
3 They're going to lose the election.
4 I'm not going to work for a month this summer. I need a holiday.
5 The house doesn't have heating. You're going to be cold in there.
6 Is the weather going to be OK?
7 Look at the snow! There are going to be accidents on this road.
8 I'm going camping with some friends this weekend.

▶ TRACK 224

1 they're
2 there are
3 you're
4 we're
5 you're
6 We're going to take an exam next week.
7 We're going to have a lot of fun.
8 You're going shopping later.
9 They're going to win.

▶ TRACK 226

1 Can you help me in a minute?
2 It was lovely weather when I was there.
3 It happened after I left her.
4 I can have the car when I need it.
5 I'm going there in a few weeks.
6 I get angry when I'm tired.

▶ TRACK 227

A: So, Ivan. It was lovely to meet you.
B: You too, Fei.
A: Thanks for everything.
B: It was a pleasure.
A: I made you something to remember our time together!
B: Oh, what lovely photos! Thanks.
A: That's OK. It's been great.
B: I'm going to put them on the wall in our kitchen.
A: I'm happy you like them.
B: I'll help you put your bags in the taxi.
A: Oh, be careful! Don't hurt your back!
B: Wow – they are heavy! What do have in there?
A: I bought a lot of gifts for my family.
B: Yes – a lot! So, Fei. Stay in contact. Don't forget us!
A: I won't.
B: Have a good journey.
A: I hope so. I'll call you from home.
B: OK. Say hi to you family.
A: I will.
B: Bye now.
A: Bye.

▶ TRACK 229

1 Don't forget to call them.
2 I'll go and get something to drink.
3 I'll send someone to look at it.
4 I can't go now, but I'll do it later.
5 Do you know a good place for lunch?
6 I don't want to have fish and chips.

NATIONAL GEOGRAPHIC
L E A R N I N G

National Geographic Learning,
a Cengage Company

Outcomes Beginner
Hugh Dellar and Andrew Walkley

Vice President, Editorial Director:
John McHugh

Executive Editor: Siân Mavor

Editorial Project Manager: Laura Brant

Development Editor: Stephanie Parker

Head of Strategic Marketing EMEA ELT:
Charlotte Ellis

Product Marketing Manager: Victoria Taylor

Head of Production and Design: Mike
Burggren

Content Project Manager: Ruth Moore

Manufacturing Manager: Eyvett Davis

Cover Design: Lisa Trager

Interior Design and Composition:
emc design ltd.

For permission to use material from this text or product,
submit all requests online at **cengage.com/permissions**
Further permissions questions can be emailed to
permissionrequest@cengage.com

Student Book and Class DVD:
ISBN: 978-0-357-03399-9
Student Book and Class DVD and OWB PAC
ISBN: 978-0-357-04343-1

National Geographic Learning
Cheriton House
North Way
Andover
UK
SP10 5BE

Locate your local office at **international.cengage.com/region**

Visit National Geographic Learning online at **ELTNGL.com**
Visit our corporate website at **www.cengage.com**

CREDITS
Although every effort has been made to contact copyright holders before publication, this has not always been possible. If contacted, the publisher
will undertake to rectify any errors or omissions at the earliest opportunity.

Photos
Cover AllisonGinadaio/iStock/Getty Images.
Front Matter
2 (tl) AshTproductions/Shutterstock.com; (tl) Philippe LEJEANVRE/Moment/Getty Images; (cl) Adrian Buck/Alamy Stock Photo; (cl)
AllisonGinadaio/iStock/Getty Images; (bl) Skreidzeleu/Shutterstock.com; (bl) nui7711/Shutterstock.com; **4** (tl) wavebreakmedia/Shutterstock.com;
(tl) Barry Winiker/Getty Images; (cl) Golubovy/Shutterstock.com; (cl) Marcos Mesa Sam Wordley/Shutterstock.com; (bl) Harry KiiM/Shutterstock.
com; (bl) Ververidis Vasilis/Shutterstock.com;
6 (tl) AshTproductions/Shutterstock.com; (tr) Mohd Hafiez Mohd Razali/EyeEm/Getty Images; (c1) Standard Studio/Shutterstock.com; (c2) Iakov
Filimonov/Shutterstock.com; (cl) Pietus/Shutterstock.com; (cr) Carlos Banyuls/Shutterstock.com; (bl) Monkey Business Images/Shutterstock.com;
(br) WAYHOME studio/Shutterstock.com; **7** (tl) Klaus Tiedge/Blend Images/Getty Images; (cl) Monkey Business Images/Shutterstock.com; (bl) AP
Images/Jonathan Brady; (br) Jorge Salcedo/Shutterstock.com; **8** (t) Greg Elms/Lonely Planet Images/Getty Images; (cr1) Michael Ochs Archives/
Getty Images; (cr2) DIMITAR DILKOFF/AFP/Getty Images; (cr3) DEA PICTURE LIBRARY/De Agostini/Getty Images; **10** (tc1) Tetiana Yurchenko/
Shutterstock.com; (tc2) Toronto-Images.Com/Shutterstock.com; (tr1) monticello/Shutterstock.com; (tr2) Min C. Chiu/Shutterstock.com; (tr3)
MakaBaka/Shutterstock.com; (c) REPORTERS ASSOCIES/Gamma-Rapho/Getty Images; **12** lechatnoir/E+/Getty Images; **14** (tl) Philippe LEJEANVRE/
Moment/Getty Images; (tr) Evelyn Chavez/Shutterstock.com; (cl) Monkey Business Images/Shutterstock.com; (cr) all_about_people/Shutterstock.
com; (bl) tazzymoto/Shutterstock.com; (br) Monkey Business Images/Shutterstock.com; **15** (tl) steve estvanik/Shutterstock.com; (cl) macroworld/
E+/Getty Images; (c) Claudia Totir/Moment/Getty Images; (cr) Ryan McGinnis/Alamy Stock Photo; (bl) Serg Zastavkin/Shutterstock.com; (br)

Printed in China by RR Donnelley
Print Number: 02 Print Year: 2019

Shutterstock.com; (cl) Kevin Mazur/One Love Manchester/Getty Images; (cl) pdrocha/Shutterstock.com; (c) NASA; (cr1) duncan1890/iStock/Getty Images; (cr2) Peter Horree/Alamy Stock Photo; (cr3) NurPhoto/Getty Images; (br) Juanmonino/E+/Getty Images;

DVD videos

Video 1 photos (1) Bogdan Khmelnytskyi/Shutterstock.com; (3) Scott Hortop Life/Alamy Stock Photo; (5) arabianEye/Getty Images; Video 2 photos (2) MAHATHIR MOHD YASIN/Shutterstock.com; (4) Boston Globe/Getty Images; (5) Romankonovalov/Shutterstock.com; (7) Mikhail Gnatkovskiy/Shutterstock.com; (8) Simon Mayer/Shutterstock.com; Videos 3, 4 and 6 National Geographic; Video 5 Paulina Almazan

Illustrations

108 Ricardo Bessa/Folio Art; 45 Clive Goodyer/Beehive Illustration; 80 (r), 84 (bl) Irina Golina-Sagatelian/Beehive Illustration; 8 (ml, bl), 9 Phil Hackett/Eye Candy Illustration; 13 Daniel Limon/Beehive Illustration; 64 (ml), 70 (b), 106 (b) Arpad Olbey/Beehive Illustration; 16 (c) Dave Russell; 39 Gary Venn/Lemonade Illustration; 30 (bl) Dan Widdowson/The Bright Agency.

Acknowledgements

The publishers and authors would like to thank the following teachers who provided the feedback and user insights that have helped us develop *Outcomes* Beginner: Silvia Carchano Alcina, EOI Gandia, Gandia, Spain; Lara Alvarez, Newham College of Further Education, London, UK; David Byrne, EC London, London, UK; Sarah Donno, Edinburgh College, Edinburgh, UK; Eder Garces, EC London, London, UK; SoYeong Kim, EC London, London, UK; Luz Stella Hernández Ortiz, Universidad de La Sabana, Chia, Colombia; Melissa Perkins, EC London, London, UK

Authors' acknowledgements

Thanks to our editors Stephanie Parker, Dona Velluti, Laura Brant and Siân Mavor. Also thanks to John McHugh, Dennis Hogan, and NGL for their continued support and enthusiasm for the *Outcomes* series.

Thanks also to all the students we've taught over the years for providing more inspiration and insight than they ever realised. And to the colleagues we've taught alongside for their friendship, thoughts and assistance.